Edexcel AS English Language and Literature

Val Bissell　　**Mary Jay**　　**Mike Royston**

STUDENT BOOK

Consultant: Jen Greatrex

Skills Coverage Map

Skill/specification coverage	UNIT 1	UNIT 2
Analysing spontaneous speech (conversation)	8–22	–
Understanding the differences between speech and writing	23, 29	99–101
Analysing e-communication (text messages, blogs)	23–30	122–128
Analysing live speech in broadcasts	30–36	130–133
Analysing the use of voice in oral narratives	35–36	–
Understanding the features of scripted language	36–43	137–41
Understanding the creation of idiolect (distinctive voice)	19–20, 41	–
Understanding the differences between scripted language and spontaneous speech	8–9, 30, 36–43	–
Analysing the use of voice in scripted drama	36–43	137–141, 142–145
Analysing the use of voice in poetry	44–51	–
Understanding personae in poems and monologues	45, 48–49	142–145
Analysing voices in narrative	52–60, 65–85	108–114
Understanding first person narrative voices in prose	52–53, 56–57, 65–73	–
Understanding third person narrative voices in prose	54–57, 80–85	–
Analysing voice in non-fiction	58–59	115–121, 122–128, 134–137
Analysing the construction of dialogue in written texts	74–79	–
How to read and analyse transcripts of spontaneous speech	9	–
Aspects of syntax, lexis, phonology and graphology that contribute to creating voice in texts	16–17, 25, 27, 29, 32	–
Understanding register and formality in spoken and written texts	12–13	–
Understanding regional dialect in spoken and written texts	19–20	–
Understanding how writers and speakers project a persona or constructed identity	28	–
Exploring the craft of writing	–	92–93, 104
Writing in different genres for specific audiences and purposes		94–101
Writing creatively for a reading audience		105–128
Writing creatively for a listening audience		129–143
Writing commentaries on your own work		114, 133, 146–153
Selecting your reading related to a topic area		102–104
Communicating clearly your responses to texts	50–51, 61–64, 78–79, 86–89	–

Contents

GCE AS English Language and Literature: Introduction

Welcome to English Language and Literature at advanced level. In this course you will explore texts from both a linguistic and literary perspective taking an integrated approach, and will also create your own texts.

The kinds of text you will explore include literary, non-fiction and media texts that are spoken, electronic, digital and multi-modal. So, in addition to prose, drama and poetry, you will explore communication through the medium of informal and formal speech, telephone calls, emails, text messages, TV and radio broadcasts and blogs – taking a 'hands on' investigative approach to texts that are part of your everyday lives.

How can I make English Language and Literature most rewarding?

To enjoy and succeed in your course you will need:

- an interest in language and how it works
- an interest in people and how they communicate with each other
- the ability to write in original, entertaining ways for readers and listeners
- an enjoyment of reading – everything from novels and stories to soap scripts and websites
- an enquiring mind that likes to find patterns in things.

What will I learn?

Unit 1 – Exploring Voices in Speech and Writing. For Unit 1 you will sample a wide range of fiction and non-fiction, including transcripts of conversations, radio broadcasts, TV chat shows, play extracts, novels, travel writing, electronic communication such as texts and emails, and poetry.

You will study a novel or a collection of short stories. You will look at one aspect of it, 'voice', and how this connects up with your study of speech and writing in other contexts. 'Voice' applies to both the writer's way of telling you the story and the way in which the characters speak. You'll examine how a writer creates individual voices and how these are used to engage and influence the reader.

This means that you will learn about the differences between speech and writing; the features of conversation and scripted speech; how narrative voice is used in written and oral texts; how distinctive voices are created in texts, for example, through the use of dialect and different levels of register (formality); and how audience, purpose and context influence the choice of language.

Unit 2 – Creating Texts. The central focus of Unit 2 is on two pieces of creative writing. One will be something that the audience will read, such as an extract from a piece of non-fiction; an extra episode from a novel you are reading and studying; an obituary of one of the characters; an episode rewritten as a newspaper report. The other piece will be something that an audience will listen to, such as an interview with a character from one of the texts studied, a radio script for an additional scene or a dramatised extract. You will show your understanding of the writing process by writing a commentary on each piece.

Your creative writing will grow out of your wider reading on a topic and you have a completely free choice of texts to study, as long as this includes one piece of prose fiction and either one play or poetry text. The emphasis is on your development as an independent reader, writer and thinker.

How will I be assessed?

Unit 1 is assessed by an external exam.

30% of your A level course is assessed by a 2 hour 15 minute exam. You have to comment on:

- three previously 'unseen' texts from speech, e-communication, broadcasting or literature
- an extract from a modern novel you have studied and relate this to other parts of the book.

Unit 2 is assessed by coursework.

20% of your A level course is assessed by your teacher. You have to create your own texts for a reading and a listening audience. In consultation with your teacher you will choose your own topics for writing, then add a commentary explaining your purposes and how you achieved them.

Throughout, you will develop your understanding of how the literary and linguistic elements of texts work, and develop your writing skills as writers for different audiences and purposes. These will be rewarding and valuable skills for the future – whether you are giving a presentation at a business meeting or writing a piece of journalism from one of the world's hot spots.

Jen Greatrex, Edexcel

How to use this book

This **Student Book** is divided into Unit 1 and Unit 2. **Unit 1** supports your work for the AS exam. **Unit 2** supports your work for the AS coursework component.

The **Teaching and Assessment CD-ROM** provides additional support, including commentaries and further texts, questions and exemplar responses. It can be used alongside this book.

Unit 1. Exploring Voices in Speech and Writing: an outline

Unit 1 in the Student Book is divided into two sections, reflecting the two sections of the exam.

Section A: Voices in speech and writing (pages 8–64). Section A provides you with the tools that you need to examine the way spoken and written language works. Section A also introduces you in a systematic way to the types of text you have to know about for the unseen question in your exam. The final part helps you prepare for Section A of the exam by giving you a sample paper and analysing the questions and their requirements.

Section B: Voices in literature (pages 65–89). Section B helps you to prepare for the part of the exam on your prescribed novel or short story collection. It covers the different aspects of voice you could be asked about in your exam, and guides you towards analysing the text in the way examiners expect. The final part helps you to prepare for Section B of the exam by giving you a sample paper and analysing the questions and their requirements.

Unit 2. Creating Texts: an outline

Unit 2 in the Student Book focuses on your coursework. It is divided into four main sections.

Section A: The writing process (pages 92–104). The first section will help you to decide what you would like to write about for your coursework tasks and how to go about doing it. It will also answer important questions about the creative writing process.

Section B: Writing for a reading audience (pages 105–128). This section gives you guidance on how to write effectively for a reading audience. You will explore a range of texts in different genres, as well as sample responses, and practise writing your own.

Section C: Writing for a listening audience (pages 129–145). This section gives you guidance on how to write effectively for a listening audience. You will explore a range of texts in different genres, as well as sample responses, and practise writing your own.

Section D: Writing your commentaries (pages 146–153). The final section gives you guidance on how to write your commentaries.

The two middle sections are free-standing: you can begin with the task of your choice or even work on the two tasks in parallel.

Tackling the exam

Each unit in the Student Book includes features and activities to help you to consolidate your learning and prepare for the exam. The features include guidance about assessment objectives, sample exam questions and sample student responses with critical comments. Go to the Edexcel Examzone website http://www.examzone.co.uk/home/ for more information about preparing for Edexcel exams. There's everything from practice exam papers that you can download to information on how exams are marked – and you'll also find plenty of revision tips along the way!

- Section A of the exam provides three short unseen texts. You have one hour to answer three questions on them.
- Section B of the exam allows you about one hour to answer one essay question on your prescribed novel or short story collection.

For the coursework unit you will hand in a folder containing two pieces of your own writing, plus a short commentary on each piece. One is for a reading audience and the other is for a listening audience. Both pieces of writing are informed by wider reading in a topic area.

Unit 1

Exploring Voices in Speech and Writing

Unit introduction

In Unit 1 of Edexcel AS English Language and Literature you will:

- learn how to analyse a range of spoken and written texts
- explore the differences between spoken language and writing
- examine the way writers create and use voice in literature
- study the uses of voice in one modern novel or a collection of short stories
- increase your understanding of why context is important to the way texts work.

The course

What you will do in the exam (2 hours 15 minutes)

There are two questions. You will be asked to:

- comment on three previously 'unseen' texts from speech, e-communication, broadcasting or literature
- analyse the use of voice in your prescribed novel/short story collection by commenting on an extract and relating it to the book as a whole.

What will the examiners be looking for?

Examiners use three assessment objectives (AOs). They are, in summary:

Assessment objective	What this means in practice	Percentage of marks
AO1 Select and apply relevant concepts and approaches from integrated linguistic and literary study, using appropriate terminology and accurate, coherent written expression.	You have to use: • suitable linguistic frameworks – toolkits to examine the way spoken and written language works • suitable linguistic terms • a style of writing that is clear and fluent.	30%
AO2 Demonstrate detailed critical understanding in analysing the ways in which structure, form and language shape meanings in a range of spoken and written texts.	You have to apply to spoken, written and electronic texts: • an understanding of how their language conveys meaning • an understanding of how their form and structure convey meaning • an understanding of how language, form and structure combine to convey meaning.	50%
AO3 Use integrated approaches to explore the relationships between texts, analysing and evaluating the significance of contextual factors in their production and reception.	You have to show: • an integrated Lang-Lit approach to analysing texts • an ability to compare and contrast texts • a knowledge of the context of texts and why it is important.	20%

Examiners will also be looking for evidence of:

- your ability to show how language features influence a reader or audience
- your ability not just to 'spot' language features but also to *explain* how they shape the meaning of a text
- detailed, not sketchy, knowledge of your prescribed novel or short story collection with a focus on the concept of voice
- original thinking.

Section A: Voices in speech and writing

Section A provides you with the 'tools' of language analysis you need for Unit 1 and the other unit(s) in your AS (A2) course. You need to become confident in using these in order to progress.

Section A introduces you in a systematic way to the types of text you have to know about for the unseen question in your exam. This unseen question may include texts chosen from a very wide range. It is important to cover them all.

Section B: Voices in literature

Section B helps you to prepare for the part of the exam on your prescribed novel or short story collection.

It covers the different aspects of voice you could be asked about in your exam. Bear in mind that this is not a substitute for reading and making your own study of your prescribed text. There are seven prescribed texts on the specification: this book cannot and does not attempt to cover 'all you need to know' about yours. Rather, it guides you towards analysing the text in the way examiners expect and gives you plenty of practice in doing so.

How to succeed in English Language and Literature Unit 1

You can achieve a high mark on this unit by:

- getting to grips early on with linguistic frameworks and the terminology that comes with them: these need to be *learned*
- taking the initiative in finding, reading and analysing some texts for yourself: don't depend on your teacher for everything
- increasing your understanding of how texts work by writing them yourself: original writing is a tool of understanding as well as a means of expression
- focusing on the idea of voice in all your texts, including your prescribed novel or collection, and how it is central to your exams in both Section A and Section B.

A Voices in speech and writing

This section provides a foundation for your work throughout Unit 1. It introduces the **linguistic frameworks** you need in order to analyse both unseen and prescribed texts. Linguistic frameworks are the toolkits used to examine the way spoken and written language works. The first set of frameworks applies to **spontaneous conversation**.

1   Analysing spontaneous conversation

Assessment objectives

AO1 marks are awarded for selecting and applying relevant concepts and approaches from integrated linguistic and literary study, using appropriate terminology and accurate and coherent written expression (10 marks).

AO2 marks are awarded for demonstrating detailed critical understanding in analysing the ways in which structure, form and language shape meanings in a range of spoken and written texts (20 marks).

AO3 marks are awarded for using integrated approaches to explore the relationships between texts and for analysing and evaluating the significance of contextual factors in their production and reception (20 marks).

Spontaneous conversation is unplanned talk between two or more speakers. It takes place in real time, usually with the **participants** face to face.

The unseen part of the exam on Unit 1 may ask you to analyse one or more passages of spontaneous conversation. This section introduces you to:

- the distinctive features of spontaneous conversation
- a vocabulary of technical terms to describe them.

Spontaneous versus scripted conversation

Activity 1

A Here is part of a spontaneous conversation. The two participants are talking about how floods have affected their Cotswold village. PDW is a postal delivery worker. N is a newsagent. Read the passage to yourself.

(.) indicates a short pause, (1.0) indicates a one-second pause, // indicates overlapping or interruption.

N:	well, leastways the mail's comin (1.0) the mail's gerrin through
PDW: (laughs)	yeah (1.0) ave to be wearin me waders though
N: (laughs)	mm (.) real bad round Sedgeberrow I heard isn't it //
PDW:	// terrible yeah
5 N:	terrible (1.0) some of they livin down by the coach house, y'know
PDW:	coach house mmm (1.0) well it's (.) it's so er low-lyin //
N:	// down there
PDW:	insurance'll not cover it (1.0) not at all
N:	oh insurance (1.0) no, no

B Here is a scripted conversation from a radio drama series. The three characters are preparing for a friendly football match in their village. Read it aloud.

SID:	Still no sign of him?
TONY:	Apparently he went over to Felpersham to collect some silage. He must have been delayed.
SID:	Oh blimey! He's our main striker! What do we do?
5 TONY:	Keep stalling, Eddie says. And hope he turns up. If not we'll have to play Neil up front. And put Robert in midfield.
SID:	Terrific!

(Pause)	
ROY:	Come on, lads, what's the hold-up?
10 SID:	We're not ready.
ROY:	You mean you're trying to hang on till David gets here. Kick-off time was five minutes ago, Sid!
SID:	Yeah, alright!
15 TONY:	It's only a bank holiday kick about, Roy. Not the Cup Final.

1 Discuss in a small group:

   a which features of conversation **A** suggest it is spontaneous rather than scripted. Note down at least three points.

   b which features of conversation **B** show the dramatist trying to **simulate** spontaneous speech. Note down at least three points.

2 Share your ideas from the group work. Then use them to begin a class chart listing the typical features of spontaneous conversation. Put these under three headings (as shown below):

- Structural features – describing the way the **exchanges** in it are built up.

- Lexical features – describing the language used by participants in a conversation. **Lexis** is a term for the words people choose when they speak or write.

- Grammatical features – describing the way speakers combine together words, phrases, clauses and sentences to express what they mean.

Three entries have been made for you.

Typical features of spontaneous conversation		
Structural features	**Lexical features**	**Grammatical features**
• some **overlapping** speech	• some **colloquial language** or slang	• some **incomplete constructions**, eg 'well, it's …', '… not at all'

As you work through this section up to page 22, add periodically to the class chart. The text will specify where this is essential. There will be other points where making your own entries will help you build up linguistic frameworks to analyse any spontaneous conversation passage in the exam.

Using a transcript: how to read spontaneous conversation

A **transcription**, or transcript, is a printed version of everything that is said in a conversation. In a basic transcript, punctuation is left out, apart from capital letters to begin proper nouns (Jackie, Bristol) and apostrophes to indicate possession or **contraction** ('we're' for 'we are'). The following symbols are used to show how the conversation sounds:

- (.) a short pause of less than one second, often called a **micropause**

- (2.0) a longer pause, in this case lasting two seconds

- // overlapping, where one speaker starts before the previous speaker has finished

- (laughs), a non-verbal response

- underlining, to indicate a stressed word.

Reading transcripts is a skill that develops gradually. The more you practise it, the more accurately you will interpret any conversation in the unseen exam. The best advice for getting inside a transcript is:

- read it through two or three times

- read it aloud, or aloud inside your head

- use all the information you are given about the speakers and the situation they are in

- remember there is always an audience for conversation: try to visualise the listener(s) and their reaction to what is being said.

Key terms

linguistic framework
spontaneous conversation
participants
simulate
exchange
lexis
overlapping
colloquial language
incomplete construction
transcription
contraction
micropause

Take it further

Record about 30 seconds of a radio or TV interview. Practise making a transcript of it using the conventional symbols and markers.

The contexts of spontaneous conversation: who and where?

Context describes the physical and social circumstances in which a conversation takes place. It includes the identity of the speakers and the relationship between them. Context is a key influence on the form and language of any conversation: it determines how the speakers **interact**.

Activity 2

The 'conversation' transcribed below takes place in a hairdresser's. Read it through to yourself and try to hear it in your head. Then read it aloud with a partner.

| C: | Customer [middle-aged] |
| H: | Hairdresser [in their twenties] |

C: we eloped // yeah we <u>eloped</u>

H: // (laughs)

C: we went on to have six (.)

H: <u>six!</u>

5   C: yeah (2.0) one after the other

H: did you // you and him (.)

C: // yeah yeah yeah

H: one after the other // six children (.)

C: // mm it's a bit weird actually (.) I think we thought
10   we were the bloody <u>Waltons</u> // I'm not sure (laughs)

H: // (laughs)

C: yeah (.) so we did that um (.) he went off and had
(.) er he was leading a <u>double life</u> really (.) he had

another relationship while he was married to me and
15   every time I had a baby she had one // and we're still

H: // what

C: yeah (.) that's how that ended up (.) but his <u>mother</u>
knew about it as well his mother was living with us //
she

20   H: // his <u>mother?</u>

C: yeah everyone did // on his side

H: his <u>mother</u> was living with you?

C: yeah

H: and she knew // about the woman and the kids
25   down the road //

C: // yeah she used to // but

H: and she never said a word

C: and all these things came to light // afterwards,

H: // (gasp)

1 Discuss with your partner how the following **contextual factors** may have influenced this conversation. Don't be afraid to speculate: there are no absolute 'right' and 'wrong' answers here.

   a The social situation: public, private or somewhere between the two?

   b The relationship between the participants: friends, strangers or acquaintances?

   c The age and gender of the participants.

   Note down your ideas.

2 Share your ideas in class discussion. Agree on three reasons why context – the 'who' and the 'where' – will always have an important bearing on the form a conversation takes and on the participants' choice of lexis.

The purposes of spontaneous conversation: what's it for?

Clearly, the general purpose or function of all conversation is to communicate. Even when you talk to yourself, or to the cat, you are addressing a **receiver** (self, Mog) and therefore engaging in a speech act or a **speech encounter**.

However, just pointing out that people 'communicate' with each other in particular contexts will not take you very far as a Lang-Lit student. It's too vague. In order to say something interesting about the distinctive form and language of any conversation, you need first to decide on its purpose(s).

Key terms
interact
contextual factors
receiver
speech encounter
CPR

Activity 3

1 Make a table with the following headings:

Speech encounter	Topic	Context	Purpose	Receiver(s) – ie the other participant(s)
Informal chat	The X Factor	on the bus	gossip	2 friends, Zak and Jen

On your table, note down four or five conversations you have had in the last 24 hours (the one here is given as an example). Try to include a variety of contexts, purposes and receivers. Linguists often refer to these by the abbreviation **CPR**.

2 Share findings about your own conversations with the class. Consider in particular:

a Did your lexis and grammar vary depending on CPR? If so, how?

b How was the structure or pattern of your conversation influenced by CPR? Try to describe some structural features of two of your conversations that were quite different.

Activity 4

Read aloud the bits of conversation below and on page 12 with a partner. They have been lightly punctuated in the interests of easy reading.

A

A: hiya (1.0) eugh man I feel seriously rough

B: well, surprise me why don't you! you poured a gallon down your neck last night

A: yeah, don't go there (2.0) I didn't sink half as much as you, though, if I remember (.) which I don't

B: some of us can hold our liquor, Stevie boy, and some of us can't

B

A: hello there (1.0) all right?

B: yeah, I'm good

A: another video is it?

B: mmm (4.0) have you got that um that Bruce Willis one that just came out (.) er, cops, car chases (.) you know //

A: // yep, on the shelf just by you (.) there you go (.) £2.50, please, return by next Monday (2.0) OK?

B cheers (.) lovely job (2.0) see ya

C

A: so (1.0) we need a full stop to make it make sense

B: (3.0) yeah

A: and why can't we use a comma?

B: cos … um … well, cos it's a long pause

5 A: well, OK, it's a long pause (3.0) but let's also look at the (.) grammar of the sentence (2.0) now what's its (.) you should know this (.) its subject? hmm?

B: (5.0) 'running'?

A: no (2.0) that's part of the verb (2.0) look for the noun

B: (6.0)

D

A: I hereby pronounce you man and wife (1.0) you may kiss the bride.

B: (kissing noises)

Here are some **function categories** linguists use to describe conversation:

- transactional – getting something done
- expressive – giving expression to feelings
- instructional – giving information about how to do something
- phatic – socialising through 'small talk', for example, 'Lovely weather', 'How are you?'
- referential – conveying factual knowledge
- persuasive – advocating a point of view, trying to change someone's mind
- performative – accompanying an action with a 'set' form of words, for example, 'I sentence you to the maximum term the law allows'.

1 Decide which of these could apply to conversations **A** to **D** above.

2 Make up and read out brief phatic, referential and persuasive utterances with a partner. An **utterance** is simply an uninterrupted stretch of language by one speaker.

A note of caution: few discourses fit neatly into just one function category. Talk would be much duller if they did! Their purposes tend to overlap and change as a conversation goes on. So text **B** above is principally transactional but also phatic. Text **C** is principally instructional but also referential. Many conversations are multi-purpose in this way.

> **Key terms**
>
> function categories
> utterance
> register
> tone

> **Take it further**
>
> Make up several short exchanges that include more than one function. Write them down as above. Annotate them to show which functions they illustrate.

> **Writing in the exam**
>
> Start your analysis of a conversation with CPR. You will then have a relevant basis for the analysis you go on to write. Context–Purpose–Receiver defines the nature of the interaction.

> **Assessment objectives**
>
> AO3 gives 20 marks out of 50 in Section A for 'analysing the significance of contextual factors'. You will need to show a knowledge of the context of texts and why it is important.

The registers of spontaneous conversation: informal to formal

Register describes a form of language appropriate to a particular situation or context. Seeing your doctor by appointment about a serious health problem is a formal matter: the language and **tone** of your conversation will reflect this. Speaking to your doctor in an informal context such as a fun run will give rise to a correspondingly informal manner of speech.

So in conversation, register – or manner – is determined by two things:

- the relationship between the speakers
- the context or situation they are in.

In identifying a speaker's register, you need to look at the level of formality shown.

Activity 5

1 Read the following conversational snippets.

> No pudding, thanks, I'm really full.

> The sweet looks very tempting, but I simply couldn't force down another morsel.

> No, ta, I'm pigged out.

> Black Forest Gateau contains more calories than a marathon runner burns in the course of 10 miles.

a As a class, place the snippets on a continuum running from 'very formal' to 'very informal'.

b Suggest a context for each of these snippets and the speaker's implied relationship with the receiver.

2 With a partner, write three short conversations displaying different levels of formality – one formal, one informal, one semi-formal. Choose the contexts and the participants yourself. Read them out. Then consider with the whole class how formality/informality is made apparent in spontaneous conversation:

a through the choice of lexis?

b through the grammar and/or sentence construction, ie **syntax**?

c through the tone of the speaking voice, ie **intonation**?

A note of caution: think carefully before you describe a whole conversation as 'formal' or 'informal'. Many come somewhere between these two extremes. Levels of formality can also vary in the course of conversation. For example, in the formal context of an interview a skilful interviewer may switch to an informal register to help the interviewee relax or 'open up'.

Writing in the exam

Start your analysis of a conversation with Context-Purpose-Receiver (CPR) which defines the nature of the interaction. You will then have a relevant basis for the analysis you go on to write.

Key terms

syntax

intonation

tag question

The structures of spontaneous conversation: how is it built?

The main structural features of spontaneous conversation are shown in the table below and on page 14:

Adjacency pairs	Where one utterance by Speaker A leads directly to another by Speaker B, for example:
	'Great game, wasn't it?'/'Yeah, absolute classic. Awesome!'
	Adjacency pairs are the building bricks of conversation. They can take the form of greeting–greeting, request–acceptance, question–answer, etc. One common adjacency pairing is formed when an utterance ends in a **tag question**, for example:
	'You've remembered the tickets, *haven't you?*' is followed by an answer: 'No, I thought you were bringing them, idiot.'

Chaining	Where adjacency pairs are linked, allowing the conversation to proceed like the links in a chain until one speaker initiates a topic shift/transition or the conversation ends. For example:	
	'Terrible shirt, that' / 'Get lost, scruffbag! Cost me thirty quid from Top Man this did' / 'You going out clubbing, then?' / 'Nah. Just chilling with the lads down the precinct. See ya.'	
	Chaining is the structural principle on which all conversations develop.	
Non-fluency features	Where a speaker hesitates, makes a false start and self-corrects or uses a **filler** such as 'er', 'um', 'y'know' or 'right'. For example:	
	'I told her … I said to her, I told her to her face, I'm not interested in your … um … your lousy love life, right, and if you don't stop gobbing on about it, right, I'm going to scream.'	
	Fillers are not a sign that the speaker is inarticulate: they act as 'filled pauses' to allow thinking time between utterances. A **hedge** is a filler which softens the force with which something is said, often because the speaker is reluctant or embarrassed to say it, such as 'well, er …', 'the thing is, you see …', 'sort of'.	
Cooperative signals	Where Speaker A uses words and phrases, such as 'yeah', 'really?', 'oh dear!' or 'good heavens!' or makes sounds, such as 'mmm' or 'ah-ha' to give feedback to Speaker B.	
	These signals tell a speaker 'I'm listening, carry on' or 'I sympathise'. Feedback is the green light of conversations.	
Discourse markers	These are words and phrases which mark boundaries in a conversation between one topic and the next, such as 'right, ok then …', 'on the other hand', 'I was just thinking …', or 'Next thing I knew …'	
Phatic talk	Where utterances have a purely social function designed to initiate or encourage conversation: 'Excuse me, I wonder if …?' or 'You're looking well.'	

Key terms

filler

hedge

turn-taking

topic management

dominant speaker

agenda

cue

Activity 6

1 Look carefully at the list of structural features in the table above. Then re-read the hairdresser/customer conversation on page 10. As a class, identify in this conversation:

  a two adjacency pairs

  b hesitations, false starts and fillers. (suggest why the customer uses two hedges in line 12)

  c interruptions and overlaps

  d two examples of the hairdresser giving cooperative signals (also termed 'positive reinforcement' or 'back-channel behaviour')

  e two discourse markers.

2 Imagine the phatic utterances, or 'phatic tokens', that may have been made to open the conversation.

3 Role-play a spontaneous conversation between one of these pairs with a partner:

- a police officer and a suspected burglar

- a reality TV celebrity and a fan

- a teacher and a frequently absent pupil

- a dentist and a patient.

First choose a specific setting and plan a real-life context for the conversation, for example:

- the TV celebrity and the fan meet in an airport departure lounge
- the pupil and the teacher meet in a supermarket car park.

Then come out of role and discuss the way your conversation developed:

a Who started, or initiated, it?

b Who chose the main topic?

c Did the topic change as you went on?

d How did the conversation close?

e Was the **turn-taking** roughly equal or was there one dominant speaker?

These aspects of conversation are referred to as **topic management** or topic development. Activity 7 takes your analysis of this basic element of spontaneous conversation a stage further.

Activity 7

1 Refer back to the hairdresser transcript on page 10 in a small group. Answer these questions about its structure – that is, how it develops and how it is shared out between the participants. Use your role plays in Activity 6 to help you.

a Who is the **dominant speaker**? How do you know?

b Who sets the **agenda**, or topic, for the conversation?

c Who controls the turn-taking? Who offers the most turn-taking **cues**?

2 Share your ideas from the group work. Then talk more generally about turn-taking and how it works. Turn-taking is a fundamental part of conversation (although we have all met the ego-tripping bore who wants to hog the limelight). What factors do you think have the strongest influence on turn-taking? Consider:

a physical and social context, for example, the headteacher's office, a service encounter

b differences between the status or gender of the participants, for example, traffic policeman/speeding motorist, parent/child, older/younger, male/female)

c personality.

3 The terms linguists use to describe patterns of turn-taking are borrowed from debating.

a What cues do you think speakers might give to show:

- they are ready to 'yield the floor'
- they want to continue to 'hold the floor?'

b What cues do you think receivers might give to show they want to 'take the floor'?

4 Write a conversation which demonstrates some of the conclusions you came to in questions **2** and **3** about turns and the turn-taking strategies participants use. Include a typical opening (meeting and greeting) sequence and a typical closing (parting and departing) sequence. Then read it aloud with a partner.

5 Class chart – make entries on your class chart in the column headed 'Structural features'.

Writing in the exam

Structural features will be an essential reference point for analysing live conversation. Memorise the features listed in this section. For example, you might write, 'The student in the conversation uses the hedge 'well, er ...', which indicates that he is embarrassed to tell his teacher that he has not done his homework.'

The lexis and grammar of spontaneous conversation: how speakers choose to say it

Activity 8

Here is the transcript of a conversation between 11-year-old Hannah, her mother and her friend Sophie. They are talking about an accident Hannah had. They are at Hannah's home.

1 Discuss in a small group how the CPR of this conversation influences the lexical choices made by Hannah and her mother. Focus on:

  a Hannah's purpose in recounting her accident – who is her principal receiver?

  b her mother's role in the conversation

  c the informal setting, Hannah's home.

HANNAH:	well I was pretending to be Popeye walking out of the bathroom with a toothbrush in my hand in my <u>mouth</u> even
MOTHER:	I never knew you were pretending to be Popeye
5	
HANNAH:	I <u>was</u> I was going phoop phoop (.) Popeye the sailor man phoop phoop (.) and then I slipped on the floor and it just cut the insides of my mouth (1.0) and you thought it was chewing gum and started <u>pulling</u> on it and I was going <u>aargh</u>
10	
MOTHER:	it was this big bubble on her mouth like you know //
HANNAH:	and it was just //
15 SOPHIE:	// um
HANNAH:	because you know that was the cheek but it was the <u>inside</u> //
SOPHIE:	// like white
MOTHER:	yeah and (.) it just looked like a gobstopper or a big round //
20	

SOPHIE:	// chewing gum
MOTHER:	chewing gum thing you know and I said ugh and I sort of tried to
HANNAH:	pull it out and she didn't notice // I'm going
25 MOTHER:	// horrible
HANNAH:	oow like that
MOTHER:	horrible horrible wasn't it because I I (.) when I realised of course I stopped and said oh no there's something come out of Hannah's cheek
30	
HANNAH:	and they didn't (.) they left it for ages and ages (.) no they <u>actually</u> took me to casualty and they said just leave it and it'll clear by itself // or something
35 MOTHER:	// they had this theory that she could bite it off
SOPHIE:	oh that's horrible

2 Share your ideas from the group work. Then look carefully at the following list of lexical and grammatical features typical of spontaneous conversation. Make entries in the second column.

Lexical and grammatical features	Examples from the Hannah transcript
Use of informal/colloquial language	
Use of **vague language**, eg 'kind of thing', and **idiom**, eg 'down in the dumps'	
Frequent use of **common nouns**	
Frequent use of personal pronouns, eg 'I', 'we', 'you'	
Simple and undemanding vocabulary	
Deictic language or **deixis** – words or expressions that rely on the context to give meaning, eg 'this', 'over there', 'that dress'	

Ellipsis – the omission of part of a sentence that can be understood from the context, eg 'Going down town?'/ 'Maybe'	
Incomplete utterances	
Clauses linked by **coordinating conjunctions**, eg 'and', 'so', 'or', 'but'	
Non-fluency features, eg fillers, pauses, false starts, repetitions	

3 **a** Recast the first 11 lines of the Hannah transcript (as far as 'aargh') into a third person story. Use a mixture of **reported speech** and **direct speech**. Set it out and punctuate it in standard form.

b Then, as a class, look at one or two of these story versions. Discuss the lexical and grammatical changes you have made. What does this activity tell you about the lexis and grammar of spontaneous conversation and how it differs from writing?

4 Now make further entries on your class chart in the columns headed 'Lexical features' and 'Grammatical features'.

Writing in the exam

A transcript of conversation will display most of the lexical and grammatical features listed on the chart. You could write: 'The non-fluency features in A's first few utterances, where he self-corrects and uses two fillers, show that he is nervous and unsure of himself in this formal interview.' This meets the requirement of AO1 to 'apply concepts from integrated linguistic and literary study, using appropriate terminology.'

Key terms
vague language
idiom
common nouns
deictic language
deixis
ellipsis
coordinating conjunctions
reported speech
direct speech

The sounds and signs of spontaneous conversation

Participants in a conversation communicate non-verbally as well as verbally. This being so, linguistic analysis needs to take account of:

- the **prosodic features** of speech: a speaker's volume, pitch, tone, pace and stress
- the **paralinguistic features** of speech: a speaker's gestures, posture and facial expressions.

Activity 9

1 Role-play one of the following short conversations with a partner in front of another pair:

- a year 11 student breaking the news about their GCSE results to mum or dad
- mum or dad asking their 17-year-old son/daughter why they got in last night at 2 a.m.

Then re-enact the same conversation without its main prosodic and paralinguistic features. Keep your voice as neutral as possible. Avoid all gestures and facial expressions.

2 Talk as a class about how much of the interaction in your role plays depended on the non-verbal aspects of speech. Were these just an 'added extra' or were they an essential part of the meaning of what was said?

Then re-read the Hannah transcript (page 16). Infer as much as is possible and reasonable about the participants' use of prosodic and paralinguistic features.

3 Now make further entries on your class chart by creating a fourth column headed 'Prosodic and paralinguistic features'.

Speaking on the telephone

Telephone conversations have their own distinctive structures and typical lexical features. Linguistic analysis needs to take account of:

- the purposes of the telephone call: expressive? transactional? multi-purpose?
- the pre-existing relationship, if any, between participants
- the absence of face-to-face contact.

Activity 10

1 Turn your back to a partner and enact a social phone call to each other. It should last about 60 seconds.

Then make a flow-diagram to show the pattern of your conversation. Start with:

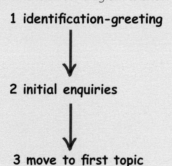

1 identification-greeting

↓

2 initial enquiries

↓

3 move to first topic

2 Review your completed diagrams in a small group. Use them to discuss the following questions:

a Was there a clear 'beginning–middle–end' structure to your calls?

b Was turn-taking more or less pronounced than in face-to-face conversation?

c Were non-fluency features, including pauses, more or less prominent than in face-to-face conversation?

d Was grammatical usage more or less formal than in face-to-face conversation?

3 Draw together your ideas as a class about the differences between a social phone call and face-to-face conversation. Then role-play transactional telephone calls between:

- a headteacher and a parent discussing a child's behaviour
- a shop assistant and a customer enquiring about a product.

Observers in the class should listen carefully and make notes about:

- opening and closing sequences
- who controls the agenda, and how this is signalled
- lexical choices, as compared with those in a social phone call.

4 Use the work you have done in questions **2** and **3** to write an analysis of the telephone transcript below. S and H are male, aged 17 to 18, and close friends.

H	hello	
S	hello is that H	
H	yes	
S	it's S	
5 **H**	oh (.) all right	
S	how are you	
H	I'm OK (.) thanks very much [*stupid voice*]	
S	good lad (.) have you seen the paper (.) the *Burton Mail*	
H	no	
10 **S**	er (.) well you're in it	
H	am I	
S	yes	
H	what	
S	well (.) you know you played well (.) didn't you	
15 **H**	yes	
S	well hey (.) you played brilliantly	
H	yes	
S	well you're in the *Burton Mail*	
H	am I	

20 **S**	yes (.) player of the match and all this lot
H	really (.) well what's it say
S	man of the match and it says (.) H laid all the goals up (.) and this lot (.) so I'll bring it round to you now (.) if you want
25 **H**	yes (.) I wouldn't mind (.) ta
S	because I'm coming past
H	ah (.) cheers mate (.) are you going out tonight
S	there's supposed to be a party at Vines (.) isn't there
H	yes I'm going with A____ I think
30 **S**	are you going
H	yes
S	good lad (.) and when you going (.) what time
H	well I'm gonna have me tea (.) then I was going to walk down to A____'s
35 **S**	OK (.) I'll be round in a bit
H	OK (.) see you in a bit then
S	OK see you
H	cheers

Varieties of spoken language: dialect, sociolect, idiolect

Read the definitions below.

Key ideas

Dialect is the term for a form of language with its own distinctive lexis, grammar and pronunciation. It is most commonly used to describe **regional** forms of language, for example, Cockney, Geordie and so on. Linguists also use it to describe **ethnic** dialects.

Sociolect is the term for a form of language associated with a particular social group defined either by age, for example, teenagers; occupation, for example, lawyers; or lifestyle, for example, rock musicians.

Idiolect is the term for an individual's unique way of speaking.

Key terms
dialect
regional
ethnic
sociolect
idiolect

Activity 11

1 Select an example of dialect or sociolect which interests you. Conduct a short investigation into it to present to the class. The areas you might look at include:

- how the dialect/sociolect originated
- who speaks it now
- whether it is a written medium as well as a spoken one
- whether it has a high or low status in society generally and among particular social group and, if so, why.

The internet will provide you with a mass of information: use it selectively. You will find audio recordings of different dialects at 'BBC Voices' and on the British Library website.

2 Make a five-minute presentation of your research findings to the class. If possible, use both audio and visual resources.

3 Now make further entries on your class chart by creating a fifth column headed 'Dialect, sociolect and idiolect'.

Take it further

Write a descriptive account of your own idiolect – your linguistic DNA. What do you think are the influences that have led you to speak as you do in an informal context and a formal context?

Some conventions of conversation: cooperating, being polite, saving face

Participants communicate through words and utterances. But they also interact by using conversational conventions, a knowledge of which they bring with them to any speech encounter and which they normally follow instinctively.

Some linguists refer to unwritten rules or 'maxims' of cooperation, which participants follow to ensure that conversations work. These are based on the premise that speakers have common goals and agreed ways of achieving them. The main maxims are:

- be truthful: the maxim of quality
- be brief – don't talk too much or too little: the maxim of quantity
- be relevant to the context of the conversation: the maxim of relevance
- be clear and unambiguous: the maxim of manner.

Activity 12

Read the following invented exchange between Ben, a year 12 student, and his teacher (T).

> T: Are you clear about the homework, Ben?
>
> Ben: I'm really looking forward to the weekend.
>
> T: Oh, right. Going far, are you?
>
> Ben: Just popping across to Florida with Sam and Sharon. My auntie, the Transylvanian transvestite, lives in LA, you know. The weather's brilliant this time of year – 40 degrees in the shade: sun, sea, snowboarding, you name it, pal.
>
> T: And the homework I've just set?
>
> Ben: Did it yesterday, didn't I? During Physics, when all the lights fused.

This conversation is 'unconventional' because Ben is not following the understood principle that participants will cooperate linguistically.

1 Talk with a partner about how Ben flouts all four maxims of cooperation. Then rewrite Ben's dialogue so that he follows the maxims.

2 As a class, illustrate from personal experience:

  a the phrases participants in a conversation use to conform to the **cooperative principle**. For example, 'I'll keep it very brief …', or 'I hate to change the subject, but …'

  b the phrases participants use to show annoyance when others flout the cooperative principle. For example, 'What's that got to do with it?' or 'Is there any point to this story?'

Some linguists suggest that participants follow the **politeness principle** if they want their conversation to succeed. The main rules of positive politeness are:

- never impose on your receiver
- always give options to your receiver
- always make your receiver feel good.

The **face theory** of conversation proposes that 'saving face' and 'losing face' play an important part in talk because participants are deeply concerned about their status. We show respect for other people's 'face' in order that they will respect ours in return. Some of the ways in which we employ positive face are:

- by following the conventions of turn-taking: for example, not hogging or butting in
- by using terms of address appropriate to others' status: for example, 'your honour' rather than 'me old mate' to a judge in court
- by speaking to others in a way that accurately reflects our social relationship with them: for example, 'Barbara' rather than 'darling' to a new acquaintance
- by using a register in keeping with the context of the conversation: for example, not using **taboo language** or telling dirty jokes in church.

Key terms
cooperative principle
politeness principle
face theory
taboo language

Activity 13

1 As a class, think of common conversational phrases people use when following the politeness principle. As a starting point, say how the politeness principle is being obeyed by these conversational phrases:

'I'd love to hear your opinion about that ...'

'Pardon me for asking, but could you possibly ...?'

'No, I think *you* ought to choose the wine this time ...'

2 Consider the face theory of conversation in a small group. Write a 20-line play in which the characters exhibit negative face in almost everything they say. Annotate it to show where and how they speak in face-threatening ways.

3 Listen to some extracts from the plays as a class. Then look back through this sub-section and decide how important the conventions you have examined are to the structure of conversations. Are you surprised to find that, according to some linguists, much of your spontaneous speech actually follows 'rules' and predictable patterns? Or do you think these linguists over-state the case?

4 Now make further entries on your class chart in the column headed 'Structural features', covering the features examined in this section.

Independent research

Conversation theory is a large area of study. Select some key names – for example, Paul Grice, Erving Gofman, Robin Lakoff – and read about how they arrived at their theories by collecting original data 'in the field'.

Writing in the exam

Try to include comments on the cooperative and politeness principles when analysing spontaneous conversation. Relate these to turn-taking and lexical choice. You might focus on cooperative signals, terms of address, concern for the status of other participants, use of an appropriate register, etc.

Summary: the key features of spontaneous conversation

Use your completed class chart to fill in a copy of the table below. Include at least five features in each of columns 1 to 3 and as many as you wish in columns 4 and 5.

Structural features	Lexical features	Grammatical features	Prosodic and paralinguistic features	Dialect, sociolect and idiolect

This table and the one on page 17 will be an essential part of your revision for the Unit 1 exam.

2   Analysing e-communication

In the unseen part of your Unit 1 exam, you may be asked to analyse the use of voice in:

- an email or emails
- a chat room conversation
- an online diary (weblog or 'blog')
- text messages.

This section introduces you to the key features of voice in electronic and digital communication. You will learn how to apply suitable linguistic frameworks to help you comment on them in the way examiners expect.

Speech versus writing

The table below lists the main differences between speech and writing. It is adapted from the work of the linguist David Crystal.

Speech	Writing
Speech happens in real time with participants normally present.	Writing is spacebound, static and permanent.
Spontaneity and speed make it hard to plan talk, leading to looser expression and some rephrasing.	Writing, because it is planned, tends to promote more compact expression and therefore more complex grammar.
Clues such as facial expression and gesture can aid meaning and allow vague expressions such as 'those', 'that', etc (deictics).	Lack of visual contact means that writers cannot rely on context to make their meanings clear: hence they need to be more explicit.
Prosodic features such as intonation, loudness, tempo, rhythm, pitch, pronunciation and tone are part of the effect of speech.	Prosodic features can only be approximated in writing – varied grammatical constructions are therefore more likely.
Certain types of informal language such as slang and obscenity are more likely in speech.	Writing can act as a record to be revisited and re-read at leisure: its lexis and grammar tends to be formal.
Speech is suited to social or phatic conversations where opinions and nuances can be expressed.	Writing includes many spatial features, some of which cannot be spoken (tables, graphs, diagrams), but has limited prosodic features.
Once something is said it cannot be unsaid or altered – speech is an event.	Writing can be redrafted later.

As you work through this section, refer to this table for each activity you do. E-communication often straddles the boundary between speech and writing. In the unseen exam you will need to identify, and differentiate between, features of speech and writing in any e-text you are given.

Emails

Activity 14

1 Think of three or four emails you have sent recently. Use them to fill in a copy of the grid below.

My emails			
Topic	Purpose	Receiver(s)	Reasons for choice of email as a medium
1			
2			

Then write the text of a short email to a friend who is away from school/college.

2 Compare your grids and your texts in a small group. Discuss the following questions.

a Are there any patterns in your use of emails?

b Why send emails in preference to telephoning or texting?

c Which features of your emails do you think resemble spontaneous conversation?

d Which features of email do you think resemble writing?

Show what you decide by making bulleted lists headed 'Speech features', 'Writing features' and 'Features of both speech and writing'.

3 Share your ideas from the group work. Then read the two emails below. Use them firstly to test out your three lists.

Email **A** is from 17-year-old Rebecca to a friend. Email **B** is to Rebecca from her mother. Rebecca's parents are visiting relatives in Bristol.

A

From:	Becky-17@email.com
To:	Chezza@email.com
Subject:	PARTAY!

Hi Chez!

Having a barbie. My place, Sat, 8ish. RU up for it? Should be gr8 - yeah!!!

Just the skool crowd, ABSOLOOTLY no parents 'n other wrinklies. Craig's coming, WELL fancies you I reckon – lol!!! (tough, he's mine!) :-)

5 Mail me yes/no/mebbe. If yes, can u bring booze and stuff? Ta.

CU, luv, Bex

B

From:	MumandDad@email.com
To:	Becky-17@email.com
Subject:	Barbecue

Hello Rebecca,

Thanks for your telephone message. About the barbecue: dad says you'll need more charcoal. Go to that garage on the A46, Truckers Stop or something similar. Firelighters on top shelf in the utility room (between light bulbs and candles).

5 I've phoned Uncle Frank and A.Doreen. They say they'll pop round to help with the cooking, etc. Let them know times a.s.a.p.

It's lovely here at Rose's. Driving to Bath tomorrow to see the sights. Dad is very sunburned already.

That's all for now, darling,

Love, Mum.

4 Compare the use of voice in the two emails, drawing items from the frameworks below. Examine:

Structural features	Lexical features	Spelling	Grammar	Graphology (the visual aspects of texts)
openings and closings (eg 'wotcha mate', 'speak to you soon')	informal/formal language	standard/non-standard spelling	sentence construction (eg simple, compound, incomplete constructions)	parenthesis (brackets)
terms of address (eg 'Dear Sid', 'sweetie')	vague language (eg 'sort of thing')	colloquial spelling (eg 'hiya', 'kool')	**sentence types** (declarative, imperative, etc.)	capitals/asterisks (for accentuation)
topic shifts / transitions	social language/slang	phonetic spelling (eg shud, praps)	prosodic features typical of speech	punctuation (standard/non-standard)
discourse markers	clippings or shortenings (eg 'soz' = sorry)			exclamations
deixis (context-dependent language: eg 'this', 'that', 'over there')	letter **homophones** or initialisms (eg omg, 'KWIM' = know what I mean)			emoticons (eg smileys)
ellipsis				

5 Write an analysis of these emails. Use the title: 'In emails **A** and **B**, how do the senders use elements of the spoken voice and the written voice? How do their choices of language reflect their different contexts, purposes and audiences?'

Write two or three paragraphs. Select features from the frameworks above. These frameworks will help you to analyse voice in any email text in your unseen exam – as long as you use them not just to *spot* linguistic features but also to *comment on their effect* in the particular text given.

Key terms
terms of address
topic shift
discourse markers
homophones
sentence types
graphology

Take it further

Use your own emails to conduct a short investigation into their typical CPR and language features. How accurate is it to describe them as 'speakwrite'?

Writing in the exam

Memorise the frameworks above before your unseen exam. They will give you a platform for analysing voice in most e-texts as well as emails.

Assessment objectives

AO1 gives 10 marks out of 50 in Section A for 'using appropriate terminology and accurate expression'. You will need to use suitable linguistic terms and demonstrate a style of writing that is clear and fluent.

Chat room conversations

Chat room conversations take place between several (sometimes many) participants. This makes them different from two-way telephone calls. The interaction is also written, though it has some of the characteristics of speech: hence 'chat'.

Activity 15

Read the chat room conversation below. The participants are four middle-aged women and one 20-year-old, Sonya87. The text is printed just as it appeared on screen. The first contributor is watching Sky News. She notices an item headlined 'Teen Party Hell'.

MARG:	Is anyone watching this? Teenage girl had a party when her parents were away and there was £20,000 worth of damage.
CRÈME-COOKIES:	omg! what did they do?
MARG:	someone posted an invite on myspace and there were loads of gate crashers. I'd of bliddy throttled her if she was mine. I am never leaving my son overnight after watching that. jeez.
CRÈME-COOKIES:	not all teenagers are like that. least not so bad anywho.
MARG:	I know all teenagers aren't like that but omg can you imagine coming home and finding your house wrecked.
KMA:	No I couldn't. The time and money I'm puttin into my house there had better be a plane watein for them! Cuz they wouldn't be able to run fast enough, I'd kill them if they even did it to some1 else's house as well!
GAERWITCH:	Them wer the days tho eh?
KMA:	They were the days but we had respect for the home we was in! I don't think my kids have got the gutts to take me on in that way. Or I'd get there gran to stop over pms.
MARG:	My son knows me well enough to not even try it.
SONYA87:	I had a party once which ended up being a free for all and I didn't even need to advertise it on myspace. It was a good party even though my mum near killed me the next day. There wasn't even that much damage done, even still never again did I have a party. Someone even fed the fish vodka, in fact that was the only damage done. lol.

1 Refer back to David Crystal's table on page 23. Discuss the following questions as a class.

   a Which typical features of the spoken voice are apparent in this extract?

   b Which typical features of the written voice does it have?

   Refer to specific examples in the text.

2 Discuss in a small group how the chat room conversation may have been influenced by the following contextual factors.

   a The participants are communicating via a keyboard, ie through writing rather than through speech.

   b The participants are not face to face.

   c The conversation is not private or **dialogic** (ie one-to-one).

   Quote details from the text as evidence. Then draw up a class list of 'Contextual factors that influence the use of voice in chatroom conversations'.

3 Compare the features of voice in the chat room conversation with those in the emails from Rebecca and her mother. Write two paragraphs. Select items from the frameworks on page 25 and the framework below.

Key term
dialogic

Structural features	Cooperation and politeness	Lexis and grammar	Graphological features
phatic utterances	signals of cooperation	formal/informal language	abbreviations
turn-taking and topic development	positive politeness strategies	ellipsis	letter homophones
adjacency pairs		deixis	
cooperative signals		complete/ incomplete utterances	
discourse markers		sentence types: declarative, imperative, etc.	
nicks (ie online nicknames)			

Take it further

Take part in a chat room conversation, making sure you observe the necessary protocols. Make a short transcript. Do the frameworks in this section provide an adequate basis for analysing voice in chat rooms? Do you need to add further features?

Writing in the exam

Accurate use of technical terms is essential, just as it is in your Section B exam. Check that you understand (and can spell) these terms as you undertake revision. AO1 gives 10 marks out of 50 in Section A for 'using appropriate terminology and accurate written expression'.

Online diaries or 'blogs'

Along with text messaging, blogging is the fastest growing mode of interactive electronic communication. Its purposes are varied and, as technology develops, they will undoubtedly change. When working on this section, therefore, bear in mind that your analysis of voice in blogs may need to be rather more tentative than for traditional types of text.

Activity 16

Read the three extracts from teenage blogs below.

A – Blog by xxbecka90xx   29 July 2005

OMG I fink im gonna call Jason! I might as well ask him out I mean he does like me!! But were close m8s I luv him to bitz I just dno if we break up then we can't be m8s after
5   why is my life so complicated? lol! HELP PLZ!!

B – Blog by fran94   4 August 2007

hey, I'm kinda new to this as I've never done it before so you guys will have to bear with me! I set up this account to write what I want when I want how I want so you know here goes!

5   I'm 13 and I live with my family in cheshire, I go to a big public secondary school and I love swimming, shopping and reading!! I just got back of holiday to Skiathos, wich is an island in greece! It was gorgeous and hot, but no luck where i am now!

C – J and me = its over HELP! by ShiningxLight
        28 May 2007

Right.

Erm. I haven't been blogging cos I've had a lot
5   going on.

I broke up with J.

His parents are getting divorced and he just got more and more quiet until he barely spoke at all.

It ended up in a huge fight.

10   Yepp. It's over … godd. Its so hard seeing him.

Cos I still love him and im so so so so so sorry … I know it must be tough for him.

He could have def done without me taking a psycho.

1   Make a bulleted list of the contexts and the possible purposes of these teenage bloggers with a partner. What conclusions can you come to about the **persona** (web personality) each is trying to project?

2   Compare these extracts with the typical features of spontaneous conversation as a class. (Refer back to your table on page 22). Create a grid showing at least three ways in which they are like, and three ways in which they are unlike, spoken communication.

Then consider how the voices in these blogs are influenced by the following factors.

  a   The participants are communicating with an unknown audience in writing.

  b   The participants are conducting an asynchronous (not happening at the same time) interaction.

  c   The participants are not receiving simultaneous feedback as they would face to face.

Read the extract below from the blog of a teenager living in Oklahoma.

Activity 17

D   Birthday and DND, 27 October 2006 at 12.57 am

My birthday was last week, and this showed just how much my parents know that they raised a computer engineer. Birthday presents included a domain name and a *wireless mouse*.

So. Yeah. Finally got a domain name. I've actually had it for a while, my dad bought it for me as an early birthday present. www.nolemonplease.com. I've been waiting to mention it because I wanted to get some more work done on it, but that hasn't happened yet. So there it is, only halfway finished. It's just a simple layout with a neat header, but it still has a small sense of elegance. All handcoded, yes, I'm proud.

To add ever more nerdiness to this post, a small group of us has started a Tuesday night Dungeons and Dragons group, and it has been really fun so far. We're still in the process of making characters sheets and stuff, and I'm excited for the actual playing part.

Anyway … bedtime.

1 Refer back to David Crystal's table on page 23 in a small group. Use a 'Speech → Writing' framework to analyse the main features of voice in blogs **A** to **D**. Make notes on a chart, like this:

	Evidence of speech mode features	Evidence of writing mode features
Blog **A**	• • •	• • •
Blog **B**	• • •	• • •

2 Share your findings from the group work. Then discuss:

  a whether the form and language of these blogs is nearer to speech than to writing or vice versa

  b suitable linguistic frameworks for analysing voice in a blog if your unseen exam contains one.

Writing in the exam

The 'Modes of Speech and Writing' table is basic to your work for both Unit 1 exams *and* for Unit 2 coursework. Using it will help you meet all three AOs for Section A. It is likely that you will be asked to comment on a spoken and a written text in the same answer, 1b.

Text messages

This section requires you to collect and investigate your own data. Text messaging is such a widespread and still relatively recent form of communication that, in the absence of established frameworks, the logical course is to construct your own.

Key terms

persona

elision

Activity 18

1 Provide evidence of your recent text messages in a small group. (You may wish to do a little screening in advance.) Then copy and complete the table below.

Teenage text messages		Examples and comments on these
Aspects of voice		**Examples and comments on these**
Structural features:	• openings and closings? • variations on adjacency pairs and chaining? • discourse markers? • ellipsis? deixis?	
Lexis:	• informal/formal? • social language? • colloquialisms? • taboo language?	
Spelling and grammar:	• contractions? • **elision**? • non-standard spellings, eg 'tonite'? • initialisms, eg 'asap'?	
Graphology:	• emoticons? trailers? asterisks? • non-standard punctuation?	

2 Share your findings from the group work. Then discuss whether you agree that, linguistically speaking, a text message is best described as 'written spoken language'. Consider these points:

> It uses a medium, the telephone, normally associated with speech.

> It uses openings and closings, and other structural features, associated with spontaneous conversation.

> It often uses the loose grammatical structures and informal lexis typical of speech.

> It uses graphological features characteristic of writing.

> It is not face to face so there is no simultaneous feedback: this is also the case with writing.

> It is preserved in print and can be re-read.

3 Analyse the use of voice in two of your own recent text messages using a 'Speech → Writing' framework. Then compare their language features with emails (see page 24). Are there more similarities than differences, or vice versa?

Take it further

Write an article for a linguistic website entitled 'The language of texting: a personal account'. Use evidence from the text messages you send and receive.

---

3 Analysing live speech in broadcasts

In your unseen exam on Unit 1, you may be asked to analyse voice in a passage of live speech from a TV or radio broadcast, for example:

- a sports commentary
- a talk show
- a phone-in programme.

This section introduces you to some key features of voice in these broadcasting **genres** and suggests appropriate frameworks for analysing them.

You need to bear in mind that, while broadcasting often presents itself as a spontaneous speech medium, the interactions between speakers are to some extent planned. Interviewers use prepared questions, talk show hosts follow a set formula, producers can edit speech in various ways, and so on. One of the points of interest in this section is to explore just how close to spontaneous conversation broadcast speech actually is, or whether some of its features have more in common with **scripted speech** covered in Section A.4.

Key terms
genre
scripted speech

Unscripted sports commentary

Sports commentary is a highly specialised broadcasting genre. Commentators are describing events that are instantaneous and largely unpredictable. They speak in monologue for a mass audience about which they can make some assumptions (common interest, shared knowledge) but which is, by definition, unknown. The frameworks you need for analysing an 'event commentary' must take these contextual factors into account, particularly for radio, where the commentator has to act as the eyes of the listener.

Activity 19

Read the transcript below. It is a passage of radio commentary on an international football match between England and Belgium in the 1980s. It has been deliberately chosen from the archive so that you can compare its linguistic features with present-day commentaries and assess whether the genre has changed in any ways over time.

> and again it's Wilkins high across the area looking for Keegan (.) Keegan gets the header in (.) not enough power (.) Ceulemans fortunately for Belgium is there to clear (.) not very far though (.) Sansom comes forward a yard in from the near touchline the England left (.) long ball from Sansom high across the area Pfaff is there (.) punches
> 5 the ball away (.) not very far but effectively (1.0) and Cools the (.) Belgian captain picks it up in space (.) far side from us the Belgian left (.) he's tackled fiercely though (.) and he loses the ball to Coppell to Brooking (.) <u>tall</u> Brooking (.) of West Ham (.) touches the ball on (.) Wilkins (.) good ball through too to Brooking (.) Brooking got four red-shirted Belgians around him (.) turns the ball back to Keegan (.) England's <u>captain</u> (.)
> 10 Keegan holds (.) still holds then starts to move forward slowly (.) goes away from van Moer's tackle (.) <u>another</u> tackle comes in on Keegan though (.) and in any case it's (.) a a (.) a foul tackle this time (.) plus a hand ball I think (.) so it's a free kick to England (.) this is halfway inside the Belgian half (.) England nil Belgium nil (.) the opening game (.) of this group for both these sides (.) and again (.) cries of 'England' ringing
> 15 round the stadium Wilkins takes the free kick short to Brooking (.) five yards outside the Belgian penalty area (.) good running by Brooking (.) down to the bye-line (.) cuts the ball back (.) Meeuws is there to head the ball away (.) not very far Wilkins trying to get the shot in Wilkins going forward <u>a chance for Wilkins here (.) and Wilkins (.) has scored for England</u> (.) oh a most intelligent goal (.) by Ray Wilkins …

1 Recast the part of the commentary from 'good running by Brooking' (line 16) to 'a chance for Wilkins here' (line 18) into a passage of descriptive writing. Use complete grammatical sentences and standard punctuation.

2 Compare your writing with the transcript. Discuss the following questions in a small group.

  a What additional words and phrases have you used?

  b Which grammatical categories do these fall into: for example, noun, pronoun, verb?

  c Which words and phrases from these lines and the rest of the transcript would you have to explain to someone who knew nothing about football?

3 As a class, share your conclusions from the group work. Then draw on the framework and notes below to make an analysis of voice in this transcript. You should give a clear explanation of *why* the features you identify are present and how they are matched to the needs of the listener.

Framework for analysing voice in sports commentaries
Specialised lexis (sport-specific terms) used continuously: • pitch-related, eg 'halfway line', 'in the area' • rule-related, eg 'free kick', 'penalty' • skills-related, eg 'flick on', 'early cross'.
Proper nouns used continuously: names of players, names of teams, names of clubs, eg 'Chelsea's John Terry, the England captain'.
Adverbials used frequently, eg 'in front of', 'across the line', 'a long way out'.
Figurative language (metaphor and simile) can feature, often drawn from the **semantic field** of warfare, eg 'fierce strike', 'cannonball shot', 'blasted it'
Connectives used rarely: clauses linked by pauses rather than conjunctions, eg 'Rooney turns (.) shoots'.
Noun phrases and noun clauses very frequent, eg 'Gerrard in space', 'Fingertip save by Robinson'. Structure of the whole commentary is clause-based.
Ellipsis and minor sentence forms used extensively, eg 'foul on Crouch', 'it's Lampard'.
Omission/deletion of normal sentence elements such as **auxiliary verbs**, eg 'Owen (is) going forward', and the articles 'a' and 'the', eg '(a) long ball from Ferdinand', 'Ashley Cole in (the) space'.
Verb tenses: simple present, eg 'he goes down in the box', or present continuous, eg 'Neville is surging up'.
Relative absence of the non-fluency features typical of spontaneous speech, eg hesitations, fillers, false starts.
Register: a combination of specialist, professional and colloquial – varies with the state of play.

4 a Make a short transcript of a football commentary on radio – no more than one minute. Use the framework above to analyse the use of voice, or voices, in it.

b Comment briefly on any linguistic differences you find between a present-day commentary and the one you examined from the 1980s, particularly if it involves an expert summariser or 'pundit'.

Writing in the exam

Beware of just 'spotting' language features in an unseen text. 'In this commentary there is frequent use of ellipsis and minor sentences', needs to be followed by 'The radio commentator is describing a high-speed game and therefore omits sentence elements such as pronouns and articles, which are less important than nouns and verbs for visualisation.'

Television talk shows

Television talk shows are filmed in front of an audience. You need to take account of this when analysing the use of voice by the host or interviewer and the guest. As always, context is key to defining the language of the interaction.

Activity 20

Brainstorm the different types and formats of interviews that are shown on television.

Place these on a continuum line of formality → informality. Where on the continuum would you put:

• interviews which elicit information and opinion, for example, with 'experts', with eye witnesses, with politicians, with 'the man in the street'?

• interviews for entertainment, for example, with actors/singers/comedians, with sportspersons, with celebrities, with 'lifestyle gurus' from fashion, cookery, gardening, etc?

Activity 21

Read the transcript below. It is taken from the talk show *Trisha*. Trisha is interviewing Trevor who has previously appeared on the programme, accused by his partner Martine of being 'one of Britain's most jealous men'. Here Trevor gives his side of the story. The interview is being conducted in front of a studio audience.

TRISHA: ok now last time we met Martine was branding you as one of Britain's most jealous men but <u>you</u> were saying you had just cause (1.0) what what is it you want to find out about Martine and what
5 she's been up to

TREVOR: if she's ever cheated on me (0.5) erm I see her on the doorstep with a friend at half one in the morning er with her arms around him and er she said nothing happened she said he wanted to come in for a <u>coffee</u>

10 TRISHA: yeah

TREVOR: at half one in the morning and er it was only three days later that she did (0.5) did admit to me that she actually gave him a <u>hug</u> and a <u>kiss</u>

TRISHA: ahhh (2.0) why didn't you do something when
15 you saw her with er her arms around this guy there and then (.) why didn't you (.) most guys would have dashed up and said get your hands off him or said something

TREVOR: because I was in a taxi (.) and I was going to let
20 her explain to me the next day

TRISHA: (2.0) ok now (.) the other thing you are angry about is this wedding dress that's been hanging in the wardrobe for how long now

TREVOR: um just over two years

25 TRISHA: and does it make you suspicious that she won't commit

TREVOR: (1.0) yeah because it's been there for 2 years (.) £1500 wedding dress and it just seems a waste (.) you know I mean obviously (0.5) if she's got
30 nothing to hide you know

TRISHA: um (1.0) and yet <u>you've</u> cheated on Martine how many times

TREVOR: three times

(audience gasps, 3.0)

35 TRISHA: did you have a break after any of those times you cheated

TREVOR: we was … we <u>was</u> together but we wasn't actually <u>living</u> together (.) at the time

TRISHA: each time that you cheated (0.5) but you weren't
40 actually together

TREVOR: well we wasn't living together we was together as fiances but we wasn't living together

TRISHA: hang about (.) you were fiances (0.5) you were living in separate places

45 TREVOR: yes

TRISHA: why did you go off with other women at those times then

TREVOR: (1.0) lonely (1.0) bored

---

1 Talk and make notes in a small group about the features of spontaneous conversation that are apparent in this exchange. Focus on:

  a topic management: how is turn-taking handled?

  b adjacency pairs, particularly question–answer

  c discourse markers

  d signals of cooperation and politeness.

2 As a class, share your ideas from the group work. Then look carefully at Trisha's role in the exchange. What evidence is there that she:

  a is using prepared questions

  b switches in the course of the exchange from positive to negative face

  c changes her register?

3 Trisha is talking to Trevor; however, she has other receivers in mind. Who are they? Discuss the implications of this for defining the CPR of this exchange.

Take it further

Watch several 'live' talk show interviews. Evaluate the extent to which they are scripted. Focus on the interviewer's cues, cooperative signals and non-fluency features.

4 Use the transcript to analyse:

   a how the structure of the interview reflects its context

   b the differences between Trisha's voice (including register) and Trevor's

   c the extent to which the interview seems formal or more like 'chat'

   d the balance of power between the participants.

   Write two or three paragraphs.

Live phone-in programmes

Look back to page 18 to remind yourself of the typical structural and lexical features of social and transactional telephone calls. As you work through this section, compare them with the voices in the transcript below.

Activity 22

Read the following transcript. It is from a phone-in programme on the Irish radio station RTE. Callers are talking about the hazards of train travel in southern Ireland. The previous caller has been complaining about the toilet facilities on high-speed trains.

> **J:** **Joe Duffy** [host, middle-aged]
> **R:** **Robert** [caller, middle-aged]

J: good afternoon

R: good afternoon Joe

J: another train story (.) when (.) last weekend

R: yes the train was coming up from Killarney erm a
5   stag party coming home after the night before (.) still
      drinking //

J: // um

R: and most of them drunk erm on a two carriage
      commuter train (.) which is not
10   the most comfortable of (.) of trains and erm

J: the Arrow trains are they the Arrow ones is it

R: yes but it basically

J: do they have toilets

R: pardon

15 J: do they have loos

R: Jesus they was plenty of toilets on the floor Joe (.) I
      didn't know where it was coming from the floors was
      soaking from drinking there was everything going (.)
      but it was a <u>disgrace</u> (.) we were rising Mallow station
20   and er security and er stationmaster <u>totally</u> ignored the
      situation

J: were they high spirits or were they annoying people

R: not at all no they guys were just (.) they were still drunk
      from the weekend

25 J: but what were they doing

R: singing chanting trying to chat up the women (.) and
      walking up and down the carriages and (.) but my point
      was that there's no security on the train and if something
      happened (.) there was bottles of cider being drank and
30   when they were drank they were left on the floor to roll
      around around the floor and only one driver on the train
      and nobody else

J: and you're saying it was a train from Killarney to (.) to
      Cork (.) one of those commuter trains (.) ok

35 R: yes it stops in Mallow (1.0) the problem they had Joe
      was that (.) the regular train was gone to Dublin for the
      match //

J: // ok ok

R: there's no security Joe it's a disgrace //

40 J: // I know I know

R: yeah

J: ok Robert thanks indeed (.) what's a bigger disgrace
      is their behaviour (.) you'd be afraid to complain I
      presume like a lot of people

45 R: but if I did complain to the lads like because because
      you know they could have got … you know and I //

J: // and you can't run anywhere you're in an enclosed
      tube

R: absolutely

50 J: ok Robert (.) safe travelling

1 Discuss the structure of this conversation in a small group.

   a Does it follow a 'beginning–middle–end' pattern?

   b Does the host, Joe Duffy, follow a standard formula?

   c How many structural features typical of spontaneous conversation can you identify?

Focus on phatic tokens, turn-taking and adjacency pairs, and non-fluency features.

2 Share your findings from the group work.

Then copy and complete the chart below.

Key features of voice in the phone-in conversation		
Structural features	**Lexical features**	**Grammatical features**

3 Use your work in questions **1** and **2** to write two paragraphs analysing the use of voices in the phone-in transcript. Consider the following questions in particular:

   a Who controls the conversation, and in what ways?

   b What similarities and differences are there between this and a social telephone call?

   c How close does this exchange come to spontaneous conversation?

Oral narratives

A substantial amount of 'air time' is taken up by people telling personal anecdotes. Think of examples from your recent viewing/listening. They are a kind of sub-genre of live speech in broadcasts. The activities below help you to build up frameworks for analysing the use of voice in oral narratives.

Activity 23

1 In groups, take turns to tell 'You won't believe this but it really happened' stories lasting up to one minute. Other members of the group should act as audience, and make brief notes about language use.

2 Discuss these questions.

   a Is there a discernible and common *structure* to these stories?

   b How is the voice of the speaker matched to, and influenced by, the audience?

   c How does the narrative form of uninterrupted utterance make it different from spontaneous speech?

Read the transcript below. Richard Madeley, the television presenter, is telling a story about his daughter Chloe on the news and talk show *This Morning*. He is talking to a guest in front of a studio audience. The programme is live.

> I'll tell you one thing (.) when we moved to London and we'd been here for about a month and we were just driving around looking at the sights and we were driving past Buckingham Palace right and Chloe's in the back of the car right (.) this is so funny um and she said there it is there's Buckingham Palace woah woah oh we should open the window oh and the Queen lives there oh look the flag's up the Queen's in there now (.) and she said is that the Queen's house then (.) and we said yeah and she said ooh fancy building a palace next to the main road

5

1 With a partner, talk about:

   a how Richard signals the start of the story

   b how he uses **embedded dialogue** to bring the story alive

   c how he links together phrases and clauses

   d how he uses features typical of spontaneous speech to hold the interest of his receivers.

2 As a class, share your ideas from the group work. Then look at the template below, which some linguists use to analyse the structure of spoken narratives.

> Spoken narrative structure can be divided into:
>
> *abstract:* a signal that the story is about to start
>
> *orientation:* establishes the context of the story, for example, what, who, when, where
>
> *action:* establishes 'what happened'
>
> *resolution:* establishes 'what happened in the end'
>
> *evaluation:* signals used throughout the story about why it is interesting/worth telling.

Discuss how well this template describes the elements of Richard's story. If you were given this oral narrative in your unseen exam, what other features of voice would you comment on?

3 Watch and listen to a recording of a comedian telling a 'funny story'. Then rewind and use the pause button to analyse:

   a how far the story fits the template above

   b the extent to which the story seems spontaneous or scripted, and how you can tell.

Report your findings back to the class.

4   Analysing voices in drama

In Section A of the exam on Unit 1, one text could be:

- an extract from a stage play, or
- an extract from a television drama, or
- an extract from a radio play.

Drama versus spontaneous conversation

This section helps you to identify the distinctive features of voice in **scripted drama** and, in particular, to compare and contrast it with spontaneous conversation.

Unlike conversation, dialogue in drama is constructed, ie scripted by a writer, to create a particular theatrical effect. Often the speech is constructed to make it *seem* spontaneous. When faced with a drama extract in the exam, therefore, you need to analyse and comment on the ways it has been crafted for an audience – unlike live conversation, which is improvised by the participants as they go along.

Activity 25

To help you begin to do this, compare the four drama extracts below with unplanned talk. First remind yourself of the key features of spontaneous conversation on your chart on page 22.

Read the extracts aloud round the class. Then do activities **1**, **2** and **3** on page 38.

This is an extract from a TV drama series, *Hotel Babylon*. The Hotel manager, Miss Mitchell, is talking to an accountant, Miss Merchant, called in to deal with staff pilfering from the hotel.

A

MISS MITCHELL: I want you to be as thorough as possible, Miss Merchant. Every bottle, napkin and peanut that can't be accounted for, I want to know about it.

5 MISS MERCHANT: Before I start a job, I always ask the question, do you trust your staff?

MISS MITCHELL: Mmm, I used to.

MISS MERCHANT: Well, then, you've been naïve. In my experience people are generally bad. They
10 lie, they steal, they copulate.

MISS MITCHELL: Well, I'm not sure I should judge them on that basis.

MISS MERCHANT: A sin is a sin, Miss Mitchell. As well as the audit, would you like me to set any traps?

15 MISS MITCHELL: Traps?

MISS MERCHANT: I could stick an extra case of wine behind the bar, some steaks in the fridge, see where it ends up in the next audit.

MISS MITCHELL: (smiles)

This is an extract from a play set in Liverpool. 10-year-old Mickey takes Linda, a girl of his own age, to meet Edward. Edward is a new friend of Mickey's and lives in a large detached house.

B

MICKEY: *(loud but conspiratorially)* Eddie … Eddie … y'comin' out?

EDWARD: I … My mum says I haven't got to play with you.

5 MICKEY: Well, my mum says I haven't got to play with you. But take no notice of mothers. They're soft. Come on, I've got Linda with me. She's a girl but she's all right.

EDWARD *decides to risk it and creeps out.*

10 MICKEY: Hi-ya.

EDWARD: Hi-ya, Mickey. Hello, Linda.

LINDA: Hi-ya, Eddie.

She produces the air pistol.

Look … we've got Sammy's air gun.

15 MICKEY: Come on, Eddie. You can have a shot at our target in the park.

LINDA: Peter Pan.

MICKEY: We always shoot at that, don't we Linda?

LINDA: Yeh, we try an' shoot his little thingy off, don't
20 we, Mickey?

They all laugh.

Come on, gang, let's go.

This extract comes from 'Her Big Chance', one of Alan Bennett's *Talking Heads* monologues written for television in the 1990s. Lesley, an actress, is talking about how she broke into films.

C

LESLEY: Now my hobby is people. I collect people. So when I saw this interesting-looking man in the corner, next thing I find myself talking to him. I said, 'You look an interesting person. I'm interested in interesting people. Hello.' He said, 'Hello.' I said, 'What do you do?' He said, 'I'm in films.' I said, 'Oh, that's interesting,
5 anything in the pipeline?' He said, 'As a matter of fact, yes,' and starts telling me about this project he's involved in making videos for the overseas market, targeted chiefly on West Germany. I said, 'Are you the producer?' He said, 'No, but I'm on the production side, the name's 'Spud.' I said, 'Spud! That's an interesting name, mine's Lesley.' He said, 'As it happens, Lesley, we've got a problem at the moment.
10 Our main girl has had to drop out because her back's packed in. Are you an actress?'

This is the opening of a play set on a remote island in Scotland.

D

The sound of water on a shore.

ROBERT: I have noticed that something draws us towards outlying islands. Some force pulls us. A quiet bay, an island in its middle – we take a small boat and we row out from the land. We circle the island, looking for a beach. We pull up the boat and light cigarettes. We walk the island's boundaries. We make a fire.

5   We sit on the beach and drink beer.

We cast our eyes back to the far shore from which we've come.

Night falls and the mainland slips into darkness.

We listen to the waves.

The island claims us.

10   *The crash of the sea on rocks.*
A cliff.
A thousand seabirds.

I have noticed from the study of maps,
The more outlying the island –
15   The further out it is in the remote ocean –
The stronger the force that pulls us towards it.

1 Share your responses as a class to these extracts. Which ones did you particularly enjoy? What did you find interesting about them?

2 In a small group, use your knowledge of live conversation to rate the drama extracts on a scale from 'very like spontaneous speech' to 'nothing like spontaneous speech'.

1 _____ 2 _____ 3 _____ 4

(very like spontaneous speech)   (nothing like spontaneous speech)

3 As a class:

  a compare your ratings with those of other groups

  b argue for your view, referring to your knowledge of spontaneous conversation

  c talk about what each writer was aiming for in constructing their spoken voices

  d talk about why they chose to construct the voices in those ways.

4 Write a short dialogue between two people which takes place in school or college, at home, or in the workplace. Here are a few suggestions:

> Two students arguing about something that happened at a party the night before.

> A parent and child talking about tidiness.

> A boss telling an employee s/he has been sacked.

Write two versions of the dialogue, with no more than six to eight exchanges between the speakers.

- In the first version, try to make it as close to spontaneous speech as you can.

- In the second version, try to keep the 'feel' of spontaneous speech but craft it more so that it could form a little moment in a staged play. Think hard about what you want to convey through the dialogue: for example, revealing something about the characters and their relationships. Make every exchange count; avoid the kind of loose, rambling talk you often find in spontaneous speech.

5 Read some of the dialogues aloud as a class. Share any fresh insights you have gained into scripted speech from writing it yourself.

6 Choose *one* of the drama extracts to focus on in more detail. Using a grid, list the features that make it seem spontaneous and the features that show it has been scripted. Give a short example of each feature as evidence.

Spontaneous	Example	Scripted	Example

Then use your grid to write one or two paragraphs about the way the dramatist scripts speech in your chosen extract.

Analysing scripted drama: key questions

For your unseen exam, it is helpful to have a bank of questions to draw on which you can apply to any stretch of scripted dialogue. This section shows you:

- what these questions are
- how to select from them so they are appropriate to the *kind* of drama text chosen
- how to use them to analyse and comment on voice in the text chosen.

Read carefully through the list of key questions below.

Key question 1

What does the dialogue show about the *relationship* between the characters?

Explore the ways in which this relationship is conveyed through the dramatist's use of the following features.

- Structural features: who sets the agenda? Who initiates topic shifts? Does turn-taking follow a set pattern or is it disrupted? Are there interruptions?
- Prosodic features: what indications are there of pitch, volume, intonation and stress (emphasis)?
- Paralinguistic features: what indications are there of the characters' body language, physical gestures and facial expression?

Key question 2

What can you tell about the *personality* of each character? How does the dramatist convey an impression of their personalities and states of mind through their individual voices, ie their idiolects?

Explore the dramatist's use of:

- a distinctive lexis for each character
- idioms, colloquialisms, standard and non-standard forms, taboo language
- ellipsis, deixis
- formal and informal registers, terms of address
- sentence types – imperative, declarative, interrogative, exclamatory.

Key question 3

What evidence is there of the dramatist emulating the typical features of spontaneous speech?

Focus on non-fluency features such as:

- false starts, self-corrections, hesitations, repetitions
- incomplete utterances
- fillers, hedges, pauses.

How do these spontaneous speech features affect the audience's response to the characters?

Key question 4

What kind of exchange is this, for example:

- social chit-chat?

- characters getting to know each other?

- characters in conflict?

- characters uncovering deep feelings?

How do the characters' voices reflect the situation they are in and the context of the drama, for example, an intimate or private dramatic context; a broader social setting?

Activity 26

As a class, read aloud the extract below. It comes from *Death of a Salesman* by Arthur Miller (1949).

Willy has been sacked from his job as a travelling salesman. Charley is a friend and neighbour with his own successful business. Here Willy turns to Charley for help. This is not the first time it has happened.

WILLY:	Charley, look … *(With difficulty)* I got my insurance to pay. If you can manage it – I need a hundred and ten dollars.	

CHARLEY doesn't reply for a moment, merely stops moving. (5)

WILLY:	I'd draw it from the bank but Linda would know, and I …
CHARLEY:	Sit down, Willy.
WILLY:	*(moving toward the chair)* I'm keeping an account of everything, remember. I'll pay every penny back. *(He sits)*. (10)
CHARLEY:	Now listen to me, Willy.
WILLY:	I want you to know I appreciate …
CHARLEY:	*(sitting down at the table)* Willy, what're you doin'? What the hell is goin' on inside your head? (15)
WILLY:	Why? I'm simply …
CHARLEY:	I offered you a job. You can make fifty dollars a week. And I won't send you on the road. (20)
WILLY:	I've got a job.
CHARLEY:	Without pay? What kind of a job is a job without pay? *(He rises)*. Now, look,

(25) kid, enough is enough. I'm no genius but I know when I'm being insulted.

WILLY:	Insulted!
CHARLEY:	Why don't you want to work for me?
WILLY:	What's the matter with you? I've got a job. (30)
CHARLEY:	Then what're you walkin' in here every week for?
WILLY:	*(getting up)* Well, if you don't want me to walk in here –
CHARLEY:	I am offering you a job. (35)
WILLY:	I don't want your goddam job!
CHARLEY:	When the hell are you going to grow up?
WILLY:	*(furiously)* You big ignoramus, if you say that to me again I'll rap you one! I (40) don't care how big you are! *(He's ready to fight)*.

(Pause)

CHARLEY:	*(kindly, going to him)* How much do you need, Willy? (45)
WILLY:	Charley, I'm strapped, I'm strapped. I don't know what to do. I was just fired.

As a class, use the key questions **1** to **4** above to analyse the way Arthur Miller constructs the voices in this extract. All of the questions are relevant.

Writing in the exam

The key questions provide you with a framework for analysing any passage of drama in the unseen exam. Remember, though, that extracts from different dramas will highlight different linguistic features and different aspects of voice.

It is important to select from the list above in light of the kind of drama you are given. During your revision, learn the key questions to ask about any drama extract you may be given from literature or broadcast sources.

Trying out the key questions on a different play

Activity 27

Here is an extract from *The Caretaker* by Harold Pinter. Read it aloud, including the stage directions.

Davies is a tramp who has been offered temporary accommodation by Aston in the house he claims to own. In this scene, Aston helps Davies to settle in.

Davies turns and peers under the sink.

DAVIES: This the bed here, is it?

ASTON: *(moving to the bed)* We'll get rid of all that. The ladder'll fit under the bed.

5

They put the ladder under the bed.

DAVIES: *(indicating the sink)* What about this?

ASTON: I think that'll fit in under here as well.

DAVIES: I'll give you a hand. *(They lift it)* It's a ton weight, en't it?

10

ASTON: Under here.

DAVIES: This in use at all, then?

ASTON: No. I'll be getting rid of it. Here.

They place the sink under the bed.

15

There's a lavatory down the landing. It's got a sink in there. We can put this stuff over there.

They begin to move the coal bucket, shopping trolley, lawnmower and sideboard drawers to the right wall.

20

DAVIES: *(stopping)* You don't share it, do you?

ASTON: What?

DAVIES: I mean you don't share the toilet with them Blacks, do you?

25 ASTON: They live next door.

DAVIES: They don't come in?

Aston puts a drawer against the wall.

ASTON: You see a blue case?

DAVIES: Blue case? Down here. Look. By the

30   carpet.

Aston goes to the case, opens it, takes out a sheet and a pillow and puts them on the bed.

That's a nice sheet.

ASTON: The blanket'll be a bit dusty.

35 DAVIES: Don't you worry about that.

Aston stands upright, takes out his tobacco and begins to roll a cigarette. He goes to his bed and sits.

ASTON: How are you off for money?

40 DAVIES: Oh well ... now, mister, if you want the truth ... I'm a bit short.

Aston takes some coins from his pocket, sorts them, and holds out five shillings.

ASTON: Here's a few bob.

45 DAVIES: *(taking the coins)* Thank you, thank you, good luck. I just happen to find myself a bit short. You see, I got nothing for all that week's work I did last week. That's the position, that's

50   what it is.

1 Select from the list of key questions the ones you think are most relevant to analysing the voices in this extract. Consider in a small group:

- the relationship between the two characters (remember they have only just met)
- the ways in which their idiolects differ
- what their idiolects show about their personalities.

2 Share your ideas from the group work.

Writing in the exam

Note that in the commentary there is precise textual reference to illustrate every point made. This is key to meeting AO2, 'demonstrate detailed critical understanding', for which there are 20 marks out of 50 in Section A.

Independent research

Find and read a one-act play by Harold Pinter, for example, *The Room*, *The Dumb Waiter*, *A Slight Ache*, *A Night Out* or *The Lover*. Use extracts to analyse the way in which characters' voices are constructed in the dialogue and the ways Pinter tries to emulate spontaneous speech.

3 Read the extracts below from a commentary on *The Caretaker* passage. Discuss how this analysis meets the requirement of AO1 to 'select and apply concepts and approaches from integrated linguistic and literary study' and the AO2 requirement to 'analyse the ways in which structure, form and language shape meanings'. Think about how this commentary:

- applies linguistic concepts to a literary text
- uses linguistic terminology accurately
- makes statements supported by clear examples from the text
- shows how the playwright tries to simulate spontaneous speech.

For most of this exchange, the dialogue takes a question-and-answer form. Turn-taking reflects the dramatic situation. Davies, a stranger in Aston's house, uses factual interrogatives ('This in use at all, is it?') and Aston, the owner, answers them with brief, undeveloped declaratives ('No. I'll be getting rid of it'). The dialogue follows a pattern of adjacency pairs typical of spontaneous conversation.

Although Aston is the 'host' in this encounter, it is interesting that he does not emerge as the dominant speaker. Up to the question about Davies's finances, the tramp leads the conversation, repeatedly using tag questions ('...is it?', '... en't it?', '... do you?') to prompt Aston to give information. Aston may be a naturally diffident character, or just wary of a man he has only recently met. His lexis is impersonal and unemotional, whereas Davies shows signs of wanting to take the conversation to a more confidential level with his emotive reference to 'them Blacks' and his concern about toilet arrangements.

The relationship changes when Aston initiates a topic shift: 'How are you off for money?' Davies at once reverts to the role of tramp, addressing Davies with the deferential term 'mister'. His embarrassment at being penniless is reflected by the non-fluency features in his utterance: 'Oh well ... now, mister, if you want the truth ... I'm a bit short'. His direct questions earlier give way here to unease and evasiveness, as the hesitations, fillers and the hedge 'a bit short' show.

Applying the key questions to a television drama

Activity 28

The extract below is from a 1998 episode of *EastEnders*. Read it aloud.

SCENE: The Queen Vic, upstairs. Night (11.57 pm)

Tiffany comes to top of the stairs. She sees Grant and Tiffany's bedroom door ajar, looks in. The bed is empty, the cover pulled back. Puzzled, she stands a moment, then hears a slight noise.
5 *She smiles to herself, exits to landing, heads to lounge, enters.*

Grant, in a coat, is crouched by the sofa, putting Courtney's shoes on. Courtney is dressed in a coat and bobble hat, ready to go out. Tiffany comes to a halt, stands rooted to the spot.

GRANT: Hello Tiffany.

10 *Sounds from downstairs, preparations for New Year, slowly escalate.*

TIFFANY: What are you doing here?

GRANT: Nice surprise, is it?

TIFFANY: How did you ...?

15 GRANT: Bail. Ever heard of it?

	TIFFANY:	You shouldn't be here. You ain't meant to be anywhere near me or Courtney.		*Pause.*
				Well, are we?
	Courtney starts to get off the sofa and move towards Tiffany. Grant pops her back on the sofa.		TIFFANY:	[*empty*] No.
20	GRANT:	You stay there darlin'.	40	GRANT:	So, you're still gonna take her?
			TIFFANY:	Please, Grant, just give her to me …
	Tiffany approaches. Grant steps forward, blocks her path.		GRANT:	Why should I? I made one mistake. One stupid, stupid mistake …
	TIFFANY:	Just give her to me.	TIFFANY:	It wasn't one mistake. Just the last in a long line
	GRANT:	I don't think so.	45	of things.
	TIFFANY:	Grant …	GRANT:	What things?
25	GRANT:	You had me locked up. You were gonna leave me there …	TIFFANY:	Take your pick. The fact is, you never really loved me.
	TIFFANY:	That ain't true. I … I sorted things …	GRANT:	That's not true.
	GRANT:	No. You were gonna go off, take my little girl away. Well it ain't gonna happen.	50	TIFFANY:	You tried, but you never had it in you.
			GRANT:	That last night … I said I loved you and I meant it.
30	*Grant picks up bag. Faint sound of countdown to New Year from Vic downstairs.*		TIFFANY:	Doesn't matter. It's too late now.
	TIFFANY:	Let's sit down, talk about it.	GRANT:	Don't you have any feelings for me?
	GRANT:	'Bout what?	55	*Tiffany looks at Grant. A long moment.*
35	TIFFANY:	You and me, everything. I'll tell the police you didn't do it.	TIFFANY:	[*upset*] No. [*gentle*] I'm sorry. Now please, just give her to me.
	GRANT:	Then what? We gonna patch things up? We gonna give it another go?		

Write an analysis of the way this exchange between Tiffany and Grant is crafted. Comment on:

- how the scriptwriter, Simon Ashdown, simulates spontaneous speech to create the characters' voices.

- the way in which this dialogue from a TV soap differs from a theatre play like *Death of a Salesman* or *The Caretaker*. Bear in mind the different context, which means that the audience is familiar with the characters and the narrative from previous episodes, there are more than 15 million viewers from a broad social spectrum, and so on.

Independent research

Read a selection of scripts from other soaps, for example, *Coronation Street*, *Brookside* or *Emmerdale*. They are published by ITV and Channel 4. Make an investigation of how tightly they are scripted to give the impression of spontaneous speech.

Writing in the exam

Before the exam, make a list of the typical features of voice in scripted drama and how these often simulate spontaneous speech. Memorise this list. In commenting on a passage of scripted drama, you could write: 'The playwright tries to simulate spontaneous speech by including some overlaps and interruptions in the dialogue. However, this is less marked than it would be in authentic live conversation since the viewing audience may lose the thread if characters repeatedly speak over one another.'

5 Analysing voices in poetry

In your unseen exam on Unit 1, you may be asked to analyse voice in a poem. Your task will be:

- to identify the kind of voice it is
- to comment on how the voice is created and conveyed.

This section introduces you to the idea of voice in poetry and helps you to analyse it using appropriate frameworks. These frameworks will differ somewhat from those you used for live conversation, e-texts and broadcasting since poetry is highly crafted, however 'loose' in structure or colloquial in style it sometimes seems. You will draw on the linguistic terms you have become familiar with but also use some **literary** terms and concepts you recognise from GCSE.

Voice in poetry

All poems have their own 'voice'. This will sometimes resemble the speaking voice typical of conversation: the conversational voice. It will sometimes be the more reflective or descriptive voice of the poet: the poetic voice.

Activity 29

1   Read the four extracts from modern poems below with a partner as if you were sitting on a bus chatting to each other. Try to catch their mood and their rhythm. Take two each.

A

The winter evening settles down
With smell of steaks in passageways.
Six o'clock.
The burnt-out ends of smoky days.

B

I could hav been a builder
A painter or a swimmer
I dreamt of being a Rasta writer.
I fancied me a farmer
I could never be a barber
Once I was not sure about de future.

C

You are the bread and the knife,
the crystal goblet and the wine.
You are the dew on the morning grass,
and the burning wheel of the sun.
You are the white apron of the baker
and the marsh birds suddenly in flight.

D

The boat docked at Liverpool.
From the train Tariq stared
at an unbroken line of washing
from the North West to Euston.

Now try performing them as if to an audience in a theatre.

2   As a class, discuss which of the extracts sound closest to ordinary speech and why.

How are your decisions affected by:

- lexis
- grammar
- line structure?

3   Read aloud the extract from another modern poem:

Talk about why the lexis here might be termed 'poetic' as opposed to 'everyday'. Focus on the poet's use of:

- figurative, or **metaphorical**, language
- rhythm
- **onomatopoeia** and **alliteration**.

After the funeral, mule praises, brays,
Windshake of sailshaped ears, muffle-toed-tap
Tap happily of one peg in the thick
Grave's foot, blinds down the lids, the teeth in black,
The spittled eyes, the salt ponds in the sleeves,
Morning smack of the spade that wakes up sleep …

4 Look back to poems **A** to **D** above with a partner. Think of adjectives to describe the tone of voice in each of them: ecstatic? bored? optimistic? depressed? and so on. What kind of person do you imagine speaking in each case? Justify your choices from the text.

5 As a homework activity collect your own extracts from four other poems that seem to represent a spectrum from 'highly poetic' to sounding like spontaneous speech. Place them on a continuum on the classroom wall: poetic → spontaneous speech.

The invented persona voice

This is an 'I' or 'me' whose voice is clearly not the personal voice of the poet. Rather, it is the voice of a character the poet creates, termed a persona.

Activity 30

Read the poem opposite by Carol Ann Duffy.

1 Make a character profile of the persona in this poem with a partner. As a starting-point, consider what Duffy tells us, or implies, about:

- the life he leads as an adult
- what his childhood was like
- his relationships with women.

2 Share your ideas in a small group. Then discuss the way Duffy's choice of language helps to create the persona's voice. Focus on:

- lexis, including pronoun use
- metaphorical language
- tone and register.

3 Share your ideas about these lexical features from the group work. Then fill in a copy of the chart below. It shows how Duffy's poetic crafting helps to create the voice of the persona.

Boy

I liked being small. When I'm on my own
I'm small. I put my pyjamas on
and hum to myself. I like doing that.

What I don't like is being large, you know,
grown-up. Just like that. Whoosh. Hairy.
I think of myself as a boy. Safe slippers.

The world is terror. Small you can go. *As I
lay down my head to sleep, I pray* … I remember
my three wishes sucked up a chimney of flame.

I can do it though. There was an older woman
who gave me a bath. She was joking, of course,
but I wasn't. I said *Mummy* to her. Off-guard.

Now it's a question of getting the wording right
for the Lonely Hearts verse. There must be someone
out there who's kind to boys. Even if they grew.

Carol Ann Duffy

How poetic crafting helps to create voice in 'Boy'		
Structural feature of the poem	Example	Effect on the reader
sentence forms (simple, compound, minor)		
line lengths		
rhythms		
stanza forms		

Key terms

literary
metaphorical
language
onomatopoeia
alliteration

Independent research

Find and read a selection of 'persona' poems by Grace Nichols (eg *The Fat Black Woman's Poems*), Tony Harrison (eg *V*) and U.A. Fanthorpe (eg *Not My Best Side*). Compare the ways in which they create the persona's voice with Duffy's technique in 'Boy'.

Assessment objectives

AO1 gives 10 marks out of 50 for 'applying concepts and approaches from integrated linguistic *and literary* study'. The literary approaches and terms used throughout this section are essential for commenting on a poem in the exam. You will know most of them from GCSE.

First person voice

This is an 'I' or a 'me' whose voice seems strongly personal. In first person poems, the lexis and register suggest that the poet is describing and/or reflecting on a significant experience.

Activity 31

Read the poem below.

> **Driving to the Hospital**
> We were low on petrol
> so I said let's freewheel
> when we get to the hill.
> It was dawn and the city
> 5 was nursing its quiet
> and I liked the idea
> of arriving with barely
> a crunch on the gravel.
> You smiled kindly and
> 10 eased the clutch gently
> and backed us out of
> the driveway and patted
> my knee with exactly
> the gesture you used
> 15 when we were courting,
> remember, on the way
> to your brother's: I like
> driving with my baby,
> that's what you said. And
> 20 at the time I wondered
> why my heart leapt and leapt.
>
> *Kate Clanchy*

1 In a small group, talk about:

a Who is the poet addressing here? Do you think it is only the reader, or is there an unnamed listener?

b What kind of voice is this? Think about its level of formalilty/informality and in what ways it is close to spontaneous speech.

c What is the context of the poem? Think about the words which build up a pattern: 'dawn', 'nursing', 'arriving', 'my baby', etc.

2 Share your ideas from the group work. Then produce together a chart describing how the voice is created in this poem, as below.

How poetic crafting helps to create voice in 'Driving to the Hospital'			
Lexis		**Structure**	
Examples of informal language typical of spontaneous speech:	Examples of figurative language:	Structural features resembling conversation:	Structural features of a crafted poem:

Use your completed chart to consider why Kate Clanchy may have chosen poetry rather than prose to capture this moment.

Third person (or 'detached') voice

This is a 'he' or 'she' voice. In third person poetry, the poet stands apart from their subject and observes the scene, shaping it into the form of a poem as a camera frames and captures an image.

Activity 32

Read the poem below.

Single Parent

Because she shares the bedroom with the baby
she undresses in the dark
and tonight her underclothes flash

and crackle in the dry air, like
5   miniature lightning, like
silver fireworks. It reminds her

of strobe lights, and her old crowd.
she trips and cracks her head on the bedstead
but of course she must not cry out.

Connie Bensley

1 Talk with a partner about:

   a the theme of this poem

   b how the lexis, including the figurative language or imagery, makes you respond to it.

2 Share your ideas from the pair work. Then copy and complete the chart below.

How the voice is created in 'Single Parent'	
lines 1–2 and lines 8–9	**lines 3–7**
Lexis:	Lexis:
Grammar and clause structure:	Grammar and clause structure:

What *contrasts* do you notice? How do these contrasts help to convey the poet's attitude to the single parent?

3 Although the poet's narrating voice is detached, her poem evokes strong emotion.

   Experiment with re-forming 'Single Parent' in a different voice. You could choose:

   - the first person voice of the single parent

   - the poet as an observer in the poem, for example, 'I saw/thought/felt …'

   - some other voice.

   What differences does this make? Is the emotional impact as strong as in the original?

Writing in the exam

If you are given a poem in the exam, always include comment on its structure, as demonstrated above. AO2 gives 20 marks out of 50 for analysing 'the way structure, form and language shape meaning'.

The dramatic monologue voice

This is a narrative or storytelling voice. A character in the story concerned addresses a listener (unseen and unheard), giving us their own view of events and revealing themselves through their speech.

Activity 33

Read the poem below.

The story here is from Shakespeare's *Macbeth*, at the point where Macbeth, having achieved the Scottish throne by assassination, has been deserted by his followers and is threatened by the English army. Lady Macbeth ('HM' in the poem) has been driven mad through guilt and walks in her sleep, obsessively washing imaginary blood from her hands. A doctor has been called in. Macbeth spends most of his time alone, sometimes speaking in soliloquy.

Waiting Gentlewoman

If Daddy had known the setup,
I'm absolutely positive, he'd never
Have let me come. Honestly,
The whole thing's too gruesome
5 For words. There's nobody here to talk to
At all. Well, nobody under about ninety,
I mean. All the possible men have buggered
Off to the other side, and the rest
Poor old dears, they'd have buggered off
10 Too, if their poor old legs could have
Carried them. HM's a super person, of course,
But she's a bit seedy just now,
Quite different from how marvellous she was
At the Coronation. And this doctor they've got in –
15 Well, he's only an ordinary little GP,
With a very odd accent, and even I
Can see that what HM needs is
A real psychiatrist. I mean, all this
About *blood* and *washing*. Definitely Freudian.
20 As for Himself, well, definitely
Not my type. Daddy's got this thing
About selfmade men, of course, that's why
He was keen for me to come. But I think
He's gruesome. What HM sees in him
25 I cannot imagine. *And* he talks to himself,
That's so rude, I always think.
I hope Daddy comes for me soon.

U.A. Fanthorpe

1 Use the chart below to explore how U.A. Fanthorpe creates the Waiting Gentlewoman's distinctive voice, ie her idiolect. Fill in the third column of the chart below as you talk in a small group.

The Waiting Gentlewoman's voice		
Language feature	**Example**	**Impression given of character**
Lexis: terms of address idioms/**social language** taboo language/slang deixis	'Daddy', 'HM', 'Himself' 'too gruesome for words' 'a super person' 'I think he's gruesome' 'buggered off' 'the setup', 'this doctor they've got in'	
Grammar: personal pronoun use minor sentences/ellipsis hedges/fillers crisp declarative sentence forms	'I', 'me', 'my' 'I mean, all this/About blood and washing. Definitely Freudian' 'I mean', 'Well' 'There's nobody here to talk to/At all'.	
Prosodic features: clipped tone stressing the adverb disparaging tone	'I'm absolutely positive' 'definitely/Not my type' 'only an ordinary little GP' 'what HM sees in him/I cannot imagine'	

2 Share your findings from the group work. Then talk about the verse form of this dramatic monologue. It is an updated form of Shakespearean blank verse. Do you think this adds anything to the way in which U.A. Fanthorpe constructs the Waiting Gentlewoman's voice?

Key questions to use in your exam

When faced with a poem in your unseen exam, the list of questions below will guide you towards making a clear and focused analysis.

Key question 1

Whose voice is speaking in the poem?

- an invented persona's voice

- a first person voice that sounds like the poet describing their own experience

- a third person, detached voice

- the voice of a character in a dramatic monologue

Take it further

Read U.A. Fanthorpe's poem 'Not My Best Side'. Write an analysis of the way it represents the speaking voice.

Key term
social language

Key question 2

What is the audience for the poem?

- the reader only

- an implied addressee, as, for example, in a love poem: 'Shall I compare thee to …'

- a character who does not appear in the poem but is assumed to be there

Key question 3

How is the voice created?

- through the lexis

- through the use of spontaneous speech features

- through the use of poetic features, for example, figurative language, free verse, stanzas, rhyme, alliteration, assonance, onomatopoeia

- through the tone and register

- through a combination of these

Key question 4

How close to, or distant from, the language of speech is the voice in the poem?

Look at:

- informal/formal lexis

- lexis typical of spontaneous speech: colloquial, idiomatic, clichéd, vague

- structural features of spontaneous speech: ellipsis, deixis, incomplete structures.

Using the key questions to write an analysis

Activity 34

Read the following poem.

> **Take One Home for the Kiddies**
>
> On shallow straw, in shadeless glass,
> Huddled by empty bowls, they sleep:
> No dark, no dam, no earth, no grass –
> *Mam, get us one of them to keep.*
> Living toys are something novel,
> But it soon wears off somehow.
> Fetch the shoebox, fetch the shovel –
> *Mam, we're playing funerals now.*
>
> *Philip Larkin*

1 Examine in a small group how Larkin constructs two different voices in this poem and the effect his technique has on the reader. Focus on the contrast between third and first person voices, in particular:

  a the third person voice of the poet.

  - What attitude does the poet's voice suggest towards the animals in the pet shop and the 'kiddies'?

  - How does the choice of lexis convey this attitude?

  b the first person voice of the children.

  - What attitude does their voice suggest towards the animals?

  - How does their lexis convey this attitude?

2 As a class, read the following analysis of the voices in this poem. Discuss how this analysis meets the requirement of AO1 to use 'concepts and approaches from integrated linguistic and literary study', and the requirement of AO2 to 'analyse the ways in which structure, form and language shape meanings'. Think about how this commentary:

- focuses on the poet's technique rather than 'what the poem is about'
- uses terms from both literary and linguistic study
- uses statements supported by specific evidence from the text
- concentrates on the creation and use of voice.

Larkin's poetic voice is used in stanza 1 to describe the animals for sale in a pet shop. The adjectives in line 1, 'shallow straw', 'shadeless glass', are balanced to emphasise that the animals are neglected, an impression strengthened by the verbs 'Huddled' and 'sleep' in line 2. Their lives are defined by what they lack, as the multiple repetition of 'no' in line 3 makes clear. They are imprisoned in an artificial environment that is the opposite of their natural habitat, a point underlined by the rhyme on 'glass' and 'grass', which draws a contrast.

Larkin's voice seems at first to be detached and unemotional. However, his compassion for the animals is brought out by sharp observation: 'Huddled by empty bowls'. By contrast, the indifference of the pet shop owner, who sees the animals merely as commodities ('Take One Home for the Kiddies'), is matched by the strident, imperative voices of the children: *'Mam, get us one of them to keep'*. They see the animals as 'living toys' without individuality ('one of them').

In the second stanza, Larkin's tone of voice becomes bitter as he reflects on the callous fate of the animals: 'Fetch the shoebox, fetch the shovel'. In the pet shop, they were treated as objects for sale; taken to a 'home' that fails to provide them with one, they are treated as playthings, equally 'novel' whether they are alive or dead. The fact that the children make no allowance for the difference is shown by *'Mam, we're playing funerals now'*. The voice here has exactly the same register, and takes exactly the same form, as that in line 4 with which it is ironically balanced. By contrast with the poet's more reflective, sympathetic voice, that of the children is self-centred and thoughtless. For them, a 'funeral' is merely a matter of 'playing'.

Take it further

Make your own collection of poems that seem to you to have interesting or distinctive voices, whether it is the poetic voice or characters' voices within the poem. You could try Emily Dickinson, Sylvia Plath, Jean Binta Breeze, Ted Hughes's 'Crow' or T.S. Eliot's 'The Waste Land'. Make notes on the way they construct voice and how they make use of spontaneous speech features *and* poetic crafting.

Writing in the exam

Note that the commentary above is focused on the poet's technique and how it is used to create voice/voices. You can show the examiner that you are doing the same by avoiding phrases like 'This poem is about cruelty to animals' and 'The poet feels sorry for the pets'. Instead, use phrases such as 'The poet's voice is created by …' or 'By contrast with the poet's voice, the children's voices are …'.

6   Analysing voices in narrative

Your unseen exam in Unit 1 may include an extract from:

- a novel or short story, or

- a work of non-fiction such as an autobiography or a travel book.

In novels and short stories, you need to distinguish between two kinds of 'voice': the voice of the narrator and the voices of characters in the story. In the light of this distinction, the exam may ask you to analyse:

- the way the narrator's voice is created by the writer, OR

- the voice of a character, OR

- the way in which dialogue between characters is used in the narrative.

This section introduces you to a range of voices in narrative. Its also acts as a bridge between Section A of Unit 1 and Section B, where the focus will be on how writers represent voice in prose fiction. The frameworks you learn to use in this section will be developed further when you undertake a detailed study of your prescribed fiction text.

First person voice: autobiographical fiction

This is the voice of the main character in a novel telling his/her own story.

Activity 35

Read the extract below from *The Adventures of Huckleberry Finn* by Mark Twain. Huck, a young boy living in the American deep south, is telling the reader about his adventures with Tom Sawyer in an earlier novel by Mark Twain.

> You don't know about me, without you have read a book by the name of 'The Adventures of Tom Sawyer', but that ain't no matter. That book was made by Mr Mark Twain, and he told the truth, mainly. There was things which he stretched, but mainly he told the truth. That is nothing. I never seen anybody but lied, one time or another, without it was Aunt Polly, or the widow, or maybe Mary.
> 5 Aunt Polly – Tom's Aunt Polly, she is – and Mary, and the Widow Douglas, is all told about in that book – which is mostly a true book; with some stretchers, as I said before.
> Now the way that the book winds up, is this: Tom and me found the money that the robbers hid in the cave, and it made us rich. We got six thousand dollars apiece – all gold. It was an awful sight of money when it was piled up. Well, Judge Thatcher, he took it and put it out at interest, and it fetched
> 10 us a dollar a day apiece, all the year round – more than a body could tell what to do with. The Widow Douglas, she took me for her son, and allowed she would sivilise me; but it was rough living in the house all the time, considering how dismal regular and decent the widow was in all her ways, and so when I couldn't stand it no longer, I lit out. I got into my old rags and my sugar-hogshead again, and was free and satisfied. But Tom Sawyer he hunted me up and said he was going to start a band of
> 15 robbers, and I might join if I would go back to the widow and be respectable. So I went back.

1 Talk to a partner, talk and make notes about:

   a your first impressions of the narrator, Huck

   b the writer's use of lexis and grammar to create the persona of a boy

   c the kind of relationship the writer sets up between Huck and the reader.

2 Share your ideas from the pair work in a small group. Then copy and complete the chart below.

Huck's idiolect		
Language feature	Example	Impression given of character
direct address to the reader	'you don't know about me'	
colloquial language	'that ain't no matter'	
regional dialect terms	'I lit out', 'some stretchers'	
conversational phrases	'as I said before'	
deixis [context-dependent language]	'Aunt Polly, and the Widow'	
repetition	'he told the truth, mainly' 'mostly a true book'	
co-ordinating conjunctions used to begin sentences	'But Tom Sawyer … So I went back'	

Add any further features you think resemble spontaneous speech and give us the impression of listening to an oral narrative.

3 Write two or three paragraphs from your own autobiographical novel, creating a distinctive voice for yourself. Include some language features from your chart about Huck and any others that help you to construct your voice. Plan your writing by:

- choosing an episode from your earlier life about which you still have strong feelings
- deciding on the kind of persona you wish to create for yourself
- deciding on how you want your reader to respond to your voice, exactly.

Independent research

Sample the style of some recent autobiographical and first person novels. Jeanette Winterson (eg *Oranges Are Not The Only Fruit*), Kate Atkinson (eg *Behind the Scenes at the Museum*), Ian McEwan (eg *Enduring Love*), Martin Amis (eg *House of Meetings*), Iain Banks (eg *The Wasp Factory*) and Nick Hornby (eg *High Fidelity*) have all written in this style. Consider the kind of relationship they construct with the reader, and how they do this.

Third person voice: 'omniscient' and 'over the shoulder'

Third person narrators are not characters in the story. They describe events by standing above the action and informing the reader 'he did this' or 'she went there'. For this reason, a third person narrator is sometimes termed **omniscient** or god-like; they are an all-knowing voice able to tell us the thoughts and feelings of the characters.

Some third person narrators are less detached than this. They stand closer to the characters in the story. They often use an **'over the shoulder'** voice, writing in the third person but giving us the inward viewpoint of a character as well as describing the context in which we see them.

Activity 36

Read the complete short story below. Ten-year-old Myop lives in the Deep South of America at a time when prejudice against black people was strong.

'The Flowers' by Alice Walker

It seemed to Myop as she skipped lightly from hen house to pigpen to smokehouse that the days had never been as beautiful as these. The air held a keenness that made her nose twitch. The harvesting of corn and cotton, peanuts and squash, made each day a golden surprise that caused excited little tremors to run up her jaws.

5 Myop carried a short, knobbly stick. She struck out at random at chickens she liked, and worked out the beat of a song on the fence around the pigpen. She felt light and good in the warm sun. She was ten, and nothing existed for her but her song, the stick clutched in her dark brown hand, and the tat-de-ta-ta-ta of accompaniment.

Turning her back on the rusty boards of her family's share-cropper cabin, Myop walked along the
10 fence till it ran into the stream made by the spring. Around the spring, where the family got drinking water, silver ferns and wild-flowers grew. Along the shallow banks pigs rooted. Myop watched the tiny white bubbles disrupt the thin black scale of soil and the water that silently rose and slid away down the stream.

She had explored the woods behind the house many times. Often, in late autumn, her mother
15 took her to gather nuts among the fallen leaves. Today she made her own path, bouncing this way and that way, vaguely keeping an eye out for snakes. She found, in addition to various common but pretty ferns and leaves, an armful of strange blue flowers with velvety ridges and a sweetsuds bush full of the brown, fragrant buds.

By twelve o'clock, her arms laden with the sprigs of her findings, she was a mile or more from
20 home. She had often been as far before, but the strangeness of the land made it not as pleasant as her usual haunts. It seemed gloomy in the little cove in which she found herself. The air was damp, the silence close and deep.

Myop began to circle back to the house, back to the peacefulness of the morning. It was then she stepped smack into his eyes. Her heel became lodged in the broken ridge between brow and nose, and
25 she reached down quickly, unafraid, to free herself. It was only when she saw his naked grin that she gave a little yelp of surprise.

He had been a tall man. From feet to neck covered a long space. His head lay beside him. When she pushed back the leaves and layers of earth and debris, Myop saw that he'd had large white teeth, all of them cracked or broken, long fingers, and very big bones. All his clothes had rotted away except
30 some threads of blue denim from his overalls. The buckles of the overalls had turned green.

Myop gazed around the spot with interest. Very near where she'd stepped into the head was a wild pink rose. As she picked it to add to her bundle she noticed a raised mound, a ring, around the rose's root. It was the rotted remains of a noose, a bit of shredding plowline, now blending benignly into the soil.

35 Around an overhanging limb of a great spreading oak clung another piece. Frayed, rotted, bleached and frazzled – barely there – but spinning restlessly in the breeze. Myop laid down her flowers.

And the summer was over.

1 Look carefully at paragraphs 1 to 5 with a partner. Talk and make brief notes about:

   a what the narrator tells us about Myop's thoughts and feelings

   b how the narrator's choice of lexis draws us close to the 10-year-old girl and her way of seeing things. Quote three or four examples.

   c how each paragraph marks a new and different stage in Myop's journey from home.

2 Compare your ideas from the pair work in a small group. Then look at paragraphs 6 to 10. Discuss the following questions:

   a What does Myop find?

   b How does the narrator signal that Myop has only a limited understanding of what she finds?

   c What does the narrator achieve by using a third person 'over the shoulder' voice in this story?

   Then, working together, rewrite paragraphs 6 to 10 in the first person so that we see all the events through Myop's eyes and hear her own voice.

3 As a class, compare the writing you have produced with the original. What differences does narrative voice make to the effect of this story, and in what ways? Why would 'The Flowers' have had a quite different effect on the reader in Myop's first person voice?

Key terms
Narrative viewpoints:
   omniscient
   'over the shoulder'

Third person voice: 'free indirect style'

Activity 37

Free indirect style is when the narrative voice is third person but adopts the thoughts and feelings of the character.

Read the extract below from Tim Winton's novel *Cloudstreet*. Sam Pickles has lost four fingers in an accident and is in hospital. His wife Dolly is unsympathetic and curses the family's bad luck. Their daughter Rose has been aware for some time of the tensions in the marriage.

> After her mother left, Rose sat by the bedside and watched him sleep. She hated him sometimes, he was so hopeless. At times she wanted to hit him, to pick up a lump of four-be-two and snot him with it. He was a grown man and yet he didn't have a pinch of sense in him. But he wasn't mean, like the old girl was turning mean. She had to put up with all these catastrophes, so maybe she had a right, but the old man still made you love him. They'd had good times together, all of them, but something sour was coming into everything, and it'd been happening all year. Everything was falling to bits. When the old man was home they fought and swore. The old girl hammered him night and day and he went out and lost money. Even now she didn't know whether to put a cool hand on his brow or shake him by the throat. He looked so pale and busted. Oh, he'd made her laugh so many times, making a dill of himself to make her happy. He remembered what she liked, he told her adult things sometimes, and stories from his stockriding days. Rose saw through him; she knew he was always going to be useless, but she loved him. Hell, he was her father.
> Sam began to snore. Rose pressed her lips together and waited.

1 In a small group, compare the voice in the last two sentences with the voice in the rest of the extract.

   a What indications are there that the writer, for much of this extract, is presenting Rose's thoughts to us directly?

   b Quote particular phrases which sound like Rose's thoughts expressed in her own idiom.

   c How can you distinguish between Winton's narrative voice and Rose's voice? How fine a line is it?

2 Share your findings from the group work. Then consider the reasons why writers may choose an 'internal' third person style like this rather than a first person style. Think about:

- taking the reader inside a character's mind to understand their thoughts and feelings more intimately

- creating empathy between the reader and the character(s)

  BUT

- still remaining detached enough to show differences between one character's viewpoint and others'

- still remaining detached enough to show that a character's viewpoint is limited, biased, immature, etc.

Take it further

Write several paragraphs of a story in the third person, which uses a mixture of the omniscient narrator's voice and free indirect style. Your purpose is to illustrate the main conclusions you came to in your class discussion about the use of free indirect style as a narrative technique.

Writing in the exam

If you are given an extract from a novel or short story, make sure you identify the voice (or voices) in it correctly. Is it a first person narrator? A character or characters? A third person narrator? A combination of these?

Dual or multiple narrative voices

Novelists construct multiple voices through dialogue, the direct speech of characters embedded within a narrative. This will be a major focus of your work for Section B of the exam: see pages 65 to 89 below.

Novels can also incorporate more than one narrative voice where the story is broken up into sections and told by different first person narrators.

Activity 38

1 Note down the titles of any novels you know in which:

  a the narrative includes letters, diaries or documents written in voices other than the narrator's

  b the novel has a frame story told by a principal narrator, within which are the narratives of several other characters told in their own voices.

2 Consider what a novelist might want to achieve by using a variety of narrative voices in the ways listed above. As a class, think about:

- creating suspense or mystery

- interpreting the same events from different viewpoints

- involving the reader more closely with the lives of the characters.

Activity 39

Read the extract below from Zoe Heller's novel, *Notes on a Scandal*. The first person narrator is Barbara, a middle-aged teacher. Sheba, her younger colleague, is having a relationship with one of her pupils.

1 March 1998

The other night at dinner, Sheba talked about the first time that she and the Connolly boy kissed. I had heard most of it before, of course, there being few aspects of the Connolly business that Sheba had not described to me several times over. But this time round, something new came up. I happened to ask her if anything about the first embrace had surprised her. She laughed. Yes, the *smell* of the whole thing had been surprising, she said. She hadn't anticipated his personal odour and if she had, she would probably have guessed at something teenagey: bubble gum, cola, feet.

When the moment arrived, what I actually inhaled was soap, tumble-dried laundry. He smelled of scrupulous self-maintenance. You know the washing-machine fug that envelops you sometimes, walking past the basement vents of buildings? Like that. So clean, Barbara. Never any of that cheese and onion breath that the other kids have ...

Every night since we came to Eddie's house, Sheba has been talking to me like this. She sits at the kitchen table looking out on the green darkness of Eddie's garden. I sit across from her, watching her nervous fingers score ice-skating loops in the plastic tablecloth. It's often pretty strong stuff she tells me in that newsreader's voice of hers. But then, one of the many things I have always admired about Sheba is her capacity to talk about low things and make them seem perfectly decent. We don't have secrets, Sheba and I.

The first time I saw him undress, you know what I thought of, Barbara? Fresh garden vegetables wrapped in a clean white hanky. Mushrooms fresh from the soil. No, really. He was edible. He washed his hair every night. Imagine! It was limp with cleanness. The vanity of adolescence, probably. Or, no – perhaps the anxiety of it. His body was a new toy still: he hadn't learned to treat it with the indifferent neglect of adults.

1 In a small group, compare Barbara's voice with the voice of Sheba which she quotes to us. Use the notes below.

Barbara's voice	Sheba's voice
lexical choices: 'the first embrace', 'personal odour'	lexical choices: 'soap, tumble-dried laundry', 'Mushrooms fresh from the soil'
level of formality: 'the Connolly business', 'her capacity to talk about low things'	level of formality: 'The first time I saw him undress', 'He was edible'
sentence construction: 'The other night at dinner, Sheba talked about ...'	sentence construction: 'You know what I thought of, Barbara?', 'No, really', 'Imagine!'

2 Share your findings from the group work. Then discuss:

a how the two voices reflect the different characters and values of Barbara and Sheba

b what effect on the reader the contrast between these two voices has. For example, do you feel more sympathy for one character than the other? What is the effect on you of the absence of a first person narrative voice?

Voice in non-fiction: travel writing

Activity 40

Read the extract below from Bill Bryson's *Notes on a Small Island*. Bryson is travelling round Britain and has reached Oxford. He is not impressed.

Oxfordshire County Council

My gripe with Oxford is that so much of it is ugly. Come with me now down Merton Street and I will show you what I mean. Note, as we stroll past the backs of Christ Church, the studied calm of Corpus Christi, the soft golden glow of Merton, that we are immersed in an architectural treasure house, one of the densest assemblages of historic buildings in
5 the world, and that Merton Street presents us with an unquestionably becoming prospect of gabled buildings, elaborate wrought-iron gates and fine seventeenth- and eighteenth-century townhouses. Several of the houses have been mildly disfigured by the careless addition of electrical wires to their facades … but never mind. They are easily overlooked. But what is this inescapable intrusion at the bottom? Is it an electrical substation? No, it is
10 the Merton College Warden's Quarters, a little dash of mindless sixties excrescence foisted on an otherwise largely flawless street.

Now come with me while we backtrack to Kybald Street, a forgotten lane lost amid a warren of picturesque little byways between Merton Street and the High. At its eastern extremity Kybald Street ends in a pocket-sized square that positively cries out for a small
15 fountain and maybe some benches. But what we find instead is a messy jumble of double- and triple-parked cars. Now on to Oriel Square: an even messier jumble of abandoned vehicles. Then on up Cornmarket (avert your gaze; this is *truly* hideous) and finally let us stop, exhausted and dispirited, outside the unconscionable concrete eyesore that is the University Offices on the absurdly named Wellington Square. No, let's not. Let's pass back
20 down Cornmarket, through the horrible, low-ceilinged, ill-lit drabness of the Clarendon Shopping Centre, out on to Queen Street, past the equally unadorable Westgate Shopping Centre and the central library with its heartless, staring windows and come to rest at the outsized pustule that is the head office of Oxfordshire County Council.

1 With a partner, copy and complete the chart below.

Bryson's narrative voice: how does it convey his attitude to Oxford?		
Narrative device	**Textual illustration**	**Bryson's purpose and the effect on the reader**
direct address to the reader		
use of contrast		
use of imagery (simile and metaphor)		
use of pejorative (depreciative) language		
varied sentence lengths and structures		

2 Share your findings from the group work. Then imagine this narrative is to be used as the basis for the soundtrack of a TV documentary, *Bill Bryson's Oxford*. Talk about:

a what (if anything) you would change about the writing, and why

b what tone of voice you would want Bryson to use at particular points. Pick out words and phrases he should emphasise, give a certain intonation to, speak slowly, speak more quickly, etc.

3 Write EITHER a first person narrative OR a TV documentary soundtrack about a place towards which you have strong feelings, positive or negative. Annotate your writing to show how you created the voice of the piece and the effect you meant it to have on the reader or viewer.

Writing in the exam

If you are given an extract from non-fiction, focus on the way in which the writer's voice conveys their attitudes. The table on Bryson's narrative voice above directs you to the kind of language features to look for in any non-fiction text.

Voice in non-fiction: autobiography

Activity 41

Read the extract below from Clarissa Dickson-Wright's autobiography *Spilling the Beans*. The writer is best known for her appearances with Jennifer Paterson on the TV cookery programme *Two Fat Ladies*. She was trained as a lawyer at Gray's Inn with Tony Blair, the former Prime Minister. At the start of this extract she is visiting the Great Orme in Llandudno during filming of her TV series.

I stayed at the St Tudno hotel where the crab risotto was so good I ate it three nights out of five. We went up the Orme on the funicular railway with a choir singing all the way: it was enchanting. I was reminded of a young man who was at Gray's Inn with me, who was also Welsh and had a voice like an angel, rather at odds with his face which showed his other
5 passion – for rugby. After dining in Hall he would walk home singing quietly to himself, but as his voice would have filled the Albert Hall without a microphone he was often arrested for being drunk and disorderly. One day I was in Marlborough Street Magistrates' Court waiting for my case to come up when my friend was brought up. The beak, in order to teach him a lesson, happened to fine him more money than he had on him. Looking about, my friend saw
10 me. 'Hang on a minute, sir,' he cried with delight, and looking across to counsel's benches shouted, 'Hey Clarrie, lend us a tenner.' Greatly embarrassed I did and off he went. He's a judge now and a pillar of the community but he knows who he is and I hope he's still singing …

This [the filming in Llandudno] was in 1997, the year you elected Miranda [Tony Blair] with
15 a landslide, but curiously I find so few people who own up to voting for him. I remember writing in *Scotland on Sunday* that this would prove a disaster. I was never conned by our Tone, not even a little, and I think anyone who remembered him from when he was younger knew what a slippery customer he was. The previous year Jennifer and I had been presenting prizes at the Comedy Awards and oddly enough so was the Leader of the Opposition as he
20 was then. No one was talking to him in the green room and he was roving about rather like those people at cocktail parties who don't know anyone and so are for ever hailing some illusionary friend at the other end of the room and striding purposefully through the crowd, only to repeat the performance a few minutes later. I took the opportunity to speak to him. I doubt he remembered me although he said he did, and it was like talking to a psychopath,
25 where nothing moved behind the eyes and there was this constant attempt to work out what the other person was going to say and allude to it first, as if scoring brownie points to prove his cleverness. I am not easily frightened and yet I found him a very frightening man.

1 In a small group, analyse the writer's voice in these three parts of the extract:

- when she is recounting her experience in Wales
- when she is recounting her story about her friend from Gray's Inn
- when she is recounting her experience at the Comedy Awards.

How does the voice change in the course of the extract? How are these changes signalled:

a through the writer's choice of lexis?

b through the way the reader is addressed and positioned?

c through changes in verb tenses?

d through the writer's mixture of indirect and direct speech?

2 Share your conclusions from the group work. Then consider the *structure* of this piece which, like most autobiographies, is based on memories. How would you describe the structure:

- tightly constructed?
- loosely constructed?
- rambling and unstructured?

How does its structure help create the writer's distinctive voice?

Independent research

Other non-fiction texts you might sample include: *The Railway Man*, Eric Lomax; *An Evil Cradling*, Brian Keenan; *Some Other Rainbow*, John McCarthy and Jill Morrell; *Long Walk to Freedom*, Nelson Mandela.

Key questions for the exam

When faced with a passage from fiction or non-fiction in the unseen exam, the list of questions below will guide you towards making a clear and focused analysis.

Key question 1

Whose voice is speaking in the extract?

- the first person narrator

- a character, or characters, in the narrative

- the third person narrator: for example, omniscient, 'over the shoulder' or free indirect style

Key question 2

How is the voice created?

- through the choice of lexis

- through the use of spontaneous speech features

- through the dialogue: for example how it is tagged and punctuated, and its extent

- through the use of literary features: for example, figurative language, clause and sentence patterns, sentences constructed to achieve a particular effect

- through a combination of these

Always be as specific as you can about lexical and literary features.

Key question 3

What is the register of the voice in the passage?

- introspective, reflective, cynical, angry, sad, etc.

- if the passage is in the form of dialogue, are the registers of the voices different? Do they contrast?

Key question 4

How is the reader's response controlled and directed?

- through direct address to the reader.

- through the way the reader is positioned by the narrator: for example, externally, internally, seeing events 'over the shoulder' of a character.

- does the narrative perspective shift within the passage?

Key question 5

What is the combined impact of all this on the reader – in other words how does the writing assist the reader in placing the characters in some sort of perspective?

7   Tackling Section A of the exam

Section A is examined through unseen texts; that is, texts that are new to you. You are allowed 1 hour to answer THREE questions on them: question 1(a) (i), question 1 (a) (ii), and question 1 (b). There is a total of 50 marks.

The unseen texts

You will be given three short unseen texts to read. They will be drawn from a list that could include the following:

A transcript of:

- a spontaneous conversation
- a telephone call
- a TV broadcast
- a radio broadcast
- an email
- a weblog
- a chat room conversation
- a speech
- an oral narrative.

A passage from:

- a novel or story
- a non-fiction book
- a drama written for the theatre, television or radio
- poetry.

There will be three questions on the unseen texts.

Question 1 (a) (i) is likely to ask you to find examples in the three texts of a common linguistic element, for example, spoken language features. [6 marks]

Question 1 (a) (ii) is likely to ask you to comment on the *function* of the examples you have chosen in the three texts or the way they help contribute to the construction of voice. [4 marks]

Question 1 (b) is likely to ask you to analyse the way *two* of the speakers or writers craft their texts. [40 marks]

> ## Assessment objectives
>
> Question 1 (a) (i) and Question 1 (a) (ii) are assessed by AO1. When you answer these questions you need to use suitable linguistic frameworks and terms and write in a clear and fluent style.
>
> Question 1 (b) is assessed equally by AOs 2 and 3. When you answer this question consider how the language, form and structure of the texts convey meaning. You will also need to show a knowledge of the context of texts and why it is important.

Activity 42

This activity is an example of a Section A exam. Read Texts **A**, **B** and **C**. Then answer the sample questions that follow.

A This is a transcript of a live conversation. A family is chatting over Sunday lunch.

M: Mother
J: Jack (14)
T: Tom (16)
F: Father

M: will someone please pass me the mustard

T: and Petrov (.) you know (.) well everyone slates him

J: yeah (.) and ummm whats his name (.) number 4 //

F: // Mellberg

5   T: // Mellberg

M: mustard

F: how can you eat that stuff (.) just the colour makes me heave //

T: // and the stink

J: they were class yesterday umm radio WM said (.) world class

10 M: mmm I love it (.) and horseradish

F: what a goal from Barry

T: goal of the month //

J: // season

M: Yorkshire anybody

15 J: // yeah

T: // yes please

F: // yeah

B This is an extract from a personal weblog.

So after another agonisingly long wait for news I get the phone call, and this time it isn't the news I want to hear. The job, as afore-mentioned, has been offered to someone else … gutted.

Kinda feels like a punch in the stomach, I really wanted it and was quietly
5   confident. So, after a two month long process I am back at square one, there are no prizes for second place and other applications have been unfruitful.

On the plus side (a very small plus side) I got some good feedback from the company who regarded me as an excellent candidate, with the correct skills. They said I was enthusiastic and professional throughout and should be very pleased
10 with my performance, which considering the number of applicants I suppose I am. What it came down to, they said, was that the other candidate had more experience and that clinched it.

Whatcha gonna do?

C This is an extract from the novel *Vernon God Little* by DBC Pierre. The narrator is a 15-year-old Texan boy blamed for a high school massacre.

> I sit waiting between shafts of light from a row of doorways, naked except for my school shoes and Thursday's underwear. Looks like I'm the first one they rounded up so far. Still, you wouldn't want to be here today. You'd remember Clarence somebody, that ole black guy who was in the news last winter. He was a psycho who dozes in this same
> 5   wooden hall, right on camera. The news said how little he cared about the effects of his crimes. By 'effects' I think they meant axe-wounds. Ole Clarence whatever was shaved clean like an animal, with jelly jar glasses and all, the type of glasses worn by people with mostly gums but no teeth. They built him a zoo cage in court. They sentenced him to death.

Read the exam advice below as a class before answering the questions. Then work together to produce your own model answers.

Question 1 (a) (i)

The texts all contain aspects of spoken language. For each text, identify THREE spoken language features and provide an example of each spoken word feature you have identified. [6 marks]

Question 1 (a) (ii)

Comment on the function of these spoken language features within Text **A**, Text **B** and Text **C**.

[4 marks]

Question 1 (b)

Text B is an extract from a weblog. Text C is an excerpt from a novel. Both include features of spoken language. The structure and content of each text is influenced by the context in which it has been produced or is received.

Examine how the writers:

- integrate aspects of spoken language into their text

- craft each text to meet the expectations of their audience/purpose/context. [40 marks]

Exam advice

Question 1 (a) (i)

This is a short answer. It asks you to 'identify' spoken language features and 'provide examples'. So you do this and write them down. You might write about Text **A**:

1 The participants overlap at times, for example:

   F: makes me heave //

   T: // and the stink

2 Jack uses a cooperative signal:

   T: everyone slates him //

   J: // yeah

3 The participants sometimes use minor sentences:

   J: number 4   T: goal of the season

Question 1 (a) (ii)

It is a straightforward matter to relate your examples to the speaker's purpose. Try it. You need only write a sentence for each, for example:

T uses a cooperative signal to show he agrees with F's comments about mustard.

Question 1 (b)

This is a longer answer. It calls for analysis and explanation. Note that there is no requirement to compare the two texts.

Here in note form are some of the points an examiner would reward for comment on Text B:

Spoken language features:

- colloquialism ('gutted')
- filler/hedge ('kinda')
- cliché ('back to square one')
- use of present tense to report an event from the past ('I get the phone call …')
- ellipsis ('… gutted')

Evidence of crafting to develop an individual voice:

- clear sense of chronology/sequence
- reference back to previous blog entries ('as afore-mentioned')
- figurative language ('feels like a kick in the stomach')
- reported speech ('They said I was enthusiastic …')

Make your own similar notes on Text **C**.

General points

Leave yourself about 40 minutes for Question 1 (b) – 20 minutes on each text. The majority of marks are for this question.

In answering Question 1 (b), you should:

- give yourself some thinking time before you write
- annotate the passages before writing but do this *briefly*: the examiner cannot mark 'rough notes'
- interpret the verb 'craft' to mean 'choose the lexis, grammar and structure of the text to create voice/meet a particular purpose'
- avoid feature spotting only: identify and explain
- use linguistic terminology (though not for show)
- remember that almost all texts have an audience and that their audience's expectations/responses help shape the text.

Writing in the exam

Remember, never write about 'what the text is about'. Always write about 'how the voice in the text is created and used'. Recite this to yourself before you open the exam paper.

B Voices in literature

This section supports you in studying your prescribed novel, or collection of short stories, for the Section B exam. The exam question on your text will focus on the way voice is constructed and used by the writer. The 'voice' could be: the voice of a first person narrator; the voice of a character, or the voices of characters; the voice of a third person narrator; or a mixture of these.

Assessment objectives

Two assessment objectives are used to assess your Section B exam answer:

AO1 (20 marks) – Select and apply relevant concepts and approaches from integrated linguistic and literary study, using appropriate terminology and accurate, coherent written expression.

AO2 (30 marks) – Demonstrate detailed critical understanding in analysing the ways in which structure, form and language shape meanings in a range of spoken and written texts.

Thus AO2 requires you to *analyse* how your author uses structure, form and language to create and convey voice. AO1 requires you to use linguistic and literary concepts and terms to *explain* how your author does this.

In the material that follows, the 'Section B texts' boxes indicate which prescribed texts each sub-section is most relevant to. However, all the activities are designed to give you practice in commenting on the creation and use of voice in narrative. Working on texts other than your own will increase your skill and confidence in analysing your author's techniques. It will also help you prepare for the unseen exam in Section A. Note that for all activities on *Dubliners*, page references to the 2000 Penguin edition (ISBN 978-0-14-118245-2) are given.

1 Analysing first person narrators' voices

Section B texts

The activities in this sub-section are most relevant to:

Paddy Clarke Ha Ha Ha

The Color Purple

Restoration

Address Unknown

Dubliners ('The Sisters', 'An Encounter', 'Araby')

The Bloody Chamber ('Puss-in-Boots', 'The Bloody Chamber', 'The Tiger Bride')

In novels or short stories, the first person narrator's voice is a fictional 'I' or 'me' created by the writer. The narrator tells his or her own story. The reader normally 'overhears' but is sometimes addressed directly. First person narratives can also be written as if in diary form or as letters.

This sub-section uses the prescribed texts to help you:

- comment on the way different first person voices are constructed

- plan and write analyses of voice in short extracts.

The first person voices of young people: *Paddy Clarke Ha Ha Ha* and *The Color Purple*

Activity 43

Read the two novel openings below.

A *Paddy Clarke Ha Ha Ha* by Roddy Doyle

We were coming down our road. Kevin stopped at a gate and bashed it with his stick.

It was Missis Quigley's gate; she was always looking out of the window but she never did anything.

– Quigley!

5 – Quigley!

– Quigley Quigley Quigley!

Liam and Aidan turned down their cul-de-sac. We said nothing; they said nothing.

Liam and Aidan had a dead mother. Missis O'Connell was her name.

– It'd be brilliant, wouldn't it? I said.

10 – Yeah, said Kevin. – Cool.

We were talking about having a dead ma. Sinbad, my little brother, started crying. Liam was in my class in school. He dirtied his trousers one day – the smell of it rushed at us like the blast of heat when an oven door was opened – and the master did nothing. He didn't shout or slam his desk with his leather or anything. He told us to fold our arms and go asleep and when

15 we did he carried Liam out of the class. He didn't come back for ages and Liam didn't come back at all.

James O'Keefe whispered, – If I did a gick in me pants he'd kill me!

– Yeah.

– It's not fair, said James O'Keefe. – So it's not.

20 The master, Mister Hennessey, hated James O'Keefe. He'd be writing something on the board with his back to us and he'd say, – O'Keefe, I know you're up to something down there. Don't let me catch you. He said it one morning and James O'Keefe wasn't even in. He was at home with the mumps.

B *The Color Purple* by Alice Walker

You better not never tell nobody but *God. It'd kill your mammy*.

Dear God,

I am fourteen years old. ~~I am~~ I have always been a good girl. Maybe you can give me a sign letting me know what is happening to me.

5   Last spring after little Lucious come I heard them fussing. He was pulling on her arm. She say It too soon, Fonso, I ain't well. Finally he leave her alone. A week go by, he pulling on her arm again. She say Naw, I ain't gonna. Can't you see I'm already half dead, an all of these chilren.

     She went to visit her sister doctor over Macon. Left me to see after the others.
10 He never had a kine word to say to me. Just say You gonna do what your mammy wouldn't. First he put his thing up gainst my hip and sort of wiggle it around. Then he grab hold my titties. Then he push his thing inside my pussy. When that hurt, I cry. He start to choke me, saying You better shut up and git used to it.

     But I don't never git used to it. And now I feels sick every time I be the one
15 to cook. My mama she fuss at me an look at me. She happy, cause he good to her now. But too sick to last long.

1 Share your responses as a class to these openings. Do they appeal to you? What immediate impressions of the first person narrators do they give?

2 In a small group, copy and complete the chart below to show what you can gather from each opening about the story, the setting and the characters. Include as much detail as you wish.

Story/characters/setting	*Paddy Clarke Ha Ha Ha*	*The Color Purple*
What's happening?		
Where's it happening?		
Who's involved?		
Who's telling the story?		

3 Compare your findings from the group work. Then turn your attention to:

  a the tone and register of both these narrative voices

  b their idiolects

  c what their idiolects show about the character of the narrators (Paddy in **A**, Celie in **B**).

Work together to fill in a copy of the chart below.

The voice and character of the narrators		
Paddy in *Paddy Clarke Ha Ha Ha*	**Celie in *The Color Purple***	**Points about character**
Lexis, eg 'We were talking about having a dead ma'	Lexis, eg 'She say Naw, I ain't gonna'	
Register (level of formality)	Register (level of formality)	
Sentence structure (syntax), eg 'Liam and Aidan had a dead mother. Missis O'Connell was her name'	Sentence structure (syntax), eg 'Left me to see after the others. He never had a kine word to say to me'	
Grammar	Grammar	
Language features resembling spontaneous speech	Language features resembling spontaneous speech	

4 Review your completed charts. Then discuss:

a How do Roddy Doyle and Alice Walker use the first person narrative voice to present Paddy and Celie respectively?

b Why do you think they have chosen a first person rather than a third person style of narration? What difference does it make?

5 Write an analysis of *one* of these openings. Show how the novelist creates the voice of the narrator and directs the reader's response to them to establish a perspective.

A first person narrative voice from the past: *Restoration*

Activity 44

Read the opening of Rose Tremain's novel *Restoration* below. Writing in the twentieth century, Tremain is trying to create the voice of a fictional male character, Merivel, who lives in London in the seventeenth century.

> I am, I discover, a very untidy man.
>
> Look at me. Without my periwig, I am an affront to neatness. My hair (what is left of it) is the colour of sand and wiry as hogs' bristles; my ears are of uneven size; my forehead is splattered with freckles; my nose, which of course my wig
> 5 can't conceal, however low I wear it, is unceremoniously flat, as if I had been hit at birth.
>
> Was I hit at birth? I do not believe so, as my parents were gentle and kindly people, but I will never know now. They died in a fire in 1662. My father had a nose like a Roman emperor. This straight, fierce nose would neaten up my face,
> 10 but alas, I don't possess it. Perhaps I am not my father's child? I am erratic, immoderate, greedy, boastful and sad. Perhaps I am the son of Amos Treefeller, the old man who made head-moulds for my father's millinery work? Like him, I am fond of the feel of objects made of polished wood. My telescope, for instance. For I admit, I find greater order restored to my brain from the placing of my hands
> 15 round this instrument of science than from what its lenses reveal to my eye. The stars are too numerous and too distant to restore to me anything but a terror at my own insignificance.

1 Discuss as a class the way Tremain constructs a realistic voice for the narrator.

Focus on:

- factual references which establish the seventeenth-century context

- Merivel's attitude to himself and how this is conveyed

- the familiarity with which Merivel addresses the reader, as if speaking aloud to an acquaintance.

Then look closely at the following aspects of lexis and grammar in the extract:

- the use of the present tense

- the use of **rhetorical questions**

- the use of conversational terms

- the use of slightly **archaic** 'old-fashioned' vocabulary and sentence constructions.

How do these features of language help to create the narrator's persona and establish his relationship with the reader?

2 In a small group read the extract below from a response on this passage. The task is to analyse how Tremain captures the voice of the narrator. Note that this is an extract, not the whole answer.

Tremain employs a range of linguistic and literary strategies to construct a plausible, engaging voice for the narrator. She creates the seventeenth-century context by having Merivel refer to his parents' death 'in a fire in 1662' and to his 'periwig'. His slightly archaic, stylised lexis and grammar also suggest a historical setting. For example, 'I am an affront to neatness' is a formal construction that we associate with the past, and the simile comparing his hair to 'hogs' bristles' confirms this, 'hog' being a term for a pig rarely used nowadays but common in earlier times.

The long complex sentences beginning 'For I admit …' again places the narrator's voice in the past. His lexical choice of 'For', meaning 'because', is typical of formal **written discourse** rather than colloquial speech. The somewhat **verbose** but balanced phrasing of the last sentence 'The stars are too numerous and distant to restore to me anything but a terror at my own insignificance' suggests a man with an educated vocabulary used to reflecting on life in an abstract, philosophical way.

The narrator's idiolect, however, has some features typical of informal speech. 'Look at me' is an **imperative** addressing the reader in a colloquial manner. Merivel seems to be speaking to us, taking us into his confidence. His tone is informal – 'My hair (what is left of it)' – and this impression is strengthened by his use of **interrogatives** such as 'Was I hit at birth?' which he goes on to answer himself, a common feature of oral narrative.

This commentary meets AO2 for 'analysing the ways in which structure, form and language shape meaning' because:

- it is specific, not vague, about the writer's use of language
- it makes statements which are supported with clear examples from the text
- it makes comments on the effect of the extract on the reader
- it recognises that it is the writer, Rose Tremain, who creates the voice of Merivel – the character is a fictional construct, not a real person.

Writing in the exam

In the exam you would have to go on to discuss how the narrator's voice is developed in other parts of the novel.

Take it further

Choose a short passage from your prescribed text which seems typical of the narrator's or the writer's voice. Follow the model on *Restoration* to make a close analysis of how this voice is created.

Key terms

rhetorical question
archaic
written discourse
verbose
imperative
interrogative

A first person narrative voice in feline form: *The Bloody Chamber*

Activity 45

Read the extract below from Angela Carter's short story 'Puss-in-Boots'. The narrator is a cat.

> Figaro here; Figaro, there, I tell you! Figaro upstairs, Figaro downstairs and – oh, my goodness me, this little Figaro can slip into my lady's chamber smart as you like at any time whatsoever that he takes the fancy for, don't you know, he's a cat of the world, cosmopolitan, sophisticated; he can tell when a furry friend is the Missus' best company. For what lady in all
> 5 the world could say 'no' to the passionate yet toujours discret advances of a fine marmalade cat? (Unless it be her eyes incontinently overflow at the slightest whiff of fur, which happened once, as you shall hear.)
>   A tom, sirs, a ginger tom and proud of it. Proud of his fine, white shirtfront that dazzles harmoniously against his orange and tangerine tessellations (oh! what a fiery suit of lights have
> 10 I); proud of his bird-entrancing eye and more than military whiskers; proud to a fault, some say, of his fine, musical voice.

1 Discuss in a small group how Carter constructs the cat's voice in this passage. Focus on:
- the cat's attitude towards himself and how Carter conveys this
- the relationship Carter creates between the narrator and the reader
- the use of conversational terms and structures
- the use of the first person and the third person.

2 Share your ideas from the group work. Then use the cat's description of himself 'for, don't you know, he's a cat of the world, cosmopolitan, sophisticated' to analyse how Carter's style and language evoke a strong impression of his vanity. Look in particular at:
- figurative language and **heightened language**
- words and phrases associated with the educated upper class
- **sentence** and **clause constructions**.

3 Write two paragraphs about how Carter creates the cat's voice. Use the bullet points in question **1** to write your first paragraph and the bullet points in question **2** to write your second.

Key terms
heightened language

sentence constructions

clause constructions

recipient

Writing in the exam
- In the exam, you would have to go on to discuss Carter's construction of voice in another story from *The Bloody Chamber*.
- Questions on first person narrative voice will ask you to analyse how the voice is constructed, *not* to say what is shown of the narrator's personality. Although the voice does help to construct the personality of the cat, you need to understand the difference between character and characterisation and focus your answer accordingly.

A first person narrative voice in letter form: *Address Unknown*

Read the extract below from Kressmann Taylor's novella *Address Unknown*. The narrative is made up entirely of an exchange of letters between the two central characters. This is part of the first letter in the exchange, written by Max, a Jewish art dealer living in San Francisco.

SCHULSE-EISENSTEIN GALLERIES

SAN FRANCISCO, CALIFORNIA, USA

Herrn Martin Schulse   November 12, 1932
Schloss Rantzenburg
Munich, Germany

My Dear Martin:
    Back in Germany! How I envy you! Although I have not seen it since my school days, the spell of *Unter den Linden* is still strong upon me – the breadth of intellectual freedom, the discussions, the music, the light-hearted comradeship. And now the old
5   Junker spirit, the Prussian arrogance and militarism are gone. You go to a democratic Germany, a land with deep culture and the beginnings of a fine political freedom. It will be a good life. Your new address is impressive and I rejoice that the crossing was so pleasant for Elsa and the young sprouts.
    As for me, I am not so happy. Sunday morning finds me a lonely bachelor without
10   aim. My Sunday home is now transported over the wide seas. The big old house on the hill – your welcome that said the day was not complete until we were together again! And our dear jolly Elsa, coming out beaming, grasping my hand and shouting "Max, Max!" and hurrying indoors to open my favourite *Schnapps*. The fine boys, too, especially your handsome young Heinrich; he will be a grown man before I set eyes upon him again.

---

1 Discuss as a class how Kressmann Taylor uses the conventions of letter writing and lexis, including register, to create Max's voice. Fill in a copy of the chart below to help you.

How Max's voice is established			
Use of letter writing conventions	**Effect on the reader**	**Choice of lexis, including register, when making:**	**Impression given of Max's character and attitudes**
The letterhead		Political references to the past	
The date		Political references to the past	
The form of address to the **recipient**		References in the German language	
The initial greetings		References to Martin's family	
The division of paragraphs		References to Martin's future life	

2 Consider the advantages and disadvantages for a writer of constructing a narrative exclusively through letters. In a small group, think about:

a the absence of a third person narrative voice

b the need to create a social context for the reader through the voices of the correspondents

c the possibilities of **juxtaposing** (setting side by side) two different voices

d the opportunity to reflect changes in relationship through **letter writing conventions** such as dates, addresses, **salutations** and **signings-off**.

If your prescribed text is *Address Unknown* or *The Color Purple*, return to this discussion as you explore further the writers' creation and use of voice.

Key terms

juxtaposition

letter writing conventions

salutation

signing-off

Writing in the exam

Two of the prescribed texts, *Address Unknown* and *The Color Purple*, are written entirely in the form of letters. If you are studying one of these, you need to be ready to analyse how your author uses the conventions of the letter form to convey voice. The activity on *Address Unknown* gives you important guidance on this.

A first person narrative voice in dialect: *The Color Purple*

Activity 47

Read the extract below from Alice Walker's novel *The Color Purple*.

In one of her letters to God, the novel's narrator Celie describes how she told her story of being sexually abused as a teenager to Shug Avery. Shug, a nightclub singer whom Celie idolises, is married to Grady. She knows that in the past Celie gave birth to two girls.

Dear God,

    Mr _____ and Grady gone off in the car together. Shug ast me could she sleep with me. She cold in her and Grady bed all alone. Us talk about this and that. Soon talk bout making love. Shug don't actually say making love. She say something nasty. She say fuck.

5   She ast me, How was it with your children daddy?
    The girls had a little separate room, I say, off to itself, connected to the house by a little plank walk. Nobody ever come in there but Mama. But one time when mama not at home, he come. Told me he want me to trim his hair. He bring the scissors and comb and brush and a stool. While I trim his hair he look at me funny. He a little nervous too, but I don't know why,

10 till he grab hold of me and cram me up tween his legs.
    I lay there quiet, listening to Shug breathe.
    It hurt me, you know, I say. I was just going on fourteen. I never thought bout men having nothing down there so big. It scare me just to see it. And the way it poke itself and grow.

15   Shug so quiet I think she sleep.
    After he through, I say, he make me finish trimming his hair.
    I sneak a look at Shug.
    Oh, Miss Celie, she say. And put her arms around me. They black and smooth and kind of glowy on the lamplight.

20   I start to cry too. I cry and cry and cry. Seem like it all come back to me, laying there in Shug's arms. How it hurt and how much I was surprise. How it stung while I finish trimming his hair. How the blood drip down my leg and mess up my stocking. How he don't never look at me straight after that. And Nettie. …
    Shug say, Wellsah, and I thought it was only whitefolks do freakish things like that.

---

1 Alice Walker presents this extract in Celie's first person narrative voice as if she is writing a letter to God. With a partner, identify the parts of the extract in which Celie:

   a describes the setting and events that happened there, eg 'Mr _____ and Grady gone off in the car together. Shug ast me could she sleep with me.'

   b reconstructs her conversation with Shug. Note that she uses the present tense 'say' to represent 'said'.

   Highlight **a** and **b** in different colours.

2 Talk and make notes in a small group about the way Celie's language differs from standard English. Describe the differences in your own words: don't worry about precise technical terms. Focus on:

- lexis: regional dialect terms? colloquialisms? **phonetic** representations of speech?
- grammar: verb tenses? ellipsis? omission of auxiliary verbs (to be, to have)? construction of negatives? pronouns?
- punctuation: **possessives**? contractions?

3 Share your findings from the group work. Celie expresses herself in African American Vernacular English (**AAVE**). Make a list of its most typical features, using the three main headings in question **2** above. Match each of these with an example from the text.

   Then discuss how Alice Walker's use of AAVE for Celie's voice helps to shape your response to her. How far do you think it works to:

   a bring out her innocence and vulnerability?

   b bring out the friendship between Celie and Shug (who also speaks AAVE)?

   c draw the reader close to her?

Independent research

If your prescribed text is *The Color Purple*, take part in a class or group research project into AAVE. Create a research plan that will allow you to find out:

- when and how it originated
- who uses it
- how widely it is spoken
- how authentic Alice Walker's representation of it in the novel is.

Summary

As a class, look back through the work you have done in this sub-section on the way writers construct first person narrative voices. Make a list of the main techniques you have identified. It could begin like this:

Writer's technique for constructing first person narrative voice	Examples	Purpose and effect on the reader
Writer creates a distinctive idiolect for the narrator, using lexis which evokes their personality and a specific social/regional/historical context.		
Writer gives the impression of the narrator speaking aloud by simulating features of spontaneous speech.		
Writer uses sentence forms and rhetorical structures that reflect the narrator's personality and mood, eg minor sentences, imperatives, interrogatives.		

Adapt this list of suggestions to your own prescribed text and what is distinctive about the writer's construction of voice in it. Add to the list as you work through the sub-sections that follow. If your text has a first person narrator, revisit this list as part of your revision.

Key terms
phonetic
possessives
AAVE

2 Analysing characters' voices in dialogue

Section B texts

The activities in this sub-section are relevant to all the prescribed texts.

Most novels and stories incorporate a range of characters, each with their own voice. These voices are presented to the reader through dialogue. In dialogue, characters speak directly to each other, hence the term 'direct speech'.

This sub-section uses the prescribed texts to help you explore:

- the ways in which characters' voices are created through dialogue
- the links between dialogue and the surrounding narrative
- the various uses writers make of dialogue.

In novels and short stories, dialogue is normally set within a **framing narrative**. This is sometimes written in the third person, sometimes in the first. You need to distinguish between the voices of the characters in *direct speech* and the narrative voice in *indirect speech*. The interplay between these two kinds of voice can be subtle and revealing in its ability to invite the reader to adopt a moral perspective.

The construction of voices in dialogue (1): *Restoration*

Activity 48

Read the extract below from Rose Tremain's novel *Restoration*. At the court of King Charles II, Merivel, the central character and first person narrator, has been placed in charge of the royal dogs. The King has two mistresses, Barbara Castlemaine and Celia Clemence, whom he wants to keep separate. His solution is to marry Merivel to one of them in name only and set her up on a royal estate in Norfolk. Thus the King will have access to her whilst avoiding scandal.

On an April morning, the King sent for me.

'Merivel', he said, 'I want you to get married.'

5 '*Married*, Sir?'

'Yes.'

'Marriage, Sire, is not, and never has been, on my mind …'

'I know. I'm not asking you to want it. 10 I'm asking you to do it, as a favour to me.'

'But –'

'Have I not done very many favours to you, Merivel?'

'Yes, Sir.'

15 '*Voilà*! You owe me at least this one. And there will be compensations. I propose to give you the Garter, so that your bride will have a title, albeit a modest one. And small but agreeable estates in Norfolk I have confiscated 20 from a recalcitrant Anti-Monarchist. So arise, Sir Robert, and go to your duty without delay or barter.'

I knelt. We were in the Royal Bedchamber and from the adjoining study 25 came the disunified tick-tocking and pinging of the clocks, which perfectly mirrored, at that moment, my own confused thoughts.

'Well?' said the King.

I looked up. The Royal visage was 30 smiling at me benignly. The Royal fingers caressed the dark brown moustache.

'Who …?' I stammered.

The King leaned back in his chair and crossed his legs. 'Ah yes. The bride. It is, of 35 course, Celia Clemence.'

The knee on which my weight was balanced trembled and then tottered beneath me. I fell sideways into the carpet. I heard the King chuckle.

40 'It means, of course, that you – and possibly she – will have to spend some time in Norfolk, thus depriving me of your respective companies now and then. But this is a sacrifice I am prepared to make.'

45 I endeavoured to right myself, but my left knee had gone suddenly numb and wouldn't support me, so I had no alternative but to lie in a kind of foetal heap by the Royal footstool.

50 'I don't,' said the King, 'need to explain myself further, do I, Merivel?'

1 In a small group, look carefully at the dialogue in this extract. What impressions does it give you of:

   a the King's tone of voice

   b Merivel's tone of voice

   c the sentence types used by each character, ie imperative, declarative, interrogative, exclamatory

   d the length of each character's utterances?

   Fill in a copy of the chart below. Several entries have been made already.

Purposes and effects of the dialogue in the *Restoration* extract		
Purpose of the dialogue	**Examples of language use**	**Impressions given of character and relationship**
1 To bring out the King's personality and mood	• his use of crisp declaratives • his use of ironic humour • his repeated use of Merivel's name	
2 To bring out Merivel's surprise and discomfiture		

2 Share your ideas from the group work. Then use your knowledge of spontaneous conversation to compare the dialogue Rose Tremain constructs here with unplanned speech. Focus on these features:

   • turn taking and **adjacency**: what pattern does it follow? how is this pattern marked?

   • the cooperative principle: does the conversation conform to the **maxims of cooperation** (quality, quantity, relevance, manner)?

   • the politeness principle: how far do the two speakers employ politeness strategies, and why?

Now look at this extract in its proper context, as part of a novel with a first person narrative voice. Consider the short passages of narration that come between the direct speech, for example, 'I knelt. We were in the Royal Bedchamber …', 'The knee on which my weight was balanced trembled and then tottered beneath me'.

How does this narration serve to contextualise the dialogue and direct the reader's response to it?

3 Write an analysis of the way the voices of the King and Merivel are created through the dialogue and the way the dialogue is set within a framing narrative. Draw in detail on the work you have done in questions **1** and **2**.

Take it further

If your set text is *Dubliners*, conduct a similar analysis to the one above of the passage that ends 'Counterparts', from the first full paragraph on page 94 to the end of the short story (2000 Penguin edition, pp93–94).

Writing in the exam

In the exam you would have to go on to develop your ideas about voices in dialogue by referring to other parts of *Restoration*.

Key terms

framing narrative

adjacency

maxims of cooperation

The construction of voices in dialogue (2): *Paddy Clarke Ha Ha Ha*

Activity 49

Read the extract below from *Paddy Clarke Ha Ha Ha*. As it begins, Paddy, the 10-year-old narrator, is recalling his reading habits when he was younger. The whole novel is made up of Paddy's memories.

> I read William. I read all of them. There were thirty-four of them. I owned eight of them. The others were in the library. William The Pirate was the best. I say! gasped William. I've never seen such a clever dog. I say! he gasped, he's splendid. Hi, Toby! Toby! Come here, old chap! Toby was nothing loth. He was a jolly, friendly little dog.
> 5 He ran up to William and played with him and growled at him and pretended to bite him and rolled over and over.
>   – Can I've a dog for my birthday?
>   – No.
>   – Christmas?
> 10   – No.
>   – Both together?
>   – No.
>   – Christmas and my birthday?
>   – You want me to hit you, is that it?
> 15   – No.
> I asked my ma. She said the same. But when I said two Christmases and birthdays she said, – I'll see.
>   That was good enough.
>   William's gang was the Outlaws; him, Ginger, Douglas and Henry. It was
> 20 Ginger's turn to push the pram and he seized it with a new vigour.
>   – Vigour, I said.
>   – Vigour!
>   – Vigour vigour vigour!
>   For a day we called ourselves the Vigour Tribe. We got one of Sinbad's markers
> 25 and did big Vs on our chests, for Vigour. It was cold. The marker tickled. Big black Vs. From our diddies to our tummy buttons.

1 Discuss in a small group what you notice about the way the dialogue in this extract is set out on the page. Consider:

  a what is distinctive about its graphology?

  b how does the writer, Roddy Doyle, signal who is speaking?

  c what is missing from Doyle's presentation of dialogue that is normally found in novels?

2 Examine how Paddy's *narrative* voice is evoked by Doyle in the paragraph beginning 'I read William' and in the passage running from 'I asked my ma' to 'our tummy buttons'. As a class, focus on the language features listed on the chart below and exemplify them by filling in the second column.

Features of Paddy's narrative voice	Examples
grammatically simple sentence forms **subject–verb–object** structure	
compound sentences rare	
repetitive syntax	
simple lexis: mainly nouns, pronouns, verbs absence of **modifiers** (adjectives and adverbs)	
fast-paced rhythms typical of speech	
imitation of adult and literary language, ie incorporation	

3 Now look closely at the passages of *dialogue* (direct speech) which Doyle integrates into Paddy's narrative. Discuss:

a what linguistic features does the dialogue have that are like Paddy's narrative voice?

b how is Doyle demonstrating that Paddy's memories of conversations mingle with his memories of events?

4 Continue this extract in Paddy's voice. (The Vigour Tribe annoys an elderly couple by stealing their underwear from the washing line. When he gets home, Paddy is in trouble for having a black V inked on his chest.) Make up the events if you wish. Include at least two passages of dialogue. Annotate your writing to show the language features you have used and the effects.

Key terms

subject–verb–object
compound sentences
modifiers

Take it further

Choose two passages from your prescribed text that are written entirely or mainly in dialogue. Practise analysing the use of voice in them by adapting the list of language features in 'Features of Paddy's narrative voice' to the characters whose direct speech your author is representing.

The construction of voices in dialogue (3): *Cloudstreet*

Activity 50

Read the extract below from Tim Winton's novel *Cloudstreet*.

Lester Lamb and his wife Oriel are having an evening meal with their family. There are six children: the boys Quick, Fish and Lon, and the girls Red, Hat and Elaine. Here they play a game of 'spin the knife' to see who will do the washing-up.

It's a circle of silver blur on the table, almost solid with motion so that you'd swear you could see their laughing faces reflected in it as it spins. They drum their hands on the tabletop, the girls screaming and
5   elbowing each other, Lon bouncing up and down on his chair, Fish clapping with a roar of glee as Quick closes his eyes and moans in dramatic apprehension. At the head of the table, Lester Lamb holds up his finger.
10   Remember, this is for who washes up tonight.
     And this week! Red says, getting her pink elbows up in the air. All this week.
     The knife never lies, you know, Lester says. It always knows best.
15   You shouldn't teach 'em such heathen stuff, Oriel Lamb murmurs with a smile. The room smells of gas, lamb stew, mildew in the wallpaper. A fire of rotten pickets snaps and quavers behind them, beginning to warm this back bedroom that's become their kitchen.
20   Jars and bottles stand on shelves made for packing cases, and dented pots and baking dishes stand about in order.
     It's slowing down! Lon cries.
     Now you can see the round-ended old butterknife
25   blade and the browning bone handle – hear it whirr.
     Slowing.

     It's you, Hat.
     Nah, it's got plenty in it, yet.
     Gaw.
30   Quick knows it'll be him; he can almost feel the metal against his skin.
     It's you, Dad.
     Nope. It's gunna be Quick, Lester says. Lookit im. He's getting out the teatowel already, aren't you,
35 mate? Here it comes again.
     Elaine!
     Wait. Waaiit!
     Oh, Gawd! Quick thumps the table.
     Quick! Arrr, Quick gets the dishes!
40   The knife never tells a fib, but it can make a bib for a squib. Here's one. Who's got a pimple up their dimple?
     Lester! Oriel returns to the stew.
     They rollick and niggle and shriek and giggle and
45 the knife goes round in the centre of the table. The fire has a hold on the room now and there is warm light between bodies and noise.
     It's … aaagh … it's Eee-laine! Arr, pimple up yer dimple, Ee!
50   Is not.
     Carn, Ee, fair cop, says Hat.
     Yeah, says Quick, the knife doesn't lie.

1 With a partner, identify the parts of this extract which are:

a in the direct speech of the characters

b in the third person narrative voice.

Highlight each in different colours. Then look at another pair's decisions. Debate those that may be difficult to decide.

2 In a small group, use the chart below to analyse the distinctive features of the characters' voices in this extract, focusing on how Winton makes them resemble spontaneous conversation.

Voices in the *Cloudstreet* extract	
Features of spontaneous conversation	**Example and comment on the effect created**
idioms and colloquial language (Australian **vernacular**)	
phonological features (including **phonetic spelling**)	
incomplete constructions	
grammatically simple sentences	
ellipsis and deixis	
non-fluency features	

3 Compare your findings from the group work. Then make notes for a class analysis of this extract, showing how Tim Winton constructs the voices of the Lamb family. Include comment on:

- how the writer deliberately blurs the distinction between narration and dialogue

- the possible reasons why he does this.

How to comment on the construction of voices in dialogue

Activity 51

Read the following response to the *Cloudstreet* extract above. The task is to analyse how Tim Winton creates and uses the voices of the characters. Note that this is an extract, not the whole answer.

There are eight characters in this extract, all members of the Lamb family. Winton's purpose here is to evoke a scene of family togetherness, symbolised by the kitchen setting, the fire and the 'warm light between bodies and noise'. Hence the voices of the characters, though individualised by name, are presented as a kind of collective chorus rather than as belonging to separate people.

This impression of close intimacy is enhanced by the way in which Winton's narrative voice seems to blend in with the voices of the family. It is difficult to distinguish between narration and dialogue: 'It's slowing down, Lon cries / Now you can see the round-ended old butterknife blade … / Slowing.' The narrator presents himself almost as part of the family, using the same present tense and (at times) the same animated speech rhythms as the characters: 'Nah, it's got plenty in it yet / Gawd / Quick knows it'll be him.' The use of the second person, 'Now you can see', also draws the reader into the family circle.

The narrative is set out on the page to capture the sense of raucous excitement in the kitchen. Direct speech tags are almost non-existent, adding to the sense of voices tumbling out in quick succession, and the short exclamatory phrases are as much like quick bursts of noise as coherent speech: 'Elaine! / Wait. Waaiit! / Oh, Gawd!' In this extract, dialogue and visual description are effectively merged.

1 Discuss in a small group how well this response meets AO1 by:

  a identifying a range of linguistic and literary features

  b using linguistic terminology accurately and appropriately

  c being written clearly.

2 Discuss in a small group how well this response meets AO2 by:

  a focusing on form and language

  b supporting general statements with specific examples

  c dealing with the details in the text.

Writing in the exam

In the exam you would have to go on to analyse Winton's creation and use of voice in other parts of the novel.

Summary

Activity 52

1 Look back through the work you have done in the sub-section on the ways writers construct their characters' voices in dialogue. As a class, make a list of the main techniques you have identified. It could begin like this:

Writer's technique for constructing voices in dialogue	Examples	Purpose and effect on the reader
Writer creates a distinctive idiolect for the characters, using lexis which evokes: • their personality • a specific social/regional/historical context.		
Writer marks the dialogue in particular ways to direct the reader's response to: • what is said • how it is said, eg use of conventional or unconventional punctuation for direct speech, speech **tags**, graphology (appearance on the page).		
Writer relates the dialogue to the surrounding narration to guide the reader's response to the characters who are speaking by defining the overall perspective or viewpoint.		

2 Adapt this list of suggestions to your own prescribed text and what is distinctive about the writer's construction of voice in it. Add to the list as you work through the sub-sections that follow.

Key terms

vernacular

phonological features

phonetic spelling

non-fluency features

tags

3 Analysing third person narrative voices

The third person narrative voice is that of the writer; the storytelling voice which uses the 'he/she/they' form. Look back to Section A.6 'Voices in narrative' (pages 52 to 60) to remind yourself of the different stances a writer can take up in relation to the reader: omniscient, external, 'over the shoulder', internal.

This sub-section draws on the prescribed texts to help you comment on the uses and effects of the third person voice. It focuses on:

- the way third person narration establishes *viewpoint*
- the way third person narration guides and controls the reader's response.

Section B texts
The activities in this sub-section are most relevant to:
The Bloody Chamber
Dubliners
Cloudstreet

Identifying third person narrative voice and viewpoint: *The Bloody Chamber*

Activity 53

Read the opening passage of Angela Carter's short story 'The Courtship of Mr Lyon' below.

> Outside her kitchen window, the hedgerow glistened as if the snow possessed a light of its own; when the sky darkened towards evening, an unearthly, reflected pallor remained behind upon the winter's landscape, while still the soft flakes floated down. This lovely girl, whose skin possesses that same, inner light so you would have thought that
> 5 she, too, was made all of snow, pauses in her chores in the mean kitchen to look out at the country road. Nothing has passed that way all day; the road is white and unmarked as a spilled bolt of bridal satin.
> Father said he would be home before nightfall.
> The snow brought down all the telephone wires; he couldn't have called, even with
> 10 the best of news.
> The roads are bad. I hope he'll be safe.

1 Look at each of the six sentences in turn. Complete a copy of the chart below in a small group to help you identify voice and viewpoint in each sentence.

The opening of 'The Courtship of Mr Lyon'	Voice	Viewpoint
Sentence 1	third person, omniscient narrator	detached, external
Sentence 2		
Sentence 3		
Sentence 4		
Sentence 5		
Sentence 6	first person narrator	involved, internal

2 Compare your findings from the group work. Then discuss:

   a where are there changes of tense?

   b whereabouts does the narrator step outside the story to address the reader directly?

   c which sentences resemble fairy tale/fable in content and style?

3 What reasons do you think Carter may have had for introducing these shifts in narrative voice and viewpoint at the start of her story? How is the reader's response being manipulated? Sub-section 4 below returns to this story. You might want to glance ahead to it now.

> **Writing in the exam**
> You may be asked to comment on shifts in narrative perspective in the course of your prescribed text. If so, focus your answer on (i) how the voice changes (ii) how the point of view changes (iii) the effect of these changed on the reader.

Third person narrative voice and viewpoint (1): *The Bloody Chamber*

Activity 54

Read the extract below from Angela Carter's short story 'The Werewolf'. The story uses the traditional tale of Little Red Riding Hood as a reference point.

> Winter and cold weather.
>
> Go and visit grandmother who has been sick. Take her the oatcakes I've baked for her on the hearthstone and a little pot of butter.
>
> 5 The good child does as her mother bids – five miles' trudge through the forest; do not leave the path because of the bears, the wild boar, the starving wolves. Here, take your father's hunting knife; you know how to use it.
>
> The child had a scabby coat of sheepskin to keep out the cold, she knew the forest too well to fear it but she must always be on her guard. When she heard that freezing howl of a wolf, she dropped her gifts, seized her knife and turned on the beast.
>
> 10 It was a huge one, with red eyes and running, grizzled chops; any but a mountaineer's child would have died of fright at the sight of it. It went for her throat, as wolves do, but she made a great swipe at it with her father's knife and slashed off its right forepaw.
>
> The wolf let out a gulp, almost a sob, when it saw what had happened to it; wolves are less brave than they seem. It went lolloping off disconsolately between the trees as well as it 15 could on three legs, leaving a trail of blood behind it. The child wiped the blade of her knife on her apron, wrapped up the wolf's paw in the cloth in which her mother had packed the oatcakes and went on towards her grandmother's house. Soon it came on to snow so thickly that the path and any footsteps, track or spoor that might have been upon it were obscured.
>
> She found her grandmother was so sick that she had taken to her bed and fallen into 20 a fretful sleep, moaning and shaking so that the child guessed she had a fever. She felt the forehead, it burned. She shook out the cloth from her basket, to use it to make the old woman a cold compress, and the wolf's paw fell to the floor.
>
> But it was no longer a wolf's paw. It was a hand, chopped off at the wrist, a hand toughened with work and freckled with old age. There was a wedding ring on the third finger 25 and a wart on the index finger. By the wart, she knew it for her grandmother's hand.
>
> She pulled back the sheet but the old woman woke up, at that, and began to struggle, squawking and shrieking like a thing possessed. But the child was strong, and armed with her father's hunting knife; she managed to hold her grandmother down long enough to see the cause of her fever. There was a bloody stump where her right hand should have been, 30 festering already.
>
> The child crossed herself and cried out so loud the neighbours heard her and came rushing in. They knew the wart on the hand at once for a witch's nipple; they drove the old woman, in her shift as she was, out into the snow with sticks, beating her old carcass as far as the edge of the forest, and pelted her with stones until she fell down dead.
>
> 35 Now the child lived in her grandmother's house; she prospered.

1 As a class, consider the ways in which this extract differs from the version of 'Little Red Riding Hood' you know. Think in particular about:

- how the story ends
- how Carter presents the child to us
- how Carter presents grandmother to us.

2 With a partner, divide the extract into two parts. Part 1 runs from the beginning to '… the wolf's paw fell to the floor'. Part 2 runs from 'But it was no longer a wolf's paw' to the end.

   a Working separately, make brief notes about:

- Carter's use of third person narration to tell the story. What perspective is used: the omniscient author's? the girl's? the grandmother's? a combination of these?
- Carter's descriptive language. What impressions and effects do you think she intends to give?

   b Then share your findings. Are your responses the same? Use specific details from the extract to justify your ideas.

3 Share your conclusions from the group work. Then discuss where you would place this extract on a continuum with 'detached, external third person narration' at one end and 'involved, internal third person narration' at the other. To help you reach your decisions, recast a few sentences from Carter's story using the first person viewpoint of (i) the girl, and (ii) grandmother.

Take it further

If your set text is *Dubliners*, conduct a similar analysis to the one above of the passage that ends 'Eveline', from the middle of page 32 to the end of the short story (2000 Penguin edition, pp32–34).

Third person narrative voice and viewpoint (2): *Cloudstreet*

Activity 55

Read the extract below from Tim Winton's novel *Cloudstreet*. Sam Pickles has lost part of his hand in an accident and has been taken to hospital. His daughter Rose and his younger sons Ted and Chub are already with him. Sam's wife Dolly has been informed. The extract begins with her arrival at the hospital.

Rose and the boys were there. The boys let off whispering by the window and stood straight. They were rangy, sundark kids. Rose was by the bed. She didn't look up. Sam was asleep with his white fist bound up in a salute or a warning – she didn't know which. A private room in the new wing. Government money, she thought. We couldn't
5 afford this.

Four fingers and the top of his thumb, Rose said.

Christ.

Dolly saw it was his right hand. His bloody working hand. A man could hardly pick his nose with a thumb and half a pointer. They were done for; stuffed, cactus.
10 Thank you, Lady Luck, you rotten slut. It was probably time now to pack a bag and buy a ticket, but hell, there was the kids and everything. The whole town knowing. How would she live?

He bin awake?

Nup.
15 The boys, Ted and Chub, scratched themselves and pulled at their shorts.

We go down the jetty? He's not gunna wake up.

S'posed to be in school, youse.

We'll be back dreckly. Dad might be awake, eh.

Oh, ya mays well.
20 Don't drown from cryin, Rose said, from the bedside.

Dolly stood in the room with her daughter. You had to watch this kid. She was getting to be a clever little miss. And she was Sam's through and through. She was hot in the face like she was holding something back. Dolly wondered what she knew. She's a kid, I'm a woman. The only thing we've got in common these days is a useless man.
25 Dolly'd always gone for the useless ones. But this was the living end.

The room smelt of new paint and phenyle. Dolly tried to spot a mirror but there was none.

The woman and the daughter do not speak. The crippled man does not stir. The breeze comes in the window and stops the scene from turning into a painting.

Writing in the exam

Be alert to the way your author represents the thoughts and feelings of a narrator or a character, their inner voice. This is often conveyed through the use of free indirect style, as in the example from 'Cloudstreet', but it can be done in other ways: make a checklist as part of your revision.

1 With a partner, identify the dialogue (ie direct speech) in this extract. What allows you to do so? Why do you think it is unpunctuated?

2 Look at the third person narrative passages as a class. Consider:

  a how much of this extract presents the situation from Dolly's viewpoint

  b how the narrative viewpoint changes in the last paragraph. Can you suggest a reason for this?

  Then look carefully at the way the paragraph beginning 'Dolly saw it was his right hand' is written. How does it represent Dolly's thoughts and feelings directly – her *inner voice*? Why do you think the writer chooses to use this 'free indirect style' of narration here?

3 Write a short piece of fiction in the third person which includes a character's unspoken thoughts. Avoid using 's/he thought', 's/he felt', etc. Add comments at the end about how well this technique worked for you in creating the voice of your character.

Take it further

Read from the collection *Dubliners* one or more stories that make use of free indirect style in the narration, for example, 'A Painful Case', 'The Boarding House' or 'Clay'. Write an analysis of how James Joyce constructs his characters' voices through this technique.

An exercise in commenting on third person narrative voice:
The Bloody Chamber

Activity 56

Read the extract below from Angela Carter's short story 'The Courtship of Mr Lyon'.

This story is a modern version of Beauty and the Beast, the traditional fairy tale. In the final part of the story, Beauty returns to the Beast's mansion. She has been told that he has pined away with love for her since she left him to rejoin human society and is near to death. Here Beauty is being guided to the Beast's bedchamber by his spaniel.

Beauty found a candle to light her way and followed the faithful spaniel up the staircase, past the study, past her suite, through a house echoing with desertion up a little back staircase dedicated to mice and spiders, stumbling, ripping the hem of her dress in her haste.

5   What a modest bedroom! An attic, with a sloping roof, they might have given the chambermaid if the Beast had employed staff. A night light on the mantelpiece, no curtains at the windows, no carpet on the floor and a narrow, iron bedstead on which he lay, sadly diminished, his bulk scarcely disturbing the faded patchwork quilt, his mane a greyish rat's nest and his eyes closed. On
10   the stick-backed chair where his clothes had been thrown, the roses she had sent him were thrust into the jug from the washstand but they were all dead.

The spaniel jumped up on the bed and burrowed her way under the scanty covers, softly keening.

'Oh, Beast,' said Beauty. 'I have come home.'

15   His eyelids flickered. How was it she had never noticed before that his agate eyes were equipped with lids, like those of a man? Was it because she had only looked at her own face, reflected there?

'I'm dying, Beauty,' he said in a cracked whisper of his former purr. 'Since you left me, I have been sick. I could not go hunting, I found I had not the stomach to kill the gentle beasts, I could not eat. I am sick and must die; but I
20   shall die happy because you have come to say good-bye to me.'

She flung herself upon him, so that the iron bedstead groaned, and covered his poor paws with her kisses.

'Don't die, Beast! If you'll have me, I'll never leave you.'

1   Use the questions below to help you analyse the use of voice in this extract with a partner.

   a Which aspects of Carter's third person narrative voice remind you of fairy tales?

   b Which aspects of the dialogue between Beauty and Beast remind you of children's literature?

   c What is the viewpoint here, and how does Carter create it?

   d How do you think Carter wants the reader to respond to this episode?

2   Write two paragraphs analysing the way Carter combines third person narrative with dialogue to manipulate the reader's response. Say what you think Carter's purposes are and how well she achieves them.

Summary

As a class, look back through the work you have done in this sub-section on the ways writers create and use the third person narrative voice. Make a list of the main techniques you have identified. It could begin like this:

Writer's technique for constructing third person narrative voice	Examples	Purpose and effect on the reader
Writer uses an 'omniscient' style to present characters and events in a detached, objective way with little or no authorial comment.		
Writer uses an 'over the shoulder' style to convey a character's viewpoint: we see things through their eyes and are drawn closer to them as a result.		
Writer uses 'free indirect style' to evoke a character's thoughts and feelings: we are projected inside the character's mind and made to identify with them.		
Writer combines detachment with some form of internal narration: allows for comment and evaluation on the writer's part as the narrative perspective shifts.		

Adapt this list of suggestions to your own prescribed text and what is distinctive about the writer's construction of voice in it.

Remember that the narrative method does not have to be consistent in using only one technique, but can move from one method to another. Writers often slip in and out of different techniques, thus combining, for example, the more detached third person narration with free indirect style. These shifts are important in the impact they have on the reader.

4   Tackling Section B of the exam

The exam allows you about one hour to answer one essay question on your prescribed text.

You will have a clean copy of your text with you.

There are 50 marks out of a total of 100 for the whole paper on Unit 1.

Assessment objectives

Two assessment objectives are used to assess your Section B exam answer:

AO1 (20 marks) – Select and apply relevant concepts and approaches from integrated linguistic and literary study, using appropriate terminology and accurate, coherent written expression.

AO2 (30 marks) – Demonstrate detailed critical understanding in analysing the ways in which structure, form and language shape meanings in a range of spoken and written texts.

Thus AO2 requires you to *analyse* how your author uses structure, form and language to create and convey voice. AO1 requires you to use linguistic and literary concepts and terms to *explain* how your author does this.

Sample questions

Here are sample questions on three of the prescribed texts.

A *Paddy Clarke Ha Ha Ha*

Extract: 'We didn't do the barn' (page 11) to 'They didn't know' (page 12)

Using this extract as your starting point, you should:

- explore Doyle's manipulation of language to capture the voice of a 10-year-old boy

- examine how the manipulation of language contributes to the effectiveness of the novel as a whole.

B *The Color Purple*

Extract: 'Harpo want to know what to do' (page 35) to 'But he keep on trying' (page 36)

Using this extract as your starting point, you should:

- explore Walker's use of language to capture the voice of Harpo and one other character of your choice

- examine how the voices of these characters have been shaped by the society around them.

C *Dubliners*

Extract from 'Eveline', from second full paragraph on page 30 to end of first paragraph on page 31 (2000 Penguin edition).

Using this extract as your starting point, you should:

- explore Joyce's use of language to develop the voice and perspective of Eveline and her attitude to life in Dublin

- examine how Joyce's development of voice and perspective combine to reflect life in Dublin in 'Eveline' and one other story of your choice.

You need to give the same amount of attention to each bullet point. The first bullet point requires you to focus on the given extract. The second bullet point requires you to refer to the novel as a whole (or to another story in your collection). If you limit your answer to the given extract and do not refer to the text as a whole, you will lose marks.

How to plan your answer

Having identified the focus of the first part of the question, look carefully at the second bullet point to see which aspect of 'the text as a whole' you need to go on to discuss. It could be, for example:

- how the writer's creation and use of voice contribute to the effectiveness of the whole novel
- how the writer's use of voice develops in the course of the novel
- how the writer's creation and use of voice reflect social context in the whole novel
- how the writer's creation and use of voice reflect the use of genre in the whole novel, for example, fairy tale in *The Bloody Chamber* or the epistolary novel in *Address Unknown*.

Choose two or more extracts from your novel/collection to provide material for addressing the second bullet point. Mark these in your text. Then make brief notes about how you will use them. For example, if you were asked to examine how Celie's voice develops and changes in the course of *The Color Purple*, you might focus on:

- how she acquires a more independent/confident voice through her friendship with Shug
- how she acquires a wider viewpoint after she begins corresponding with Nettie and how the voice in her letters reflects this
- how she acquires a more assertive voice in her dialogue with Mr _____ when she discovers his duplicity and decides to stand up to him
- how her developing relationship with Shug and Nettie allows her to acquire a distinctive feminist voice.

How to build up your answer

Address the first bullet point by making a detailed analysis of the given extract in the light of the instruction. Remember that this will always require you to comment on the writer's creation and use of voice.

Activity 57

Read the response on page 88 on how Roddy Doyle captures the voice of a 10-year-old boy in the following extract. It addresses the first bullet point. Paddy is describing how he and his friends pretend to run the Grand National across their neighbours' gardens. Note that this response could be developed further.

> – They're off!
> Aidan didn't do any more commentating after that.
> The first fence was easy. McEvoy's wall into Byrne's. There was no hedge. You just had to make sure that you had enough room to swing your legs. Some of us could swing right over without our legs touching the top of the wall – I could – but you needed loads of space for that.
> 5 Across Byrne's. Screaming and shouting. That was part of it. Trying to get the ones at the back caught. Off the grass, over the flower bed, across the path, over the wall – a hedge. Jump up on the wall, grip the hedge, stand up straight, jump over, down. Danger, danger. Murphy's. Loads of flowers. Kick some of them. Around the car. Hedges before the wall. Foot on the bumper, jump. Land on the hedge, roll. Our house. Around the car, no hedge, over the wall. No more screaming;
> 10 no breath for it. Neck itchy from the hedge. Two more big hedges.
> Once, Mister McLoughlin had been cutting the grass when we all came up over the hedge, and he nearly had a heart attack.
> Up onto Hanley's wall, hold the hedge. Legs straight; it was harder now, really tired. Jump the hedge, roll, up and out their gate.
> 15 Winner.

In this extract, Roddy Doyle constructs Paddy's first person voice by using a range of linguistic strategies which simulate spontaneous speech. The passage is written in the past tense ('This first fence was easy' ... 'it was harder now') but the impression is of events happening in the present ('Around the car, no hedge, over the wall'), a typical feature of oral narrative. Paddy is reliving the Grand National in his memory and the shift into present continuous tense 'Trying to get the ones at the back caught' conveys the vivid immediacy of the race as he recalls it.

The sense of excitement, of everything happening at breathless speed, is further evoked by Doyle's use of minor sentences for Paddy's narrative voice: 'Danger, danger. Murphy's. Loads of flowers'. The effect here is of a sports commentary with a non-stop rhythm, an impression enhanced by the context-bound (deictic) language: 'McEvoy's wall into Byrne's ... Across Byrne's'. Ellipsis is also a strong structural feature of Paddy's sentences, capturing the feeling that in the hectic scramble to the finish he has 'no breath for it'. The elliptical final sentence 'Winner' is set out on the page as a separate line, its graphology underlining the fact that at the end of the race Paddy and his friends are exhausted but still competitive and happy.

1 As a class, use AO1 and AO2 to assess this response. Then add to it points of your own which also meet the requirements of these assessment objectives.

2 Read the following extract and then the response that follows on how Paddy's voice develops and changes in the course of the novel. Then, as a class, use AO1 and AO2 to assess this response. Add to it points of your own which also meet these assessment objectives.

In the second half of the story, Paddy's parents have problems in their marriage. They decide to separate. Paddy is distraught and plans to run away from home. Note that this response could be developed further.

> I never got the chance to run away. I was too late. He left first. The way he shut the door; he didn't slam it. Something; I just knew: he wasn't coming back. He just closed it, like he was going down to the shops, except it was the front door and we only used the front door when people came. He didn't slam it. He closed it behind him – I saw him
> 5 in the glass. He waited for a few seconds, then went. He didn't have a suitcase or even a jacket, but I knew.
> My mouth opened and a roar started but it never came. And a pain in my chest, and I could hear my heart pumping the blood to the rest of me. I was supposed to cry; I thought I was. I sobbed once and that was all.
> 10 He'd hit her again and I saw him, and he saw me. He thumped her on the shoulder.

As the novel nears its end, Doyle constructs Paddy's voice differently to reflect the trauma caused by the break-up of his parents' marriage. The extract beginning 'I never got the chance to run away' on the final pages is narrated in a much more reflective, subdued voice. Paddy's viewpoint is now more detached and introspective than in earlier parts of the book: 'Something; I just knew: he wasn't coming back.' Here the focus is on himself in relation to his father as a separate individual, no longer in relation to the 'da' he has always taken for granted.

Through the compound sentences and more formal punctuation, Doyle shows Paddy thinking more deeply: 'I was supposed to cry; I thought I was.' The narrative voice here expresses itself in a crafted way typical of writing rather than through the structures of spontaneous speech. There is more awareness of the reader, of Paddy consciously addressing us and trying both to understand and to share his feelings: 'He didn't have a suitcase or even a jacket, but I knew.' In describing episodes like the Grand National race, the rhythms of Paddy's voice were lively and animated, characteristic of a young boy's spontaneous speech. Here they are steadier and more controlled, suggesting a mature level of consciousness in the delivery of a shaped text. Paddy's voice has grown up.

Take it further

In the novel/collection you are studying, find two passages from different parts of the text where the narrator's or writer's language differs significantly. Write an exam-length analysis of the passages to show how and why it does so.

Devising your own questions

As a class, use the sample questions on page 86 to devise three possible exam tasks on your own text. Their focus must be on the creation and use of voice.

Write a collective response to one of these, referring as you do so to AO1 and AO2. Then, taking no more than one hour, write individual answers to the other two. One of them should be marked by a partner. The other should be marked by your teacher.

Final revision

Here is a list of tips to memorise immediately before you take the exam.

When analysing the given extract in the first half of your answer, concentrate on:

- the specific focus of the question: for example, 'uses language to capture the voice of a child', 'uses language to shift the narrative perspective'

- how the writer creates voice, not just the kind of voice it is: ie analyse the style, don't describe the content

- finding as much detail as you can and commenting on it systematically: avoid trying to say everything at once

- using linguistic terminology.

When referring to other parts of the text in the second half of your answer, concentrate on:

- the specific focus of the question: answer the examiner's question, not your own

- literary features as well as linguistic features

- being selective in the points you make: you can't cover everything in a limited time

- using linguistic terminology.

Relevance to the question and to AO1 and AO2 are what will gain credit in the exam. Length alone will not. You should be able to write a full and relevant answer in two to three sides, provided you analyse voice throughout and do not simply describe 'what the text is about'. How, not what, should be the focus of the whole of your answer.

Unit 2

Creating Texts

Unit introduction

Unit 2 is the coursework unit for Edexcel AS English Language and Literature. In this unit, you will:

- build on your work in Unit 1 by reading widely in a single topic area
- use your reading as a stimulus to create your own texts
- produce a coursework folder of 2000–2500 words, consisting of:
  - ♦ one text for a reading audience
  - ♦ one text for a listening audience
  - ♦ one commentary for each text that you produce.

The course

You can make a free choice of literary and non-literary texts from *one* of the five topic areas in the table below. Your choice must include one prose fiction text and one drama OR poetry text. Examples of suitable texts are also shown on the table.

In your coursework folder

You will also use a wide range of reading to stimulate ideas and approaches for your own original writing.

- One piece of original writing for a reading audience, about 1750 words (24 marks)
- One commentary on your text for a reading audience, maximum 500 words (16 marks)
- One piece of original writing for a listening audience, about 750 words (24 marks)
- One commentary on your text for a listening audience, about 500 words (16 marks)

Topics	Examples of suitable texts
Entrapment	**Prose:** *The Collector*, John Fowles **Drama/poetry:** *The Secret Agent*, W. H. Auden
Dystopia	**Prose:** *The Handmaid's Tale*, Margaret Atwood **Drama/poetry:** *Accidental Death of an Anarchist*, Dario Fo
Women's Lives	**Prose:** *The Well of Loneliness*, Radclyffe Hall **Drama/poetry:** 'Warming Her Pearls', Carol Ann Duffy; 'Not in My House', U. A. Fanthorpe
Gothic and Supernatural	**Prose:** *Dracula*, Bram Stoker **Drama/poetry:** *The Raven and other Favourite Poems*, Edgar Allen Poe
Journeys and Pilgrimages	**Prose:** *Cloud Atlas*, David Mitchell **Drama/poetry:** *Our Country's Good*, Timberlake Wertenbaker; *The General Prologue to the Canterbury Tales*, Geoffrey Chaucer

What the moderators are looking for

Your coursework will be assessed first by your teacher and other members of the English team. Then it will be assessed by an external moderator from the exam board. They will be looking for:

- two distinctly different pieces of original writing that have been deliberately shaped to meet the needs of a) a reading audience and b) a listening audience
- use of varied and effective literary and linguistic devices
- evidence of a clear understanding of audience and purpose for each text

- evidence of understanding and appreciation of the texts you have read as a stimulus for your own writing
- clear and thoughtful commentaries on your own writing, explaining how the work was shaped and the intended effects
- a personal interest and engagement with the writing tasks.

Moderators use four Assessment objectives (AOs) to mark your coursework – AO1 and AO4 to assess the original writing and AO2 and AO3 to assess the commentaries.

Assessment objective		What this includes in practice
AO1	Select and apply relevant concepts and approaches from integrated literary and linguistic study, using appropriate terminology and accurate, coherent written expression.	You need to demonstrate that: • you have studied linguistic and literary techniques and approaches • you can use key terminology accurately and effectively • you can write coherently and accurately.
AO2	Demonstrate detailed critical understanding in analysing the ways in which structure, form and language shape meanings in a range of spoken and written texts.	You need to show that you understand how and why writers make deliberate choices in the language they use and in how they organise their texts.
AO3	Use integrated approaches to explore relationships between texts, analysing and evaluating the significance of contextual factors in their production and reception.	You need to show: • your ability to make comparisons between the literary and linguistic techniques used in different texts • that you understand that texts are affected by their contexts (ie when they were written, who they were written for and who their audiences were).
AO4	Demonstrate expertise and creativity in using language appropriately for a variety of purposes and audiences, drawing on insights from literary and linguistic studies.	You need to: • be clear about your purposes and who you are writing for • select literary and linguistic techniques that are suitable for your tasks and audiences.

How you will be assessed

A maximum of 48 marks are awarded for the two tasks you choose to submit in your coursework folder, 24 marks for your text for a reading audience and 24 for a text for a listening audience. A maximum of 32 marks is given for the two commentaries, 16 marks for each.

How this book will help you

In this book, Unit 2 is divided into four main sections.

The first section will help you to answer important questions about the creative writing process and to consider what you would like to write about for your coursework tasks and how to go about doing it.

The two middle sections look in more detail at writing for a reading audience and writing for a listening audience. They are both free-standing: you can begin with the task of your choice or even work on the two tasks in parallel. You will be introduced to suitable texts and tasks, and given guidance on how to write effectively for reading and listening audiences. You will be able to read, listen to, and explore a range of model texts in a variety of genres and follow up advice about independent research. There are short analytical and writing activities to practise and examples of work by other students to read.

The final section gives you guidance on how to write your commentaries.

How to succeed in English Language and Literature Unit 2

- 'Learn to read as a writer; to write as a reader.'
- Be businesslike – writing is a craft and needs plenty of practice.
- Be curious – read or listen to as much as possible.
- Get started – expect your first draft to be disappointing.
- Look for constructive advice – professional writers, fellow students and your teachers can all offer guidance.
- Dare to be creative – experiment with fresh techniques.
- Have pride in your finished product – make sure all the fine details are polished.

A The writing process

In this section you will explore some important questions relating to creative writing, which will lead you to consider what you would like to write about for your coursework tasks. You will also need to consider how the style and presentation of each text will be determined by its audience, purpose and form. For each text you will experiment with different style models before writing up a final version, demonstrating the importance of planning, drafting and editing. You will also show your knowledge of literary and linguistic techniques by writing a commentary, explaining the choices you made in your creative writing.

1   The creative process

Your coursework tasks give you the opportunity to use your own interests and experiences as inspiration for your creative writing. You can pursue existing inspirations or you can develop ideas that arise through your stimulus texts and wider reading. The all-important trigger can come in any shape or form, and produce many different types of written work. Take a look at the activity and painting below, which show how various different texts and approaches could emerge from the same stimulus.

Activity 1

1   In a small group, look at the painting below. To see it in full colour, visit http://www.artic.edu/aic/collections/artwork/111628

Nighthawks (1942) by Edward Hopper

Each member of the group should choose one of the following tasks and write about 250–300 words, using the painting to inspire the writing:

- the opening of a detective story
- a diary extract
- a letter

- an advertisement
- an extract from a film review
- a short stretch of dialogue.

2   Now share your writing with other students in the group who chose the same task. What do you notice about the pieces of writing? What are the similarities and what are the differences?

3   Report back to the rest of the group and compare your findings.

An excellent way of approaching Unit 2 is to form a small informal group with members of your class who are interested in the same kinds of reading and writing activities. You will be able to provide support and encouragement to each other by discussing ideas about texts, your reading and your writing, and by offering constructive advice and feedback.

Activity 2

1 Individually, fill out sections A, B and C in a table like the one below.

A: What I read	B: What I watch
C: What I listen to	D: What I would like to write

2 Present your ideas with a partner or small group.

3 Working individually again, start to list some ideas in section D. You will, of course, be able to add more as the course progresses.

Getting started

Although you may have a number of ideas about the sort of things you would like to write, it can be difficult to get started and actually write something on a blank page. In the box, there are ideas for short pieces of creative writing and ways to help you start.

Creating a writing environment

- Overcome any fear of the blank page by writing anything, just to get you started. Write down any words, expressions and ideas that come to mind in connection with your chosen topic.

- Try out some text adaptation activities, for example, take a short extract from one of your literature texts and rewrite it as a radio play, or choose an extract from your drama text or a scene from a poem in your poetry text and rewrite it as the opening to a detective horror story.

- Brainstorm ideas with other members of your group or form a small group to write spontaneous pieces of creative writing.

- Watch a section of a film or reread a section of a literature text that you found inspiring.

- Try to create an environment where you feel able to write – it won't necessarily be the most obvious situation.

- Take tips from professional writers. They employ a huge variety of strategies to get the creative process going, for example, writing notes in pencil or coloured pens before transferring them to the computer; recording initial ideas on tape; working in public places like cafés and gardens; playing music in the background.

- Take a notebook wherever you go and jot down ideas when you have them.

Professional writers usually begin by asking the question 'Who am I writing for?' Even writers of fiction have an implied audience in mind. So you need to think about your intended audience and purpose. Ask yourself:

- who are my readers or listeners?

- what are their expectations, ie what do they want from my text?

The next sub-section will give you some guidance.

2 Writing for audience and purpose

Identifying the audience and purpose

With any type of writing, it is important to be clear about who your audience is and what your purpose is in writing for that audience. The purpose is the effect you want to have on your audience, what you want them to do or feel. As a writer, you can choose to write for an infinite number of different types of audience and purpose.

In addition, a text does not exist on its own, but needs to be considered in the situation or **context** where it will be read or heard. So you also need to ask yourself these questions:

Assessment objectives

A04 will reward you for writing interesting and effective texts that show you have understood the requirements of your intended audience.

* where will your audience be?

* why are they reading or listening to your text?

* how are they reading it?

Here are some examples of different contexts in which texts are consumed by audiences:

* reading of a short article or story on a train journey

* listening to a radio item while travelling in a car

* watching TV at home

* reading newspapers in a leisurely manner at the weekend

* searching the internet for information and reviews

* walking around a museum or gallery listening to an audio guide

* listening to a speech in a hall or conference centre

* reading a weblog or website home page

* listening to a podcast while walking in the street.

All these different contexts (and many more), as well as the audience and purpose, will obviously affect the language, presentation and structure of a text.

Activity 3

1 With a partner, read the short extracts below and on page 95 and discuss the possible audience, purpose and type of text for each one.

A

September 16

dear diary

just sittin in my room really tired but im not ready to sleep yet. went up town with Cheryl today didn't buy anythin tho but tried on all the clothes in the posh shops that we can't afford – was a right laugh.

B *The Independent*, 26 February 2007

FIRST NIGHT

THE GOSSIP

Heading the NME's [*New Musical Express*] annual Cool List of music icons gave singer Beth Ditto a platform, but on her band's return to the UK, they made a storm all on their own. In a scene dominated by identikit performers, Ditto, and her band, The Gossip, stand out a mile.

C The Daily Play by Mark Ravenhill,
The Guardian, 9 August 2007

*Dan is being treated for cancer in hospital. Anna, his
girlfriend, is loving but maybe a bit too controlling.*

5 DAN: I asked if you'd brought a newspaper.

ANNA: And I said no because a newspaper is too
        depressing and you won't get better if you're
        reading newspapers.

DAN: You did say that and I was angry with you.

10 ANNA: And you were angry with me. Which wasn't
        good for you. And there was a croissant.

DAN: Which also came out of a machine and had a
        bit of chocolate in the middle.

ANNA: I'm sorry I couldn't do any better. Plastic
15   cup and (*laughs*) plastic croissant.

DAN: Ah well.

ANNA: Ah well.

DAN: And I said: I need to see the news.

ANNA: And I said no.

D

How to make Indian tea in 20,000 steps

Step 1. Rise at dawn. Now walk more than three miles
to the nearest water supply.

5 Step 11,000. Wait to fill your bucket in the blistering
107˚F heat. Begin your homeward journey carrying
over four gallons of water.

Step 20,000. Make yourself a well-earned cup of tea
10 before you begin your day's work. But only if you've
got enough water left for cooking, bathing, growing
food and providing water for your husband, children
and grandchildren.

You can help in one simple step.

E

Interviewer: Why are you doing the London Marathon?

Andrew Lincoln: Barnardo's asked me and my mum's
doing it, too. She started running at 60 and I thought I'd do
5 it with her out of solidarity. It was never something
I really wanted to do. My knees are buggered but the more
training I've done, the more I've got into it.

F Franca Rame, *Waking Up*

Half past six – oh God, I'll be late.

   Bloody thing, why didn't it go off?
   (*Runs to the cot*) Come on, baby, time to start the day.
   Wake up Mama's honeybun. Time to get up. (*Picks
5 baby up*)

   You're wet! Oh, you little pisspot and I'm in such
   a hurry! How can you be wet again? I got up and
   changed you three hours ago.

G *Tatler*, February 2007

So this is the Maldives, the biggest beach story of
the decade: 1200 desert islands spread like sequins
across the vast turquoise skirt of the Indian Ocean.
5 It's freakishly perfect. Disco-blue waters, some of the
most heartbreaking diving in the world and beaches
so blonde you want to slap them.

H *Hollyoaks*

Inspector: according to Mr O' Brien,
you'd been looking after Mr Cunningham
for the past (.) four weeks or so when
5 he had his first heart attack

Clare: yeh (.) I have

Inspector: can't have been easy (.) I
mean (.) there's a kid involved (.)
Max's younger half brother Tom (.) you
10 managed to look after him as well

Clare: I did get some help with him (.)
Max's friends Tony and Dom

I Buffy's Back, GQ, August 2007

Recommended lowbrow beach reading: the eighth
season of *Buffy the Vampire Slayer*, distilled into a
comic book series. Expect explosive fonts. £1.90
5 each. www.closeencounters.co.uk

2 Copy and complete the table below, filling in the audience, purpose and type of text columns. Add a brief explanation of your decisions for each extract, based on the evidence of the language and any structural or presentational features used.

Text	Audience	Purpose	Type of text	Evidence
A	the writer	to record the day's events	personal diary	informal language, eg ellipsis, slang, references to personal details without explanation

3 Share your ideas with the whole group. Is there agreement about the audience and purpose of each text? If not, why not?

4 Collect and record the types of feature used to identify audience and purpose.

Clearly a similar topic can be treated very differently depending on the writer's purpose and intended audience. The next two activities explore this idea further.

Activity 4

1 Read the following two extracts, which deal with the topic of junk food and obesity. In both of these texts the writers are aiming to persuade, but think about the different ways they go about this and about who their audiences might be.

A *Bliss* magazine, Spring 2007

JUNK FOOD BRITAIN

We reveal the shocking truth about your diet.

FOOD FOR THOUGHT

5 Let's face it, we all love a bag of chips, but a shocking 89% of teens are eating a diet too high in junk and too low in fruit and vegetables. The nasties lurking in junk food do huge damage to our health and looks, and most of us don't even realise it's happening. Even if you're lucky enough to eat badly and stay slim, experts believe a junk food
10 diet makes you more likely to develop cancer and diabetes. And scoffing just a couple of burgers twice a week means eating an extra 59,808 calories a year – enough to put on over half a stone in weight!

B *Panic Nation* by S. Feldman and V. Marks

The present obsession with obesity has resulted in any food providing a
5 high calorie content being labelled as 'junk'. It is obvious nonsense: cheese is good food, as are fish and chips and hamburgers. It is not the particular food that makes people fat, it is the
10 amount of it that they eat.

The whale is hugely fat – it is covered in fatty blubber – but it eats only plankton. It is fat because it eats lots of plankton, not because plankton
15 contains many calories. A person gorging themselves on fruit would become fat more quickly than one eating the occasional hamburger.

2 Discuss the following questions with a partner.

   a What type of audience is each text aimed at?

   b How do the writers attempt to convince their readers by the way they address them and by their use of information and statistics?

3 Identify some specific features that helped you to make your decisions.

4 Did you find either of the texts convincing and effective? Why?

Writing for different audiences and purposes

The kind of analysis on audience and purpose you have been doing so far will help you write your commentaries on your own work (see pages 146–153). Now apply your understanding of audience and purpose to your own writing.

Activity 5

1 Choose one of the texts from Activity 3 and rewrite it for a different audience and purpose. Write only a similar amount to the original text.

2 Exchange your new text with a partner's. Try to identify the audience and purpose of your partner's text. Discuss your thoughts.

- Which features of the text led you to your conclusion?
- How correct were you in identifying the audience and purpose?
- Which features of the text did you think were particularly effective?
- Were there parts that could have been improved?

Take it further

Do some research into different types of magazine and leisure publication. Choose one you would like to write for and write an article on a subject of your choice, which you feel would be of interest to the target audience. If the magazine accepts submissions, you could send in your article. Don't expect it to be accepted necessarily, but it might be interesting to have some feedback from the editors.

Writing your commentary

Keep a record of texts you have read, making notes on their significant features and your responses to them. This will remind you of reading that you could refer to in your coursework and give you practice in noticing the kind of features you might write about in your commentary.

Before you decide on the audience, purpose and genre (type of text) of your own pieces of writing, it is useful to think of as many examples as possible, and see how they relate to each other. Then you'll be aware of lots of options for your own choices.

Activity 6

1 Working in pairs, make three lists like the ones started below and add as many kinds of audience, purpose and genre as you can. Aim to find at least six of each.

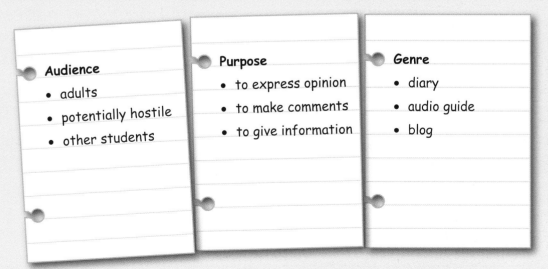

Audience
- adults
- potentially hostile
- other students

Purpose
- to express opinion
- to make comments
- to give information

Genre
- diary
- audio guide
- blog

2 Add suggestions about how you can relate your list to your chosen topic or, if you have not chosen one yet, various possible topics.

3 Share your findings with the rest of your group, recording and adding to your lists on a flip chart.

4 Now begin to think about your own writing choices.

    a Select an audience, purpose and genre that interest you and that relate to each other. Draw up a table like the one below, adding a fourth column to indicate whether the text is to be read or listened to.

Audience	Purpose	Genre	Form
Male teenagers	To evaluate/inform	Music review for magazine	Read

    b Add to the table until you have a substantial list of possible writing projects.

The lists in the following box give you a wide range of valuable ideas for making your choices for coursework tasks.

Audiences

- general or specialist
- known or unknown
- your peers
- adults
- children
- male
- female
- people who share your beliefs and values
- a potentially hostile audience

Purposes

- to write as the expert
- to provide information
- to express opinion
- to reassure
- to comment
- to provoke
- to challenge
- to promote/advertise
- to exchange information
- to evaluate
- to express attitude or emotion
- to report
- to narrate
- to warn
- to advise
- to reassure

Genre

- playscript
- monologue
- radio play or adaptation
- speech
- story
- diary or journal
- letter
- blog
- email
- text message
- review
- audio guide
- written news report
- TV or radio news report
- newspaper article, feature or editorial
- magazine article

3   Writing for readers and listeners

How would you show your understanding of the differences between speech and writing in your own work? You could look at page 23 in Unit 1 to remind yourself.

You need to be aware of the different devices and strategies writers use when they write for reading and listening audiences. You may also need to think more carefully about how a written text that is to be spoken is produced, as it may not be such a familiar task to you as producing one to be read. Getting the language, devices or strategies wrong for the purpose can make either type of text unsuccessful.

The next activity gives you some ideas about the key differences between written and spoken texts.

Activity 7

Texts **A** and **B** are both about the same event.

1 Working with a partner or in a small group, one person should read text **A** aloud, so that you can experience it as a listening audience. Then read text **B** individually.

2 Re-read the texts with the annotations and answer the questions around each text.

Key
(.) = micropause
(1) = timed pause

Starts with key word

Active verb – Find the other examples.

A Channel 4 News

Tornadoes wreak havoc across UK

Studio presenter: storms have torn through parts of southern and central England (.) many buildings have been damaged by the strong winds (1) the severe weather struck parts of the country around seven this morning (.) some homes are without power but no injuries have been reported so far (2) in Farnborough (.) Hampshire (.) police say at least ten houses have been damaged (.) including some with severe structural damage (2) a mini tornado struck in Northampton (.) where an empty school bus was hit (.) there were similar scenes in Nuneaton where 20 homes have been damaged (.) another violent storm hit Luton (.) ripping through gardens and tearing tiles off roofs

Present tense verb – What is the effect? Find another example.

Switch to outside interview with a woman whose house had been hit.

Female interviewee: it came round this large tree here [pointing] (.) and there was loads of leaves with it (.) the whole air was full of leaves

What is the effect of the eye-witness report?

Reporter: ok (.) and you hid in the bathroom

Female interviewee: I did (.) as the trampoline went up in the air I didn't wait to see where it landed (.) we just (.) my daughter and I just hid in the bathroom

Return to studio.

Colloquial description – Why has the presenter chosen this informal approach?

Studio presenter: welcome to Graham Forrester from the Met office (.) pretty horrible stuff if you had been close to one of these (.) what causes them

What is the contrast between the earlier eye-witness account and the contribution of the technical expert?

Graham Forrester: The cause was intense (.) **very** intense cold front (.) basically (.) and the winds associated with it

Studio presenter: we have about 30 of these tornadoes a year (.) there seems more of them (.) is something going on with the climate

What is the purpose of this stressed word?

Graham Forrester: don't think so (.) the UK is one of the places for getting the most tornadoes (.) although more severe storms are forecast with climate change

Studio presenter: thank you very much (.) Graham Forrester (1) if you've got any pictures of the tornadoes you can mail them to us (.) you can find details on our website

Informal speech feature of contraction – Find any other examples.

Conventional elliptical features of headline – Find at least one other example of ellipsis. What is the effect of using this grammatical technique?

Tornadoes at breakfast leave trail of destruction

South and Midlands wake to devastating storms

Winds took seconds to rip roofs from houses

Matthew Taylor

Tornadoes and gale force winds ripped through towns and villages in southern and central England yesterday morning, damaging scores of homes.

Families described how they woke to see trees being uprooted and roof tiles and chimney pots flying through the air as winds of 70 mph hit the region. Up to 10 separate tornadoes were reported in towns from Hampshire to Cambridgeshire as a cold front moved north-east across England.

Active verb in continuous present – Find another example and comment on the effect.

Frank Mikos told how he woke in Farnborough, Hampshire, to find his home 'rocking from side to side'. He said 'The entire flat just felt as if it was about to take off – just like that scene in the *Wizard of Oz*. The noise was absolutely tremendous. I thought the windows were about to come crashing in.'

Emergency services said 10 of the 20 homes affected in Mr Mikos's street had suffered severe structural damage.

Mr Mikos added: 'The devastation is unbelievable. Slates, bus shelters, all just blown everywhere.' Several garages in the area also had their roofs torn off, with debris crashing on to the cars inside.

Terry Parrott described how he saw the tornado approaching as he was getting ready for work. 'I looked out of my bedroom window and could see this huge whirling thing come through between the two houses and it lifted the garage roofs up,' he said. 'It just picked everything up, even stuff that was nailed down. It was incredible, and then after 90 seconds it was all gone, all over.'

How do the language choices convey the scale of the episode?

What is the effect of identifying a specific eye witness?

What is the effect of this reference?

3 Collate the features you have identified in a table like the one below. Some features have been identified for you.

Text A	Text B
• immediate start to news item	• headlines and sub-headings
• intonation features of pauses and stressed words	• speech quoted to provide eye-witness accounts
• contraction, eg 'don't think so'.	• verbs and adjectives used for dramatic effect eg 'tremendous', 'crashing', 'huge, whirling thing', 'incredible'.

4 Discuss the similarities between the two reports. What are the main differences in the strategies each writer uses to engage the interest of their target audience?

Although there are differences in register and language, there are similarities in the reporting of the event in Texts **A** and **B**. They include:

- making use of eye-witness accounts
- emphasising dramatic aspects of the situation through the language used
- appealing to the 'human interest' angle by interviewing ordinary people.

The writers of both texts make sure there is a constant focus on the needs of their target audience.

Remember that whether you are producing a text for a reading or a listening audience, it must be easy to follow and appealing to read or listen to. Let's look more closely at the features writers use to break up written and spoken texts to make them more appealing and readable, to give signposts to the reader and to link the sections and give the text **cohesion**.

Take it further

Choose a current news item and produce short texts in two different genres, eg a report for a free newspaper distributed to commuters in city centres and an item for presentation on a children's TV news channel. Remember to focus on the needs of your audiences as you write.

Activity 8

1 Working in a small group, collect examples of different types of short texts for reading audiences, eg leaflets, magazine articles, adverts, pages from a children's reference book.

2 Read the texts together and identify the features that have been used to present them in an appealing way. List your ideas in the first column of a table like the one below.

Features in written texts	Features in spoken texts
• paragraphs • white space	

3 Share your list with other groups and add any extra points to it.

4 Add a comment about the effect of each device, for example, to add emphasis, to highlight points, to summarise or to make distinctions.

   In the same way you will need to provide these cohesive links in spoken texts.

5 Now find examples of texts for a listening audience, eg speeches, news reports, scripts for documentary or drama programmes on TV or radio, playscripts.

6 Read these texts aloud and, on your table, list the features used to make each one appealing to a listening audience. Add comments as before.

7 Compare and refine your lists with the help of other groups.

You can now use your lists of features as a reminder of how writers present texts for both reading and listening audiences.

Key term
cohesion

Making preparations and choices

To stimulate your coursework writing, you can choose to study any literary and non-literary texts from one of the topics below, as long as you remember to include one prose fiction text and one drama or poetry text.

Entrapment   **Dystopia**   *Women's Lives*   **Gothic and Supernatural**   **JOURNEYS AND PILGRIMAGES**

Activity 9

1 Working in a small group, choose one of the topics above and brainstorm ideas for texts related to it. Record your ideas on a diagram like the one below.

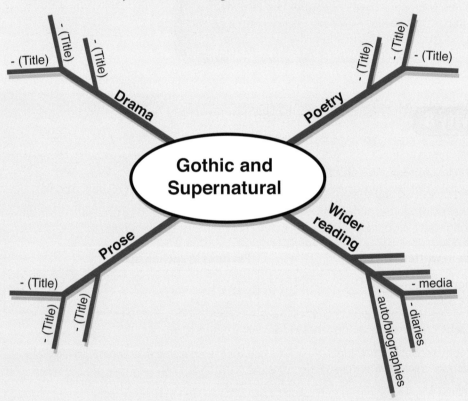

2 Individually, select two texts suitable for detailed study from your diagram:

   a choose one prose fiction text

   b add one drama or poetry text to complement your fiction text.

Keep your diagram as a reminder of the types of wider reading you can use to stimulate ideas and approaches for your own writing. Throughout the course, read as many different types of writing for reading and listening audiences as you can, to experience and explore a wide range of literary and linguistic approaches and techniques. If you can, take copies of the texts you read – or extracts from them – so that you can identify and comment on interesting features. You could also keep a diary of the texts you read and your responses to them.

You don't need to study your wider reading in as much detail as your chosen prose fiction and drama or poetry texts, but it will provide examples of good, and maybe some bad, models of writing. This will help build up your knowledge and increase your confidence, help you write your commentary and open up many creative possibilities for your own original writing.

At this stage in your coursework preparation, you do not need to make any decisions about your final tasks. Instead, take the opportunity to read, write and discuss ideas and approaches with your teacher and other members of your group. Give yourself time to read, study and reflect on your chosen texts. Take the opportunity to read widely, discover new texts and practise different types of writing without any assessment. This is the time to have fun exploring the craft of writing, finding out how professional writers work and following your own interests.

A contemporary writer Kirsty Gunn made this comment on the art of writing:

> Writing is a world. It's a place we inhabit entirely when we're there – putting words down on the page, letting sentences connect and form on computer screens. We can't imagine, when we're writing, that there's any other reality than this – the world of the story we are making, the writing we have made.

When you have chosen your texts, make a copy of the table below and use it to record the details. You can add to the wider reading section as you find new texts to read and investigate.

Unit 2: Creating texts		
Prose fiction	Title	Author and source
Drama or poetry	Title	Author and source
Wider reading	Title or type of text	Author and source

Writing your commentary

Make sure you record the title and author, as well as the source, of each text you read, so that you can find it again or refer to it accurately again. This will be invaluable because you have to include a bibliography in your coursework folder to provide evidence of wider reading and research.

Producing your coursework folder

You need to produce one text for a reading audience of about 1750 words and one text for a listening audience of about 750 words. You also need to write a commentary on each text, with a maximum of 500 words each, to explain and comment on the writing process.

The moderators can award a total of 80 marks for your coursework:

- 24 marks for your text for a reading audience
- 24 marks for your text for a listening audience
- 16 marks for each of your two commentaries.

You can earn high marks for your creative texts by:

- showing confidence in identifying audience and purpose and writing fluently and confidently to produce coherent, controlled texts (AO1)
- showing creativity in the production of a text and demonstrating expertise in selecting and using literary and linguistic approaches, drawing on insights from literary and linguistic studies (AO4).

You can gain high marks on your commentaries by:

- explaining and commenting on an interesting range of literary and linguistic techniques in stimulus texts and in your own writing; demonstrating some sensitivity and perception in discussing how form and language shape meaning, showing detailed critical understanding (AO2)
- showing awareness and exploring the significance of contextual factors in relation to literary and linguistic choices; exploring and offering detailed comment on the influence of the stimulus texts on your own writing (AO3)

For the assessment objectives in full, see page 91. Guidance on how to provide evidence for the assessment objectives in your original writing and commentaries is given throughout the rest of this unit.

Planning, drafting and editing

Key term
constructive criticism

We have looked at some aspects of planning, but drafting and editing are equally important elements in producing your coursework. All professional writers treat these tasks seriously, and you should do the same. Find someone in your group whom you can trust to give you good **constructive criticism** – and be prepared to do the same for them. In that way, you can try out your ideas on someone else and then improve your original draft as much as possible – that's the beauty of coursework.

Redrafting

When you have completed writing your original texts for the first time, ask yourself the following questions. Then you can redraft your work, incorporating any necessary changes.

- Does the text fit my purpose?

- Does it cater for the needs of my intended audience? Re-read or listen to your text from their perspective.

- Is it cohesive – does it read logically and is it clear and easy to follow?

- Are the technical terms (the spelling and punctuation) used accurately? Take the time to check and correct any mistakes before you ask someone else to look at your work.

- Try to re-read or listen to your text from the perspective of your target audience.

- Use any feedback you receive from other members of the group.

Editing

You have been given a specific word count for each of your pieces of original writing and for your commentaries (see the box on page 90). If you write at excessive length, the extra words will not be assessed so it is very important to remember the word counts. You will probably find it difficult to keep your first drafts within the word count, but you still have the opportunity to edit your writing to make sure it is the correct length, just as professional writers do.

To make decisions about how and where to edit your work, re-read your work carefully and listen to the opinions of others in your group. You should, of course, also discuss your plans with your teacher before undertaking your editing.

You may not need to cut whole sections of content. Instead, re-read your work critically to see how it could be written more economically and concisely. For example, you could, and probably should:

- delete any irrelevant or repeated material

- find a way not to repeat words and phrases, unless you are doing it deliberately as a rhetorical device

- avoid vague words like 'quite' or 'almost'.

You may be surprised by how much you can reduce the number of words in this way.

Giving constructive criticism

If someone in your group asks for your assistance in reviewing their writing, try to take the same thoughtful, constructive approach you hope they will take with your writing. You might find the following ideas helpful.

- Does the writing suit its purpose?

- Imagine you are a member of the target audience. Does the writing appeal to you and meet any needs you might have from it? Give an honest account of the effect the writing had on you.

- What do you like about the writing? What features work really well?

- What do you think could be improved? Are there parts that are difficult to follow or where it lost your interest?

- Comment on the use of specific examples of literary and linguistic features.

- Ask questions that will prompt the writer to think of other options that might work well.

Adopting a critical approach like this will also help you improve your own writing.

B Writing for a reading audience

In this section you will investigate the conventions of writing for a reading audience and explore some model texts in different genres, focusing on the short story, biography or autobiography, and weblog. You will also practise planning and writing pieces in these genres.

Your text for a reading audience will have to meet the requirements for:

AO1: showing confidence in identifying audience and purpose and writing fluently and confidently to produce coherent controlled texts (8 marks)

AO4: showing creativity in the production of a text for a reading audience and demonstrating expertise in selecting and using literary and linguistic approaches, drawing on insights from literary and linguistic studies (16 marks)

1 Introduction

You can choose from a wide variety of options for both writing tasks, but in some ways your piece of writing for a reading audience gives you more scope because it is longer than your writing for a listening audience (1750 words rather than 750). Remember that your choice of task must be related to your study of your chosen topic and the ideas suggested by your stimulus texts.

Considering the issues

First, decide on your purpose and audience. This will help you choose the appropriate tone to use, so that you can establish the kind of relationship with the reader that you are aiming for and will determine some of the techniques you use.

Now the type of text (genre) you want to write will also start to become clear. All these decisions that you have taken so far will start to determine the types of **literary** and **linguistic devices** you should use to engage your reader and show off your writing skills to the full. The extent to which you will need to use **graphological** and **layout features** will depend on the genre of the text you decide to write, but, whichever genre you choose, the presentation of your text should capture and maintain the interest of your reader.

Choosing your task

The choice is infinite, but below are some examples of texts in different genres for a reading audience. Remember to discuss the choice you are considering with your teacher.

- A short story inspired by one of your chosen texts

- A chapter or sequence for a sequel to your chosen prose text

- A newspaper or magazine article inspired by your chosen prose or poetry text

- Entries for a weblog written by one of the characters in one of your chosen texts

- A diary extract written by a minor character in your chosen prose fiction or drama text

- A review of an exhibition, event, film or play relating to your topic, for example, a review of a film version of your prose fiction text, where you explore and comment on how well the text has been adapted and how it might help (or distract from) a study of the text

Comparative reviews of texts in two different genres, for example, a film or stage adaptation of one of your chosen texts, where you explore and comment on the different perspectives and interpretations offered by the different approaches

> **Key terms**
> literary devices
> linguistic devices
> graphological features
> layout features

- A web page exploring a particular aspect of one of your chosen texts, for example, how the writer of your prose fiction text has developed character or theme or how the writer of one of your literary texts has used the context of the time it was set in.

Activity 10

1 Choose a scene or extract from your chosen drama or poetry text and rewrite it as a diary or weblog entry by one of the characters. Think about the impression you want to make on your audience and about ways you can develop the character.

2 Compare your writing with the original text, noting the differences in perspective that are created by the change of genre.

3 Ask someone in your group to read your text and give you feedback on how it affected them. Does the response from your reader match your original intention?

Take it further

Ask at least two other people to read and give you feedback on the text you wrote for Activity 10. If possible, choose people who are different in age, gender and interests. Make notes on their feedback. Do you think that the way each person responded to the text was affected by their particular perspective? Why is that?

Creating a consistent voice

You will know from your work on Unit 1 that writers try to create a particular **voice** or tone for their writing so that they can establish a relationship with their audience. The voice will differ, of course, depending on the purpose of the text: for example, you may wish to stimulate the imagination of your readers or to persuade, reassure or advise them. So the voice that you choose may suggest a close, friendly relationship or it could be more detached and impersonal. Remind yourself of some of the different voices used in the texts in Unit 1 and the particular stylistic techniques the writers used to achieve them.

Activity 11

1 Working with a partner, read text **A** which is a travel blog

   a Read and think about the notes around the article.

   b Can you identify any other distinctive features that will appeal to a reading audience?

   c Discuss the voice that comes through in the article. Jot down your thoughts on the voice and your response to it, adding evidence from the article to support your views.

A www.getjealous.com/benandjess

BenandJess Round the World

Angkor Wat at sunrise-Cambodia

The journey was an experience in itself. The road is allegedly so bad because Bangkok Airlines pay the government to not improve it, ensuring their constant stream of passengers. The sights along the way were both amazing and a huge culture shock. After the relatively Westernised Thailand, Cambodia is just a country of rice fields and huts. The simplicity of life overwhelmed us – from five year old girls fishing, to eight year old boys washing water buffalo, all in the same muddy rubbish-bin of a river. The third face of Cambodia hit us in the form of Siem Reap, a grubby little place but with a few streets in the middle filled with really cool bars and great restaurants – Touristville. We spent the next day walking around and appreciating the things on offer. Had a FAB lunch in Blue Pumpkin, all white leather sofas and imported Argentinian wines, then cocktails at night on the aptly named Bar Street. Our favourtie bar was hilariously called 'Angkor What?', where we sat watching the throngs of Americans and Chinese get accosted by tuktuk drivers.

word blending

capitalising of colloquial abbreviation

picks up on pun in name

use of dashes increases paces

neologism

2 Still working with your partner, now read an extract from a magazine article in which Noel Gallagher talks about meeting Tony Blair after his first election victory.

a Identify the distinctive features that will appeal to a reading audience. Some suggestions have been given.

b Write a short commentary on how the voice comes across in the extract and your response to it, adding evidence from the article to support your views. Conclude with your thoughts on the overall effect.

Celebrity names, prominently displayed

B: GQ Magazine, August 2007

Noel Gallagher stays up late with Tony Blair

Quoted speech

'We were chatting to Tony', said Noel. I said to Tony. 'It was brilliant … we stayed up till seven o'clock in the morning to watch you arrive at the HQ. How did you manage to stay up all night?' … he leant over and said 'Probably not by the same means that you did.'

Anecdotal style

Humourous approach

3 The writers of these texts are also aware of context – both texts are short items in popular magazines. What do they deal with and how are they intended to be read?

Activity 12

Choose one of the texts in Activity 11 and continue it in the same style, writing about 100 words.

Writing your commentary

You can achieve high marks in your commentary by explaining and commenting on an interesting range of literary and linguistic techniques in stimulus texts and your own writing, and demonstrating some sensitivity and perception in discussing how form and language shape meaning, showing detailed critical understanding (AO2). For example:

The use of quoted speech in text B makes the reader feel as if they are actually listening to the conversation between Tony Blair and Noel Gallagher. Using their actual words also captures their personalities effectively.

You must also show awareness and explore the significance of contextual factors in relation to literary and linguistic choices, and explore and offer detailed comment on the influence of the stimulus texts on your own writing (AO3).

Key terms
neologism
voice

2   Short stories

Writing short stories gives you the chance to use your imagination and to create a fictional world where you are in control. It is exciting to decide how your characters behave and what happens to them and you can become a kind of creative director, making decisions and implementing changes as you wish. So writing a short story might be an attractive task for you. You will be familiar with the genre and you will almost certainly have ideas about themes, characters and settings that you would like to put into practice.

But writing a short story is not an easy option. You will need to research and study the art of short story writing to make sure that your own writing is effective and to achieve the best results. You may be eager to start writing, but the reading is equally important. A prize-winning writer once said that all writers need to spend more time reading than writing, so read a variety of stories both before and while you are writing your own.

Start by considering the range of genres available to short story writers, for example:

- classic detective: stories of Dorothy L. Sayers

- ghost stories: M.R. James, *Stone Knights*

- horror: Edgar Allan Poe, *The Tell-Tale Heart / The Pit and the Pendulum*; Daphne Du Maurier, *The Birds*

- historical narrative

- love story

- fantasy

- science fiction: Ray Bradbury, *The Sound of Thunder*; Arthur C. Clarke, *No Flowers for Algernon*

- gritty realism or 'slice of life' story

- magic realism (a blend of realistic elements with surreal elements): Angela Carter, *The Bloody Chamber / The Tiger's Bride*.

Independent research

Read a wide selection of short stories in different genres by classic and contemporary writers. Start with some of the short texts for Unit 1 (eg page 54). Here are some more suggestions of writers:

- Graham Greene, for the well-made short story

- Edgar Allan Poe, for the classic horror story

- M. R. James, for the classic ghost story

- Raymond Carver, for detective fiction

- Val McDermid, for modern crime fiction

- Ian McEwan, for stories that subvert the reader's expectations

- Ruth Rendell, for contemporary psychological crime fiction

- Margaret Atwood, for intriguing stories, often on gender issues

- Michel Faber, for a range of stories with diverse genres and approaches.

You will probably be able to add other stories to your reading list and you may also feel that some do not fit neatly into any one genre. Many contemporary short stories involve **genre-blending**, for example, taking a story that incorporates elements of sci-fi or the supernatural into a realistic modern urban setting. (For examples of this type of writing, see the collection of modern horror stories published by Comma Press: www.commapress.co.uk.)

Writing an effective short story

Effective short stories provoke, question and/or involve the mind of the reader in some way. Many short story writers try to evoke a sense of 'reality' that readers can relate to. They might do this by exploiting the spoken word through the use of the following techniques:

- dialogue

- first person narrative

- **interior monologue**

- features of colloquialism and informality.

A short story also needs **shape** to engage the reader and give a sense of satisfaction in reading it. In simple terms, a short story needs a beginning, a middle and an end, just like any other story, and there should be an element of **exposition** to set the scene. However, also like other stories, a short story becomes much more engrossing if there is a contradiction or change in the direction of events, which acts as a **catalyst** for a conflict or problem. This develops the plot and reveals more about the characters, and ultimately leads to a type of **resolution**, or climax. Some stories have an unexpected twist, or reversal of expectations, at the end; others may leave the reader with unanswered questions, mixed emotions or disturbing thoughts.

Writers take different approaches to the narrative structure of their short stories. You could also use any of the suggestions below effectively:

- chronological unfolding of events
- a series of revelations
- flashbacks
- keeping some part of the story back
- including a thread of implications throughout the story.

Now let us look at how a selection of writers use the key features of voice, characterisation, description and plot development to write effective openings to short stories.

Key terms
genre-blending
interior monologue
shape
exposition
catalyst
resolution

Activity 13

1 As you read the following openings of short stories, think about any features that make them appeal to you. Make brief notes about which openings you enjoyed reading and which make you want to read the rest of the story. Don't worry about technical terms at this stage – just focus on your immediate reactions.

A 'The Copper Peacock' by Ruth Rendell

It was over in an instant. A flash of orange out of the green hedge, a streak across the road, a thud. The impact was felt as a surprisingly heavy jarring. There was no cry. Anna had braked but too late and the car had been going fast. She pulled in to the side of the road, got out, walked back.
    An effort was needed before she could look. The cat had been flung against the grass verge which separated road from narrow walkway. It was dead.

(line 5)

Ambiguous use of pronoun

Main character introduced

Abbreviated clauses separated by commas

Omission of unimportant grammatical features

Short sentence for effect

Builds up tension

Revelation of the event

Short sentence for impact

B From 'The Darkness of Wallis Simpson' by Rose Tremain

In those days there was a madhouse in our village. Its name was Waterford Asylum, but we knew it as 'the Bin'. It appeared to have no policy of selection or rejection.
    If you felt your own individual craziness coming on, you could present yourself at the door of the Bin and the kindly staff would take you in, and you would be sheltered from the cruel world. This was in the 1950s. A lot of people were suffering from post-war sadness. In Norfolk, it seemed to be a sadness too complete to be assuaged by the arrival of rock'n'roll.

(lines 5, 10)

C From 'Reconciliation' by Polly Clarke

It's my first day. I cycled here in my trainers and I have forgotten my shoes. It's a building like a pile of cardboard boxes. My trainers definitely will look weird with my skirt, so I don't mind if I walk in bare feet.

    I hurt my feet – mountaineering, I'll say. It's cold and raining. A thirty foot Christmas tree draped in lights rears in front of the main entrance, but it doesn't cheer the place up. 'Mountaineering?' asks the
5 fat girl in personnel doubtfully. Yes, I say, in Scotland. I'm wearing the clothes I slept in. It saved me 20 minutes this morning and meant I could sleep a little longer. My outfit is a skirt and lycra top so there's no creasing, so who would know? My brilliant time-saving idea of dry-washing my hair is less successful. I sprinkled talc on my scalp and rubbed it in as I'm sure I read somewhere and then attempted to brush it out, but it has clumped at the roots and I know I look as if I have been renovating a house and my head has not
10 recovered from bringing down the ceiling.

D 'Grateful' Jane Rogers

For what we are about to receive, may the Lord make us truly grateful.

    That's at school. When it's your turn you have to scrape your table's leftovers into the bucket. Wrinkled brown gravy dried to the plate but slimy underneath. Cold white potato lumps. Chewed gristle and bits of rind. Everyone leaves prunes and custard thick and yellow dribbling across the dish when you tilt it like two
5 runnels of snot from a kid's nose up to its mouth. When you scrape the plates more smells come up from the undersides of the food as it plops into the bucket. You think about the people who are hungry. There's a famine in Ethiopia.

    OK. When they talk to you they have no idea. No idea that you might have a grain of intelligence. No idea that you're not just some sad bimbo whose diet went wrong.

2 Now share your ideas with the rest of your group. Try to reach some agreement about what makes a successful short story.

3 As a group, discuss the following questions.

    a Text **A** begins with a dramatic episode and presents the reader with a situation that is clearly going to be a catalyst. How does the writer focus on the possibilities for plot development?

    b How does the writer of text **B** use language to describe the setting and create atmosphere? Explain the effect of the italicised phrases.

    c How does the writer of text **C** build up the character of the writer? Consider the choice of narrative voice, the physical descriptions of the character and any clues to indicate her psychological state.

    d The writer of text **D** uses a first person narrative voice to establish a 'confessional' tone. Identify some of the linguistic techniques that invite the reader to share her feelings and experiences.

4 Individually, write a short written response to each of the openings, using evidence from the extracts to support your points.

Activity 14

In Activity 13, text **C** gives you a rapid exposition and a catalyst. How does the story end? There are endless possibilities.

1 To test this out, each member of your group should write a quick outline of how the story could be developed. Then share all your outlines.

2 Choose one outline and write the next two or three paragraphs in the story, remembering the elements discussed on page 109 and writing in a similar style to the original.

Take it further

Choose either text **C** or **D** from Activity 13 and rewrite it in third person narrative. How does this change of narrative perspective affect you as a reader?

The next activity gives you the opportunity to investigate the elements of characterisation, voice and plot development in a complete short story, written by contemporary novelist and screenplay writer Hanif Kureishi. It demonstrates what can be achieved with taut, concise writing: it is economical (only 696 words), selective and fast-paced; it uses a narrative voice that involves the reader; and there are elements of descriptive writing to set the scene.

Activity 15

1 Read the short story below and explore some of the key features of short stories by responding to the following prompts.

a Identify the narrative voice.

b Identify the structure of the narrative.

c What is the duration of the story?

d Identify the catalyst for the key event.

e What type of ending has the story been given?

f What perspective has the reader been given?

g How would you describe the genre of the story?

h List the features of the story that you found effective.

The Dogs

Overnight it had been raining but to one side of the precipitous stone steps there was a rail to grip onto. With her free hand she took her son's wrist, dragging him back
5 when he lost his footing. It was too perilous for her to pick him up, and at five years old he was too heavy to be carried far.

Branches heavy with sticky leaves trailed across the steps, sometimes blocking their way so they had to climb
10 over or under them. The steps themselves twisted and turned and were worn and often broken. There were more of them than she'd expected. She had never been this way, but had been told it was the only path, and that the man would be waiting for her on the other side of the area.
15 When they reached the bottom of the steps, her son's mood improved and he called 'chase me'. This was his favourite game and he set off quickly across the grass, which alarmed her, though she didn't want to scare him with her fears. She pursued him through the narrow wooded area
20 ahead, losing him for a moment. She had to call out for him several times until at last she heard his reply.

Their feet kept sinking into the lush ground but a discernible track emerged. Soon they were in the open. It was a common rather than a park and would take about forty
25 minutes to cross: that was what she had been told.

Though it was a long way off, only a dot in the distance, she noticed the dog right away. Almost immediately the animal seemed bigger, a short-legged compact bullet. She knew all dogs were of different breeds: Dalmatians and
30 Chihuahuas and so on, but she had never retained the names. As the dog neared her son she wondered if it wasn't chasing a ball hidden in the grass. But there was no ball that she

could see, and the little speeding dog with its studded collar had appeared from nowhere, sprinting across the horizon
35 like a shadow, before turning in their direction. There was no owner in sight; there were no other humans she could see.

The boy saw the dog and stopped, tracking it with curiosity and then with horror. What could his mother do but cry out and begin to run? The dog had already knocked her
40 son down and began not so much to bite him as to eat him, furiously.

She was wearing heavy, loose-laced shoes and was able to give the dog a wild blow in the side, enough to distract it, so that it looked bemused. She pulled the boy to her, but it
45 was impossible for her to examine his wounds because she then had to hold him as high as she could while stumbling along, with the dog still beside her, barking, leaping and twisting in the air. She could not understand why she had no fascination for the dog.
50 She began to shout, to scream, panicking because she wouldn't be able to carry her son far. Tiring, she stopped, and kicked out at the dog again, this time hitting him in the mouth, which made him lose hope.

Immediately, a big long-haired dog was moving in the
55 bushes further away, racing towards them. As it took off to attack the child she was aware, around her, of numerous other dogs, in various colours and sizes, streaming out of the undergrowth from all directions. Who had called them? Why were they there?
60 She lost her footing, she was pushed over and was huddled on the ground, trying to cover her son, as the animals noisily set upon her, in a ring. To get him they would have to tear through her but it wouldn't take long, there were so many of them, and they were hungry too.

2 Now compare your exploration with the discussion of the text below.

The writer has used the narrative perspective of the omniscient author. He is distant from the main character, referring to her only by the third person pronouns 'she' and 'her', and her son is referred to as 'the child'. What effect did this have on you? Did you have a sense of frustration that you could not identify with the characters because of the lack of personal name or did this anonymity and detachment from the characters create a sense of mystery and unease? Have you considered writing a short story without naming your characters?

The narrative structure is chronological, with one event unfolding after another. The whole of the action takes place rapidly, possibly in the space of minutes. What did you identify as the point where you knew something was going to go wrong? The catalyst for the action could be the appearance of the first dog, although implications of danger are threaded through the narrative, for example with the state of the steps, the obstacles in their way, the unknown area, the distance to cross the common. Did you find the ending disturbing, given the inevitability of what is about to happen? Does it leave the reader feeling unsettled?

The reader is given an overview of all that takes place, rather like watching scenes unfold in a film. It may not surprise you that the writer, Hanif Kureishi, has also written screenplays for films.

The genre of the story is modern horror. It does not deal with classic horror and images of the supernatural, but instead presents the reader with some of the fears and dangers of the real world around us.

Writing your short story should be a stimulating and enjoyable experience and you will need the opportunity to experiment and try out different approaches. A great activity to use as a 'warm-up' exercise is to begin by trying to write some flash fiction. What is **flash fiction**?

- It is short, usually fewer than 150 words, like a haiku in prose.

- It is also known as **micro-fiction**, **postcard fiction**, **short-shorts**.

- It can be any genre you like.

- It is written by professional writers like Margaret Atwood and Raymond Carver.

- It is useful to capture an intense moment in understanding or a **revelation**.

Flash fiction is also good practice for you as a budding short story writer because it focuses the mind and helps you to limit word length – you have to get the greatest impact with the fewest words.

Here is an example of flash fiction, which was published in a magazine and written by Christie Watson, a non-professional writer.

'Snowdrops'

Labi arrived at Heathrow in darkness long after it should have been dawn. 'Asylum', he said repeatedly to the pounded yam-coloured woman, and tried to focus on her security badge, rather than the thick strap of black underwear inching away from her blouse. He was led into a room containing nothing bar a frayed carpet, two plastic chairs and window jarred open with a large yellow book.

He poked his hand through the gap in the window and felt a glassy snowdrop melt on his ringless wedding finger. He imagined his wife walking uphill in the midday sun, the citrus plastic bowl balancing on her cornrows slowly leaking cholera water.

Key terms

flash fiction

micro-fiction

postcard fiction

short-shorts

revelation

Activity 16

'Snowdrops' is only 111 words long.

1 Write some flash fiction in less than 150 words, taking the subject matter or your approach from your chosen texts.

2 Working in a small group, share and critique your writing.

Take it further

Keep on writing flash fiction at any suitable moment. You don't need to show your work to anyone else, but you may collect interesting ideas to stimulate your own writing. If you are interested in having your flash fiction published, the magazine *Mslexia* welcomes contributions.

Independent research

As a group, compile your own anthology of short stories in different genres. Each group member could contribute a favourite story, as long as it illustrates some of the distinctive features of short story writing. Make some notes on the features and identify techniques you find effective. Use the anthology and your notes as a resource to return to during your coursework.

Planning and drafting your short story

You need to make some key decisions before you start to draft your story, so the planning stage is extremely important. You will have gathered lots of ideas, but remember that your story must have developed from your chosen topic area and show evidence of inspiration from your stimulus texts.

Once you have the inspiration for your story and are ready to plan it, try to decide on:

- which genre or blend of genres is most suitable
- the most appropriate narrative voice (ie first or third person)
- the number and type of characters: it's usually a good idea to limit yourself to two or three
- the narrative structure you think will work
- how you will represent spoken language (eg dialogue, reported speech, interior monologue)
- the main event or catalyst
- a paragraph by paragraph outline
- the most effective type of ending (ie a resolution or an open ending).

You may not be able to decide on all of these features initially but do keep them in mind.

When you have completed the first draft of your story, try to leave it for 24 hours before reviewing it. This will help you to judge it with fresh eyes. It would also be an excellent idea to ask a member of your group to read your draft and give you constructive feedback.

Make notes on the feedback you receive and annotate you draft with your ideas for revising it. Keep your notes as a reminder of why and how you made changes to your story, so that you can explain your decisions in your commentary.

Make the most of this opportunity to revise and really polish your short story.

Writing your commentary

Keep any drafts and evidence of revisions to use while writing your commentary.

Activity 17

1 Put together your plans for a short story of approximately 600–700 words, taking into account all the key elements for success that you have studied (see pages 108–113 and the list above).

2 Write your first draft. Then review your work and ask for constructive criticism from someone else in your group, before deciding on your revisions.

3 Finally, revise your short story so that it is as effective as possible.

Writing your commentary

Activity 18

Read the following extract from a short story. The story was inspired by the topic Gothic and Supernatural and was influenced in particular by *Dracula* by Bram Stoker and *The Bloody Chamber*, the collection of short stories by Angela Carter.

Next to the melancholy castle the wide silver lake shone though there was no moon in the sky. The darkness was a velvet blanket wrapping the night over the land. The shadowy pine trees and the castle were hidden in the blackness but the lake was shining and sinister, like poisonous mercury. The Duke was standing at the edge of the lake staring at the water. He stood in the same place every night, fading into
5 the blackness as if he wasn't really there. It was like the smooth, glinting water was more solid than him.

Although she could not see her father, she knew he was there as she looked out of the window towards the water. He had once been a powerful General in the army of the kingdom. He had worn a blood-red coat as he rode his horse into battle. His silver sword had shone like the buttons on his shoulders and the medals on his chest. But something was weakening him. Every night he stood by the lake and every
10 morning he looked paler, transparent as water, worn out like an old nightshirt.

She heard the creak of the door downstairs and knew that her father had come back into the castle. His footsteps were quiet on the stairs, like a mouse or a shadow. She ran down the stairs and down to the edge of the lake, not daring to touch the water. The lake twinkled evilly like a witch's eye. She saw herself in the reflection of the water but she could not see anything else. The castle loomed behind,
15 but the lake only saw her.

Imagine that, as a reader, you have been asked to give advice to the writer on the effectiveness of their story. Working in a small group:

- discuss what you found effective about the extract

- discuss any particular literary or linguistic techniques you felt worked well and any points in the story where you felt it could have had more impact or been improved in some way

- agree on a list of points to feed back to the writer.

Writing your commentary

Remember to write about how your choice of language shapes the meaning of your story, in a similar way to this example:

Making the male characters in the story seem weak and powerless was a key aim, along with emphasising the power and strength of the female characters. The pejorative modification of the father 'paler, transparent as water' supports this, as does personifying the lake to make the surrounding natural world dangerous and evil, 'shining and sinister'. The simile 'worn out like an old nightshirt' creates imagery to have the effect of him becoming a broken man.

3 Biographies and autobiographies

Go into any major bookshop and you will see that the biography and autobiography shelves are crammed with new titles. This genre often features at the top of the bestseller lists. Why? Because people obviously enjoy reading about the lives of others.

Biography is an account of someone's life. The person could be living or dead, and is most likely to be, or have been, a famous historical figure or a more recent celebrity. When someone writes about their own life with a view to publishing, they are producing an **autobiography**, or memoirs, as politicians like to call them. Many people write their autobiography on their own, but celebrities like models and footballers often have the help of professional ghostwriters.

Writing a biography or autobiography can be an absorbing and exciting task as you have the opportunity to write about character, setting, plot, etc. with all the information readily available. So in some ways the job of a biographer resembles that of a novelist, except they don't have to invent the material. What the biographer does have to do is select, shape and present the details of the subject's life in a way that both informs and intrigues the reader at the same time.

Choosing a subject can also be fascinating. Avoid choosing a celebrity or famous historical person, as a great deal will already have been written about them and your biography needs to be original and to have developed from your topic. Instead, start by considering your family and friends. Is there a member of your family who has had interesting experiences, an unusual occupation, travels, or memories of past events that would be of interest to others? Is there anyone among your friends who is talented in a particular field such as sport or music? If you choose someone you know as your subject, you will be able to begin your preparation with an interview. (See page 120 for suggestions about how to do this.)

To help you decide whether writing a biography or autobiography is the option for you, read as many as you can. Limit yourself to reading short extracts so that you can read widely and get a flavour of lots of different styles and approaches. Continue your research if you do decide on this option, to help you gather ideas for your own writing. Libraries and newspaper supplements are a good source of material – and don't forget to read the obituaries as they are a type of mini-biography.

Independent research

Follow up these suggestions for wider reading.

The writer Peter Ackroyd has written several successful biographies about literary and artistic historical figures, eg *Dickens. Path to the Silent Country* and *The Dark Quartet* are fascinating biographies of the Brontë sisters and their brother by the novelist Lynne Reid Banks. Biographies of contemporary public figures include *Blair Unbound* by Anthony Seldon.

Very different sorts of people write autobiographies. You might look at *The North Face of Soho* by Clive James; *The Slow Train to Milan*, which is an autobiographical novel by Lisa St Aubin de Teran; or *Persepolis*, an exciting autobiography in graphic novel form about a young girl's experiences living in Iraq, by Marjane Satrapi.

Fact and opinion

What do you think are the primary purposes of biography and autobiography writers? The main purpose of a biographer is to convey factual information about their subject and, although an autobiographer might have some other ulterior motives, that is one of their main purposes too. The writer will also try to entertain in some way in order to keep the reader engaged and they might use their writing as a forum for their own personal opinions.

Biography and autobiography involve a blend of **fact**, **opinion** and **speculation**, so it is important for you to be able to distinguish between these elements and be aware of the writer's **perspective** or **bias**.

Key terms
biography
autobiography
fact
opinion
speculation
perspective
bias

Activity 19

1 Read the extract below. As you read, highlight or annotate a copy of the text, to distinguish between the facts and those points that offer a personal opinion or pure speculation.

From *Queen Mother* by Penelope Mortimer

The cool, showery weather at the beginning of August 1900 came as a relief after July's heatwave, particularly for women like Cecilia, Lady Glamis, waiting for the birth of her ninth child in her parents' Grosvenor Gardens apartment.

5   Exactly where in London the future Queen Elizabeth the Queen Mother was born is the subject of speculation. There is the theory that the event took place in an ambulance. The first fuel-powered buses were not in operation until that year and those, for some odd reason, were in Norfolk, so it is reasonable to assume that ambulances were horse-drawn and none too easy to summon in an emergency.

---

2 Now answer the following questions.

  a The writer describes the weather and details of contemporary lifestyle. Are these details fact, opinion or speculation? Why does she mention these details?

  b Which words does she use to indicate that she is not certain of her facts?

3 Penelope Mortimer is actually better known as a novelist. Can you identify any features that are reminiscent of novel writing? What are they and why do you think she uses them?

Creating narrative tension

In the extract in Activity 19, Penelope Mortimer used strategies more usually associated with writing fiction. Although she is well known for writing novels, she is also aware that a biography needs more than simple facts about a person's life to make it appealing. The writer has to make their subject come to life in the mind of the reader. One way of doing this is to create the same **narrative tension** as you would in fiction.

Activity 20

1 Read the extract from a biography of Napoleon below. It explores the last phase of his life when he was exiled on the island of St Helena.

From *The Dark Room at Longwood* by Jean-Paul Kauffman

Napoleon first entered this room on 18 October 1815. He is 46. What were the thoughts and feelings that filled his mind on that day? None of the books written by eye-witnesses give any satisfactory answer – those men who never took their eyes off him but never really saw him. Those who followed

5 him into exile, like his jailors, closely watched the least of his gestures but never really looked at him.

    When all's said and done, Napoleon's entry into the pavilion at The Briars was quite a banal moment in his captivity: it has no dramatic significance at all. The English behaved fairly decently towards their defeated enemy. Nonetheless, from now on, Napoleon will be a prisoner and will be given no higher title than 'General Bonaparte'. Five and a half years will pass before his death. Once

10 he stepped over the threshold of this pavilion, he lost his freedom for ever. Goodbye for the last time. Napoleon goes in … It's the end of everything.

---

2 On a photocopy of the extract, highlight and annotate the use of:

- different tenses
- dramatic statements and short sentences
- time sequences
- techniques to create a sense of mystery.

3 How does the writer try to create tension to intrigue his readers?

Positioning the reader

Key terms
narrative tension
position

You will already have realised that writers of auto/biographies are not neutral – they usually have an opinion about their subject and they purposefully use literary and linguistic techniques to try to **position** their readers to share their opinion. Often their intention (either deliberately or subconsciously) is to encourage the reader to sympathise, or even empathise, with the subject.

Activity 21

1 Re-read the extract from the biography of Napoleon in Activity 20, thinking about the effects of:

   a focusing on Napoleon's isolation

   b asking the reader questions.

2 Identify specific examples of the techniques the writer uses to position his readers.

3 How would you describe the perspective or point of view of the writer?

Take it further

Find an example of a biography of a famous person that is mainly factual (a dictionary of biographies would be a good source of material). Choose an extract from the text and rewrite it in a similar style to the extract in Activity 20.

Evoking a sense of place

Writers of biography and autobiography need to help their readers understand their subject's life; this includes where they lived and their surroundings, so one of the tasks of the biographer is to create atmosphere or evoke a sense of place. This does not mean writing lengthy descriptive passages, which may not be of interest to the reader, but it does mean including small incidental details that indicate how and where the subject lives or lived.

In the following activity you will explore an extract from a student's autobiography where she creates this kind of atmosphere.

Activity 22

Read the text below.

> But best of all was the garden. It was another world. The garden was long and thin and I liked to go right to the end where Granny's strange plants grew: tall, exotic, almost frightening. Grandad called it 'the jungle'. 'Have you been playing tigers in the jungle
> 5 again?' he would ask me. But I wasn't a tiger – I was a brave adventurer, crawling through the spiky green leaves on my belly like a snake, looking out for danger. Sometimes I used to sneak outside to the jungle at night. I'd lie on the damp earth, breathing in the green and dark smell of the plants and listening to the
> 10 silence of the night and my own heartbeat and tell myself that I was not afraid.

1 In a small group, discuss what you think the writer's purpose is.

2 Discuss how you would describe the style. Agree on which of the following adjectives is appropriate and why.

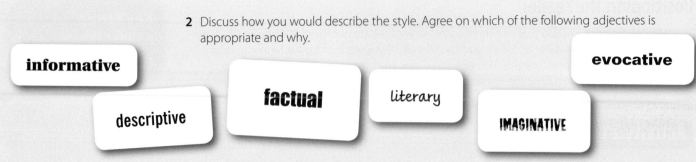

informative

descriptive

factual

literary

IMAGINATIVE

evocative

3 Individually, write a short paragraph commenting on the writer's purpose and how she tries to achieve it, using evidence from the extract to support your points.

Activity 23

Think of any childhood memory or episode that had an impact on you and write a brief autobiographical account in approximately 250 words. Aim to evoke a sense of place as in the extract in Activity 22 and to create pen-portraits of particular people.

Describing the subject

To make a biography or autobiography attractive, you need to intrigue your readers about the subject so that they are eager to discover more. This goes beyond physical description to explore their personality, attitudes and opinions – in other words, 'what makes them tick'. Ask yourself what is interesting about the subject and what, as a reader, you would want to know.

Activity 24

Read the extract below, which is the opening of a biography of Lizzie Siddall, the model for the painting of Ophelia drowning by Pre-Raphaelite painter John Millais. The painting made Lizzie famous, but at the age of 33 she committed suicide.

In this extract the writer concentrates on the physical description of her subject: it's a text full of *descriptive* adjectives and some *intriguing* background detail.

From *Lizzie Siddall: Face of the Pre-Raphaelites* by Lucinda Hawksley

The Tragedy of a Pre-Raphaelite Supermodel

The Red-Haired Model

In 1849, Lizzie was twenty years old and had lived an unremarkable life.
5   She was tall and slender with large eyes and long hair the colour of pale copper. Striking, rather than beautiful, especially with those huge, heavy-lidded eyes in such a small face, Lizzie did not conform to the contemporary ideal of beauty. Her greatest considered attributes at this date were that she had perfect deportment, fine facial bone structure and was unusual looking. A woman one
10 would look at and remember. By fashionable dictates she was too tall and her hair was red – most definitely not considered an attribute. Superstition still deemed that red hair was unlucky and associated with witches, black magic and the devil.

1 Working in pairs or a small group, decide what you think was the writer's main purpose and who you think was her target audience.

2 Individually, write a commentary on the writer's approach and the techniques and language she used. In particular, look at how she provides the reader with a description of Lizzie's appearance. Include specific examples from the extract to support your points.

3 Share your commentary with the rest of your group.

Considering audience

A clear notion of who the audience will be helps to shape any piece of writing. Who is the target audience in terms of age, gender, lifestyle and interests? Why would they want to read a particular biography or autobiography?

Activity 25

Texts **A** and **B** are both short biographies written for children. Read them and note the differences in their purpose and stylistic features.

A From *Famous People Factfile*

Elvis Presley

1935–1977

Born in Tupelo, Mississippi, USA, Elvis Presley became the most successful recording artist in the world.

He was discovered in 1953 by Sun Records, who sold his contract to RCA in 1955. By blending country music with gospel and rhythm and blues, Presley made music that attracted huge numbers of young people at a time when America was emerging from the shadow of World War II.

His first number one single was 'Heartbreak Hotel' and it was followed by a string of others. Presley caused a sensation with his dancing, which involved swivelling and gyrating his hips.

During most of the 1960s Presley also made a career in films, starring and singing in two or three every year.

In 1977 Presley died of heart failure brought on by his excessive lifestyle. His mansion, Graceland in Memphis, is now a shrine for his millions of fans throughout the world.

B From *Who's Who in Science and Technology* by Bob Fowke

Darwin, Charles Robert

He put evolution on the map

1809–82

Before Charles Darwin published his latest famous book *On the Origin of Species by Means of Natural Selection* in 1858–9, most people still believed that God created all species of living things at the beginning of the world. Lions had always looked like lions and gerbils had always looked like gerbils. Charles Darwin showed that species evolve gradually one from another, and God had nothing to do with it – at least not as described in the Bible.

Darwin was the son of a Shrewsbury doctor. In 1831 he joined a scientific expedition (1831–36) bound for South America, and the Pacific Ocean, on board the *Beagle*, as the ship's naturalist, a specialist in plants and animals. They sailed down the Atlantic Coast of South America then up the Pacific coast. In the Galapagos Islands, far off the coast of Ecuador, Darwin saw how the same species of birds living cut off for centuries on different islands had developed in quite different ways. This and many other amazing discoveries led him to his theory of 'evolution by natural selection'.

His theory lies behind all modern ideas on how different species of living things have come to be the way they are and how they will change in the future. It raised a storm of protest among religious leaders because it seemed to deny the story of creation in the Bible. Darwin's theory won out – and now he's buried in Westminster Abbey.

1 Copy and complete the chart below to help you analyse and compare the approach in both texts. What do you notice about each of the stylistic features? Some comments have been given to get you started.

Features and purpose	Text A	Text B
Treatment of facts	Mostly factual information, eg dates, ...	
Descriptive detail	Only a few adjectives, to give more information	
Other features		Dashes inject pace and add the writer's asides. The phrase '...' shows an underlying sense of humour.
Purpose		

2 Write a two-paragraph summary explaining your conclusions about the purpose of each text and how you have reached them. Remember to include evidence from the texts to support your points.

Take it further

Rewrite text **A** in Activity 25 in the style of text **B**. Your aim to is give a more personal slant on the subject and to use language to excite the reader's imagination. Ask a partner to read and evaluate your rewritten version and then make revisions in the light of their comments. Finally, write a short commentary explaining the changes you made to the original text.

Writing a biography

Your first task is to choose a subject for your biography. You might be tempted to choose a famous historical person or a celebrity, but it might be difficult to find an original approach as their life will already have been fully documented. Also, remember that your biography must be developed from your coursework topic.

As an alternative, you could choose someone you know as your subject. You need to be sure that you will have something interesting to write about, so pick someone who has achieved something worthwhile, experienced something out of the ordinary or lived through eventful times.

As a starting point, it is a good idea to interview your subject, using carefully planned questions to get information about their lives. You might even interview more than one person to give yourself a choice of subjects.

Interviewing your subject for a biography

The most difficult part of an interview can be getting started. Here are a couple of approaches that might act as an effective warm-up. Either ask your subject to write down or tell you 'five things you didn't know about me' or ask them a series of questions designed to get unusual responses, for example:

- If you were an animal or bird, what would you be?
- If you could change one event in history, what would it be?
- How would you describe the kind of place where you feel happiest?
- What is your greatest fear?
- What is your greatest pleasure?

Activity 26

With a partner, try out either or both of the ideas for starting an interview above.

a Which approach was most successful?

b Can you improve on the opening questions?

The next step is to craft the material into an extract from their biography. Use the model texts you have explored in this section to give you ideas about possible approaches and effective literary and linguistic techniques.

Activity 27

1 Working in pairs, both narrate a particular event in your life to each other while the other one takes notes. The event must have made a lasting impression on you – it might have been exciting, scary, disturbing, uplifting or life-changing, for example.

2 Individually, write an extract for your partner's biography from your notes. Use about 200–250 words.

3 Show your completed text to your subject to get their response.

> ## Writing your commentary
>
> In your commentary you need to explain the influences of your stimulus text and of the biographies or autobiographies that you used as style models.

Writing autobiography

You may decide that you would like to write an extract from your own autobiography as a coursework task. You will only be able to write a short extract in 1750 words, so you need to focus on a specific incident or experience that will give a flavour of your life and personality. Remember that the content of your extract also needs to reflect and explore an aspect of your chosen topic.

The stylistic techniques for writing biographies also apply to autobiographies. The key difference is in the narrative voice – you will be writing in the first person. (If you need to remind yourself of the differences between first and third person narrative, see Unit 1, pages 65–85.) This will allow you to express some emotion and your own opinions, but you are not writing a monologue, and your writing needs to be structured to give it some element of objectivity.

Activity 28

1 Take either the extract about the Queen Mother or the one on Napoleon on page 116 and rewrite it in the first person as if it is an autobiography (you will have to assume that the subject is still living).

2 Make notes on the changes that you made and the effects of the change in perspective.

Choosing your biography or autobiography task

When you come to choose your coursework task, remember that it must stem from chosen literary or non-fiction texts. The following generic ideas for tasks are all suitable choices, but you will need to refine them to suit your choice of subject and the coursework requirements. Above all, you are encouraged to make your own choices, in discussion with your teacher.

- Write an extract from a fictionalised biography of a minor or off-stage character from a literature text.

- Write a mini-biography of someone you know well.

- Write a mini-biography of a famous historical or contemporary person, but with an unusual perspective.

- Write an extract from your own autobiography.

4   Weblogs

If you are interested in producing **e-texts**, writing a **weblog** entry for your coursework task will be an appealing idea. The definition of a weblog is a website on which items are posted on a regular basis and displayed in reverse chronological order. '**Blog**' is an informal abbreviation of 'weblog'.

A blog is a contemporary form of text that gives writers the opportunity to reach a wide range of readers, avoiding formal criticism and preserving their anonymity. The audience is usually unknown, but the blog is instantly available to millions who are geographically, culturally and socially diverse. This can stimulate an interesting ongoing dialogue if readers are given the opportunity to comment and reply.

Blogs can have a very wide range of purposes and styles. On some, individuals or groups publish regularly updated accounts of their own or others' activities, interests and enthusiasms, rather like an online diary. Some debate global, social, political and environmental issues. Others offer fascinating creative possibilities, for example giving writers the chance to contribute sequences to short stories. So, although blogs use a specific means of communication, they include a wide range of genre – they could take the form of personal diary entries, a persuasive campaign, a debate, educational topics, study-related issues, travel writing, reviews, short story writing, etc.

A blog is immediate – what you write is what you get! A blog can be posted to reach an audience without evaluation and it can adopt any register or level of formality. Many blogs are informal, allowing individuals to share ideas and to set up a channel of communication with others.

However, that does not mean that anything goes – there are established conventions and even an etiquette for blog writing. Blogs are a series of sequential, dated entries, and each entry tends to be short – about 500 words is long enough for readers with limited time – and has a title to indicate what the subject is. Labels or 'tags' can be added to categorise entries and help readers find particular subjects quickly, for example a travel blog might have tags for all the entries about art and architecture. Many blogs include hyperlinks to guide readers to related material.

Blogs also have distinctive layout features and you can find templates for blog writing on sites such as www.blogger.com.

Writing your coursework

Even if you choose to write a blog, remember that marks will be awarded for the use of appropriate terminology and accurate, coherent written expression (AO1). So you will not be able to write a completely informal 'no rules' text. What you will be able to do is demonstrate your ability to use varied linguistic and literary techniques in a new and less conventional context for an appropriate audience.

llustration/image

masthead

**I'm an account handler...
GET ME OUT OF HERE!**

Hello, I'm Vicky and I'm going to South America for a bit to do some charity work, have a read to see what I've been getting up to

comments

« Older posts

title

7 months later....

February 17, 2008   9:30 pm

main text

Hi All

So that fateful day has cometh.... the final blog. I can't believe 7 months has gone by so quickly.

I've just left the project and what an amazing experience, I can safely say I've never done anything like it in my life. What the co-op are doing to support themselves and conserve the forest is so fantastic and it has been incredible living with them (albeit briefly) as opposed to just travelling through, whereby, in my opinion you only get to see the "nature" element, not how the "human" element underpins it. It's so great what they've managed to achieve from scratch (especially as they are so remote) and the fact that they are practically totally sustainable as-well. It really is a success story and a fantastic experience to have had.

Having said that, there have been parts which I've found quite tough. Contrary to outer impressions, I don't really mind the bugs, dirt, sporadic cold water supply, rice at every meal or gortex outfits. All those things are payoff for what you see, who you meet and (cringe coming...) kind of enhance the "experience" you have (sorry dudes!) It was the isolation that I found hardest. Having your nearest neighbour 3 hours away is the only way I can begin to describe the remoteness - or imagine nothing between London and York except trees..... Obviously that remoteness accounts for the unbelievable surroundings but when the cloud was in (as it was every day except 4) and you couldn't see 5ft in-front of you, it felt as if you were going to fall off the edge of the world. I really felt it when I was ill and they were debating getting me to a hospital and I thought "there's no way I can get myself off this mountain, and there is no way any vehicle can get to me - hmmmm" - not a fun predicament to be in and it makes you have the most enormous respect for the guys who live there.

Recent Comments

Stu: Well done VC, And Happy Birthday for Wednesday. x

nick: spider plants and dragon's blood trees all sounds very Narniaish! Can't wait for you to come back,...

gavin: Being ill without daytime telly! How does that work?

Stu: Nasty stuff. I've heard terrible things about the jungle sausage! Get well soon Vics x

gavin: Does snake really taste like chicken?

Pages
About

Archives
February 2008
January 2008
November 2007
October 2007
September 2007
August 2007
July 2007

hyperlinks

Begin with some research into the blog form. Throughout your course, read a wide range of different blogs to extend your appreciation of the diversity of purposes and stylistic approaches.

Independent research

Here are some suggestions of interesting blogs to investigate:

- The Huffington Post – www.huffpost.com – founded in Washington, this features a huge variety of postings from political and literary figures in the US

- The Greenhouse – www.demosgreenhouse.co.uk – features technological, social and sporting items

- www.myboyfriendisatwat.com – this ongoing soap opera, written by the Belgian **blogger** Zoe McCarthy, won 'Best European Blog'

- www.tokyo-girlblogspot.com – has been described as having the feel of 'a Radio 4 play' and is posted by an ex-pat Brit from Tokyo

- http://www.angelfire.com/extreme4/kiddofspeed/ – a fascinating and exciting blog by Elena Filatova, a young Ukrainian woman who motorbikes through the post-nuclear landscape of Chernobyl

- www.sino-angle.blogspot.com – an English translation of the blog by Xu Jinglei, which gives insight into the growing power of China

- http://dear-raed.blogspot.com/ – world famous 'Baghdad Blogger', a young man's diary of life in war-torn Iraq; it was so popular that it was published as a paperback book.

Activity 29

1 Working in a small group, share your responses to any blogs you have read and sites you have discovered – they could be informative, controversial or simply entertaining.

2 Start to compile a list of different types of blogs and their purposes.

Possible purposes of blogs are:

- to share personal experiences with others
- to raise awareness of certain issues
- to persuade
- to debate controversial issues
- to seek help or advice
- to educate
- to express views and opinions
- to describe personal feelings and ideas
- to write freely and creatively.

Key terms
e-text
weblog
blog
blogger

The next activity focuses on the variety in blog styles and the way the literary and linguistic features used are interrelated with the writer's purpose. The model texts are examples of well-written, literary and imaginative blogs, which could give you inspiration for your own coursework task.

Activity 30

1 Working with a partner, investigate one of the entries from five different blogs on pages 124 to 126. Make sure that at least one pair in your group investigates each of the entries. In each case:

a decide what you think the blogger's purpose is

b identify specific examples of literary and linguistic techniques that support your decision, briefly commenting on their effects

c identify any features that are specific to blogs.

The texts have been annotated with some questions and prompts for you to follow up in your analysis. You will see that some features are characteristic of other genres, because that is the style adopted by the blogger. If you think about why they used particular features, that may help you decide on the purpose of the blog.

2 Present your findings to the whole group, collecting and recording them on a whiteboard or flipchart.

3 Analyse the variety of purposes and approaches in the blogs by matching them with the descriptions below. You may feel that some fit into more than one category.

to persuade, raise awareness, demonstrate subject knowledge

to share experiences

to educate

to provoke, create debate, express strong personal opinions

to reflect and express intimate thoughts and feelings

to write creatively, to entertain

A Response to war and unrest in Beirut, from ibosblog.blogspot.com

Posted by Bob

8 August 2006

> What is the effect of this sentence?

War times are here … people have reverted to their wartime routine, waiting for long hours to get a few litres of fuel for their cars, and buying the rest from the black market at double or triple the official price. Alternate roads and make-shift bridges criss-cross the torn roads of my country, allowing access to even the most dangerous and cut-off locations.

> Find other examples of this type of emotive description.

> What is the effect of placing words in inverted commas?

My commuting time that ran for 45 minutes takes two hours these days, while home rents in 'safe' areas have doubled and one must be very lucky indeed to find even an attic to rent in some of the 'safest' areas.

Yet people are trying to bring a semblance of normality even to the most nightmarish of realities. The collective taxis called 'service', are still running, even in the most dangerous of places, albeit at a higher price per trip, and most grocers are still working, although most imported goods are hard to get. Even some pubs are open and some 'experts' are saying that alcohol and tranquilliser consumption have hit new records. People have shifted their lifestyles to endure what seems to be a very long war.

> How does this word affect the reader? Find examples of other lexical choices that make particular associations.

B Response to war and unrest in Beirut, from http://thedancingfairyblogspot.com

Posted by Fairy (the writer of this blog posted it after going to Vienna to escape the unrest in Lebanon)

9 August 2006

> Identify specific language choices that create the writer's mood.

I am so sorry to have left so many loved ones behind. I am so sorry, Beirut, to have turned my back on you in these horrible days! I am so sorry people that I'm not able to write down any positive words.

> Identify this literary technique and comment on its effect in this context

> What is the effect of this repetition?

Today, around late afternoon I slowly started to realise where I was. It's raining here and I'm freezing. People seem cold and introverted. I walked through the streets of Vienna and couldn't feel any connection anymore to this town that I lived in for seven years. I guess I never felt at home here anyway …

> What is the effect of the writer's use of the senses? Find other examples.

I'm tired, my eyes are closing but my mind is awake. When I close my eyes I see the streets of Beirut and I feel the heat of the summer, I hear the familiar noises and feel this unique familiar feeling that only Beirut is able to give me. Oh, I'm getting pathetic. I should go to sleep.

There truly is no honey on the moon these days.

> Identify one or two examples of effective **phonological techniques**.

> What is the effect of the shift in tone at these points in the text?

Key term
phonological techniques

C A green blog from http://blogs.guardian.co.uk/climate change/

The following text features extracts from an ongoing blog on climate change, posted by *The Guardian*, which invites comments and responses.

20.09.07: Green language

Alison Benjamin/Raising awareness

Carbon footprint, carbon neutral and carbon trading are no longer obscure terms bandied about by environmental anoraks. They are new entries in the latest edition of the shorter Oxford English Dictionary, which means they have officially entered the English language.

Bibi van der Zee/Reducing emissions

> *Compare the register and purpose of this entry with the one before it.*

Oh good, a carbon footprint label on my food to add to all the other labels. Shopping with small children is of course such a restful experience that I find I've plenty of time to pause and peruse the small essay written on each packet these days – no crotchety scrabbling and chucking in the trolley for me, oh no.

5 Minute Guide: Climate change

> *What is the effect of the writer's use of questions as sub-headings?*

Why does it matter?

Rising temperatures matter for several reasons: they affect rainfall patterns and make droughts more common. This is already affecting the developing world where, according to some estimates, there are already 200 million climate change refugees.

What happens next?

Climate campaigners are trying to persuade people to cut their emissions. But any climate solution needs the co-operation of governments.

> *What is the effect of this conjunction?*

The best example of this is the Kyoto Protocol, agreed in 1997, which commits developed countries to cut their greenhouse gas emissions. Yet the protocol did not have the support of the US, China and India – three of the world's biggest polluters.

D A travel blog from http://imanaccounthandlergetmeoutofhere.com/

Posted by Vicky Clarfelt, an advertising executive who left work for 6 months to volunteer in South America

3rd February 2008

> *how does the writer attempt to imitate spontaneous speech? Find other examples*

The weather is being a bit of a nightmare, and I feel like I´m undergoing a form of water torture. It´s now rained literally 24 hours a day for the last 11 days, which just gets sooooooo monotonous and, despite my trusty friend Peter Storm, I´m constantly soaked which gets pretty aggravating.

> *how does the writer try to appeal to her readers?*

Anyway, we decided to escape the rain for the weekend and go to see the Quillitoa crater lake. It was totally gorgeous and having hiked down to the lake, decided to get a mule back up to the top. Unfortunately, mine was on a suicide mission, went mental, and ran full steam into a gang of unruly, unsupervised mules on the path (1m wide, on side of ravine). In a bid to save myself I threw myself from said mule and lay on ground in style of Grand National jockey until the mule chaos had subsided. It´s obviously a spectator sport for the locals, who all stand at the top of the crater "ooohing" and "ahhing" and shouting, and clapping - mildly embarrassing. I´m now returning to the relative safety of the cloud forest with my trusty friends Peter and Berg.

> *identify features that are typical of blog writing*

Have a good week

Vicky

> *how would you describe the purpose of this blog?*

E An entertaining blog from http://yellowhighheels.blogspot.com/

Posted by Ellie Barnard, a journalism student at the London College of Fashion

Wednesday, 20 February 2008

Getting into the mind of a man

The concept of coming up with ideas for a lads mag is a slightly daunting one. Especially when it comes to trying to get into the mind of a guy who reads "Nuts". When talking to a male friend the other day, an educated city type, he admitted that he absolutely loves his weekly dose of this lads mag. I thought that this particular publication was only for the likes of guys who buy The Sun for its "articles" on page 3, but apparently I am mistaken. He told me that if he wants to read something challenging he buys a paper, when it comes to reading something to relax and unwind he'd much rather look at photos of boobs and bizarre injuries caused by male incompetence. Is this mindless form of journalism actually impressively self aware? When women read magazines, we take them seriously. We look at the fashion pages and read the real life stories and take it all in. Men don't take themselves seriously at all, a magazine doesn't need to pretend to be anything other than entertainment. So should my ideas for articles be sexist and patronising? Maybe I should just find a story which goes under each of the following headings: Naked celebrities (unobtainable women), naked real-life girls (obtainable), Cars, Scars and of course Sports. I've been left with the overwhelming feeling that this task is actually potentially the most complex yet. Mens minds might be simple, but coming up with an original idea for a lads mag is anything but.

As you have seen in Activity 30, many blogs are very well written and for the purposes of your coursework, your blog needs to be too. The next extract is from a blog written by a young female Iraqi known as Riverbend. The blog is popular because it gives a personal response to the situation in war-torn Iraq, so notice the mixing of personal narrative with political reference. The extract is also carefully crafted and seems to have been thoughtfully planned to achieve impact and to encourage empathy in the reader.

Activity 31

Read the extract from Riverbend's blog below.

Thursday April 26 2007

I remember Baghdad before the war – one could live anywhere. We didn't know what our neighbours were – we didn't care. No one asked
5 about religion or sect. No one bothered with what was considered a trivial topic: are you Sunni or Shia? You only asked something like that if you were uncouth and backward. Our lives revolve around it now. Our existence depends upon
10 hiding it or highlighting it – depending on the group of masked men who stop you or raid your home in the middle of the night.

On a personal note, we've finally decided to leave. I guess I've known we would be leaving for a while
15 now. We discussed it as a family dozens of times. At first, someone would suggest it tentatively because it was just a preposterous idea – leaving one's home and extended family – leaving one's country – and to what? To where? Since last
20 summer, we had been discussing it more and more. It was only a matter of time before what began as a suggestion – a last case scenario – soon took on solidity and developed into a plan. For the last couple of months, it has only been a

25 matter of logistics. Plane or car? Jordan or Syria? Will we all leave together as a family? Or will it be only my brother and I at first?

I know that leaving the country and starting a new life somewhere else – as yet unknown – is
30 such a huge thing that it should dwarf every trivial concern. The funny thing is that it's the trivial that seems to occupy our lives. We discuss whether to take photo albums or leave them behind. Can I bring along a stuffed animal I've had
35 since the age of four? Is there room for E's guitar? What clothes do we take? Summer clothes? The winter clothes too? What about my books? What about the CDs, the baby pictures?

The problem is that we don't even know if
40 we'll ever see this stuff again. We don't know if whatever we leave, including the house, will be available when and if we come back. There are moments when the injustice of having to leave your country, simply because an imbecile got it
45 into his head to invade it, is overwhelming. It is unfair that in order to survive and live normally, we have to leave our house and what remains of family and friends. And to what?

1 Study the text closely and identify the stylistic features that indicate careful shaping and crafting. To guide your analysis, complete the grid below.

2 Compare your findings with a partner's.

Stylistic feature	Example	Effect
Sentence types		
Verb forms and tenses		
Use of pronouns		
Type of vocabulary; and how formal or informal		
Discourse markers		
Fluency and cohesion		

Choosing, planning and writing your blog

Before you decide to choose a blog entry as one of your coursework tasks, you need to consider why a blog would be particularly suitable for writing about your chosen coursework topic. For example, you might want to create a blog for a character in one of your chosen literary texts. You could use a medium to reveal the character's thoughts and feelings, which were not available when the book was written, to provide an unusual perspective on an early or pre-twentieth-century literary text.

Below are the key issues you need to consider when choosing, planning and writing your blog. To help you to focus on how you will demonstrate your knowledge and skills in creating a blog, refer back to the section on blogs and e-texts in Unit 1 (pages 28–29) and remind yourself of the characteristic features of this type of text.

1 Think about your topic and choice of subject. Why would a blog be a good way of presenting your subject?

2 If you have not defined your task yet, look at the suggestions in the box for some inspiration. However, remember to discuss your ideas with your teacher before making a final choice.

- Write a blog about an issue connected with your chosen topic. Your approach could be to debate, offer comment and opinion, persuade, reflect, etc.

- Present your ideas about an aspect of one of your chosen literature texts in the form of a blog.

- Invent a fictitious blog for one of the characters in one of your chosen literature texts.

- Use a blog to provide comparative reviews of a text in two different forms, eg a prose text and its film or stage adaptation.

- Write a blog to persuade other students to read and study one of your chosen literature texts.

3 Decide on the purpose of your blog. It could be to inform and persuade, to describe or report experiences, to intrigue, etc.

4 Who is your audience? Obviously a weblog is in the public domain and theoretically available to anyone, but for the purposes of your coursework you need to write with a type of audience in mind.

5 Decide on the title of your blog. It is important to get this right because it is an opportunity to indicate the purpose, intended audience and content from the very beginning.

6 What presentation techniques will you use to present your blog? You will need to incorporate some simple layout features and make sure that your text is easy to read and navigate.

7 How will you structure the text? You have a word limit of 1750 words, so you have the opportunity of writing short, connected sections. However, the sequencing and chronology of your blog should be clear.

8 Next consider what tone will be appropriate. Will it be intimate and inviting your reader to share (see text **B**, page 124); more formal, sophisticated and complex (see text **C**, page 125); explicitly persuasive (see text **D**, page 125); very descriptive and reflective (see text **A**, page 124); or amusing and lively (see text **E**, page 126)? Also consider using shifts in levels of formality to create different effects.

9 Then consider your choices of language, which will depend to a large extent on your purpose and content. Another consideration is that your language should be accessible, varied and lively – Internet users have a limited attention span, so you need to capture the reader's attention and keep it. Use literary devices to provide description, visual detail or stimulating imagery for your reader.

Activity 32

1 Write a blog entry of approximately 150 words on any topic of your choice.

2 Share your blog with other members of your group.

3 Discuss and agree on the differences and similarities in linguistic and literary approach in the blogs.

Drafting and editing

As with any other text you will need to draft, edit and revise your blog to make sure it is as successful as possible. After you have written the first draft, invite other members of your group to comment on its effectiveness. Then use any constructive feedback to make suitable revisions. You will also need to consider if your text needs to be edited to take out any repetition, reorganise the structure or adjust the length.

Writing your commentary

Make a note of any changes that you make to your blog to discuss in your commentary. You will need to discuss and justify your choice of weblog as a coursework task and to indicate what you have learned about writing for the web, making reference to specific blogs you have read and showing how they influenced your approach.

C Writing for a listening audience

In this section you will investigate the conventions of writing for a listening audience and explore some model texts in different genres, focusing on speeches, audio guides, scripts and monologues. You will also practise planning and writing for these genres.

1 Introduction

The word count for your text for a listening audience (750 words) is shorter than the word count for your reading audience task to allow time for recording, testing and redrafting it. Your choice of task must evolve from your chosen topic area and study of your stimulus texts. You will also need to study a variety of texts for listening audiences in your chosen genre.

Considering the issues

What are the issues that you need to consider when producing a text to be spoken, ie delivered to a listening audience? First, you need to establish the context. Where will your audience be and how will this affect how they receive your text? For example, listening to a radio programme in the car or on a **podcast** will be different from watching a TV programme or walking around a museum with an audio guide. You also need to think about whether your audience will be listening to your text, or whether they will also be watching, or indeed listening while looking at places and objects as in a museum or gallery. It is also possible that your audience will only be able to benefit from a listening text (eg a visually-impaired visitor to a museum may benefit and expect more from an audio guide than a sighted visitor would).

The purpose of your text is just as important as in any other kind of text. Does the listener want to be informed and/or stimulated intellectually or do they want to relax, be entertained or intrigued in some way?

The context and purpose will then influence the level of formality, which will influence the tone that will establish the appropriate relationship with your audience. For example, the degree of **formality** or **informality** will be different if you are writing a political speech or a script for a soap opera.

For some spoken texts, such as persuasive speeches, voice-overs for documentaries and audio guides, you will need to use grammatical and **prosodic techniques** to provide the verbal cues and prompts needed to replace visual features. Grammatical devices such as **adverbs** and **adverbial phrases** can be used to indicate time sequences and location, for example, 'next', 'firstly', 'moving on', 'finally'. Prosodic features include:

- indicating the tone of voice and intonation by using questions and exclamations
- emboldening words and phrases to indicate those that are stressed
- indicating strategic pauses to allow time for the listener to absorb information
- introducing sound effects to create breaks (like white space and paragraphing in written texts).

In the following pages you will see these features in action when you analyse a selection of spoken texts and explore the features used to engage the interest of a listening audience.

Choosing your task

The choice is infinite, but below are some examples of texts in different genres for a listening audience. Remember to discuss the choice you are considering with your teacher.

- A persuasive speech
- A script for a scene from a radio or TV drama
- An extract from an audio-reading of a book for children
- An extract from a script for an audio guide
- An extract from a script for a documentary for either radio or television
- A monologue to be delivered on stage or television.

Your text for a listening audience will have to meet the requirements for:

AO1: showing confidence in identifying audience and purpose and writing fluently and confidently to produce coherent controlled texts (8 marks)

AO4: showing creativity in the production of a text for a listening audience and demonstrating expertise in selecting and using literary and linguistic approaches, drawing on insights from literary and linguistic studies (16 marks)

Key terms
podcast
formality
informality
prosodic techniques
adverb
adverbial phrase

2   Speeches

Speeches need to have a clear sense of context. You need to think of the place, the occasion and the type of audience present, as well as the content and purpose of your speech. You also need to consider what it is about a speech that makes it particularly suitable for addressing an issue that has interested you through your study of your chosen topic and texts.

Closely linked with the art of speech-making is the concept of **rhetoric**, although it is not confined to formal public speeches and also appears in other types of spoken and written texts. It is a technique in which grammatical and linguistic features are used to try to persuade and create emotion in an audience. The people listening to a speech are affected as much by the sound as they are by the message. Therefore, professional speech writers deliberately use rhythm, sound patterning, repetition and word images to create the desired response in the audience.

Sir Winston Churchill

Devices used for rhetorical effect	Example
First person pronouns	'I', 'we', 'me', 'us'
Possessive adjectives and pronouns	'my', 'mine', 'your', 'his', 'her', 'our', 'their', 'theirs'
Triadic structures, ie lists of three	'strong in purpose, steadfast in will, resolute in action'
Syntactic parallelism, ie repetition of the same grammatical structure	List of phrases beginning with 'change'
Conjunctions at the start of sentences	'And at all times', 'And this need'
Juxtaposition, ie balanced or contrasting phrases	'I have listened and I have learnt'
Contrasting past and future tense	'I have listened', 'I will continue to listen'
Positive abstract vocabulary	'opportunities', 'aspirations', 'potential'
Discourse markers to guide the reader through topic shifts	'As I have travelled', 'On this day'
Superlative adjectives	'the greatest'
Imperatives	'<u>Listen</u> carefully'
Words and phrases that assume shared values	'to make our nation what it can be'

Key terms

rhetoric

triadic structure

syntactic parallelism

Activity 33

The text below is taken from the first speech given by Gordon Brown when he became prime minister. He delivered it to the press outside 10 Downing Street.

1 Working in pairs, one of you read the speech aloud while the other makes notes on the techniques Brown used to hold the attention of his audience (refer to the table on page 130). Use a photocopy of the speech to make it easier to identify examples of the techniques.

2 Now reverse the process so that you both have the opportunity to approach the text as a listener.

3 Consolidate your list of techniques and examples, and add a comment on the effects of the techniques Brown used. You could do this in a table or by writing a short summary.

MY PROMISE TO BRITAIN: I WILL DO MY UTMOST

I have just accepted the invitation of Her Majesty the Queen to form a government. This will be a new government with new priorities and I have been privileged to have been granted the great opportunity to serve my country. And at all times I will be strong in purpose, steadfast
5 in will, resolute in action in the service of what matters to the British people, meeting the concerns and aspirations of our whole country.

I grew up in the town that I now represent in Parliament; I went to the local school. I wouldn't be standing here without the opportunities that I received there and I want the best of chances for everyone.
10 That is my mission: that if we can fulfil the potential and realise the talents of all our people then I am absolutely sure that Britain can be the great global success story of this century.

As I have travelled around the country and as I have listened and I have learnt from the British people – I have heard the need for change: change in our NHS; change in our schools;
15 change with affordable housing; change to build trust in government; change to protect and extend the British way of life. And this need for change cannot be met by the old politics so I will reach out beyond narrow party interest; I will build a government that uses all the talents; I will invite men and women of goodwill to contribute their energies in a new spirit of public service to make our nation what it can be.
20 And I am convinced that there is no weakness in Britain today that cannot be overcome by the strengths of the British people.

On this day I remember words that have stayed with me since my childhood and which matter a great deal today: my school motto. 'I will try my utmost'. This is my promise to all the people of Britain and now let the work of change begin.
25 Thank you.

Independent, 28 June 2007

Writing your commentary

It is a good idea to keep a Terminology Grid on which you record any new technical terms with examples and some indication of their effect.

This will build up your technical vocabulary and will be useful in writing commentaries on your own work.

Activity 34

Read the text below, which is an extract from a speech produced in response to the task of writing an election speech for the presidency of the National Union of Students.

> I do not come from a rich family. Most students in this country do not come from a rich family either, and many people have even less money. Almost everyone I speak to around in our universities has found it difficult to get money for their degree. So what
> 5 makes them carry on? Often it is only the passion of their subject and learning that helps them continue. By electing me as your president I will bring hope to anyone who has suffered the stress of worrying about money. Hope that these awful situations will not continue. I hope we are passionate enough to fight for
> 10 a better future for students, for ourselves and the students of the future. Imagine how much easier life would have been if students in the past had fought as hard as we can. Don't you wish they had?

1 Identify any examples of techniques used for rhetorical effect.

2 Make a note of any similarities and differences between this speech and Gordon Brown's.

3 Add another paragraph of about the same length in which you develop the ideas in the speech and employ some of the techniques in the table on page 130.

4 Now write a short commentary explaining the choices you made in your additional paragraph.

Independent research

Research, read and listen to other examples of speeches. You could check out speeches by famous people like Emmeline Pankhurst, leader of the Suffragette Movement (1913); Winston Churchill's wartime speeches (1940); or Nelson Mandela's speech on release from prison after 27 years. But they do not have to be political speeches; eg they could be on topics like climate change or they could be speeches delivered in your own school or college. Keep notes on the techniques they used and your responses to them.

Useful sources include anthologies of major world speeches, such as the *Penguin Book of 20th-Century Speeches*. Contemporary and historical speeches are available on the internet; searches on particular speakers will provide a variety of speeches to download. *The Guardian* offered a series of free copies of 'Great Speeches of the 20th Century' in 2007 and you can listen to audio clips on www.skreemr.com. National newspapers usually feature extracts from important political speeches immediately after the event.

Take it further

Read and compare the techniques used in famous historical and recent speeches, considering the impact of the different mediums used to broadcast them, eg Churchill's wartime speeches were recorded for radio; today's political speeches are often broadcast live on radio, television and the internet. Or, investigate and compare the literary and linguistic techniques of a speech by John F Kennedy in the 1960s and one by Tony Blair in the 1990s.

Choosing, planning and writing your speech

Before you decide to choose to write a speech as your text for a listening audience, you need to consider how your task will be linked to, or evolve from, your chosen topic. You will also need to research your material carefully – providing evidence and facts are very important for creating a convincing and authoritative voice, especially if your purpose is to persuade listeners.

Below are the key issues you need to consider when choosing, planning and writing your speech.

1. Choose an issue inspired by your chosen topic that you want to present as a persuasive argument – it could be a global or social issue or one that relates to a specific audience.

2. Decide on who you will present your speech to, eg your peers, a general adult audience, an audience of children.

3. Consider the structure, planning the entire speech from the opening address, through the main sections to the conclusion.

4. As you plan your speech, make notes of the linguistic and literary techniques you could use to appeal to listeners.

5. Now write the first draft of your speech.

6. To evaluate it effectively, either you or someone else needs to read and record it.

7. Play the speech to consider how it sounds and make notes of your first impressions.

8. Test the speech on a member of the target audience, if possible, or another member of your group. Ask them to listen to the speech initially and then read the printed version, before giving you some constructive criticism.

9. Incorporate any appropriate suggestions into your next revision of the speech, as well as your own edits to take out any errors in spelling and punctuation, unwanted repetition and adjustments for length. Keep notes of all the changes you make ready for writing your commentary. Your text will be more effective if you take the time to indicate intonation and prosodic features by emboldening stressed words and phrases.

10. Finally, rewrite your speech and then write your commentary.

Writing your commentary

Activity 35

Read the extract below from an anti-smoking speech. It was inspired by the topic of 'Dystopia' and stimulated by concerns over the number of people contracting illnesses related to smoking. It targets young teenagers who may have just begun to try smoking.

> Hot off the catwalk, here is this season's latest fashion: dull, grey skin, stinking breath, a powerful cough that brings up nasty yellow slime and of course an empty wallet. How can you get this season's look? It's easy – just take up smoking.
> 5   Smoking is bad for your health. You know that. Did you also know that it's seriously bad for your style? Before you light up next time think about this: that boy or girl you fancy doesn't think you look good. They think you look like an idiot. And don't even think about trying to pull them because you'll only be embarrassed when they tell you that you smell like
> 10 an ashtray.

1. Identify any examples of techniques used for rhetorical effect.

2. Make a note of any similarities and differences between this speech and Gordon Brown's.

3. Add another paragraph of about the same length in which you develop the ideas in the speech and employ some of the techniques in the table on page 130.

4. Now write a short commentary explaining the choices you made in your additional paragraph.

3   Audio guides

Key terms

clarity
sequencing
signposting

Many museums, galleries and historic buildings now routinely offer audio guides to their visitors. These are handheld devices with pre-recorded scripts, which complement the visual experience, so that visitors can explore and learn about particular features or exhibits while they are looking at them. Audio guides have a pause facility so that listeners can absorb information before moving on. They often direct listeners to specific points of interest in a gallery, museum or exhibition, so they are making a selection for the listener. They often provide background detail to give the audience a sense of the context, for example an audio guide for an exhibition of Picasso's paintings would include some details about the artist's life. If the audio guide is going to retain the listener's interest, it also needs to go beyond providing bare facts and inject an element of entertainment too.

If you are interested in producing a script for an audio guide, you need to consider how it could emerge from your topic and be related to your stimulus text. For example, visitors to Whitby might be interested in listening to an audio guide for a walking tour of the gothic features of this English coastal town, which focused on places and settings used in the novel *Dracula*, which is partially set there. This would suit the topic of Gothic and the Supernatural very well.

Considering practical issues

The experience of the audio guide listener is very different from that of the audience for a speech or TV or radio programme. They will be walking around, looking at things of interest *and* listening to the tape, so there are a number of practical issues in creating a successful audio guide. Above all context, **clarity**, **sequencing** and **signposting** are extremely important.

- The main focus of an audio guide is on particular items and areas of interest. General information can be given while the listener is moving from one area to another.

- The listener needs plenty of practical signposts so that they can navigate the site with ease.

- There should be short, regular pauses (possibly with sound effects) to allow the listener time to absorb the information or to turn the guide off without missing anything.

- The information needs to be presented in relatively short chunks, which are not overwhelming. Some audio guides offer information on more than one level, so that listeners can choose just the basic level and/or a more detailed approach.

- The language needs to be clear and economical, with more complex subject-specific vocabulary explained.

- Grammatical devices such as conjunctions and adverbial phrases will assist the listener's understanding and phonological devices such as repetition, rhythm and sound patterning will also be important.

Independent research

You have probably listened to audio guides on cultural trips, but if not, do take the opportunity to listen to at least one as part of your research. You can also research ideas about suitable techniques by exploring audio-visual CDs, eg it is possible to obtain virtual reality tours of famous places like the Louvre in Paris. Remember, it is not the place you are researching but the style and effectiveness of the guide, so that you can use some of the same techniques.

Activity 36

The script below consists of extracts from a handheld audio guide, which is available to visitors of Villa Kerylos, a reconstruction of a classical Greek villa in the South of France.

1 Working with a partner or in a small group, record the script or get one member of the group to read it aloud while the others listen. The bold text indicates stressed words and phrases.

2 Brainstorm initial ideas about the devices used for a listening audience – don't worry at this stage if you are not able to give them a technical label.

What is the purpose of the music?

What is the effect of the second person pronoun?

What are the associations of the word 'discover'?

What effect does this opening sentence have on the listener?

Subject-specific words are emboldened. Why is this done?

What is the effect of this phrase?

Identify the form of the verb and its purpose. Find another example.

Give the technical term for this type of phrase.

This is the modal form of the verb. Find another example later and comment on its function.

How does this phrase direct the focus of the listener?

Why has the phrase 'or forecourt' been added?

Find other examples of specific references to visual details.

What is the purpose of the fading music?

What is the effect of the conjunction 'but'?

What is the purpose here of the imperative verb?

Visit around Kerylos Villa

music (3)

Welcome to the Villa **Kerylos**. (2) The Greek villa you are about to discover was built between 1902 and 1908 on the rocky point that extends from **Beaulieu** into the **Baie des Fourmis** (.) where the sea is similar to the Gulf of Corinth. (2) *music fades out* (.)

As you enter into the semi-darkness (.) you will see the **Balaneion** opening up to your left (.) marked with the inscription **Naiades** …

When you continue into the **Proaulein** (.) or forecourt (.) you will see a mosaic with a dolphin inspired from the Trident house on Delos …

You enter the **Andron** through two doors leading to a portal with two Ionic columns made of marble (1) notice the yellow and white decorations …

Then return through the last three rooms to reach the first floor (.) *music fades out* (4) From here a corridor leads to the apartments of the masters of the house (1). On the left (.) after the display cabinet containing silverware and porcelain created for the villa (.) you enter the bedroom of Madame Reinach (.) the wife of the owner of the villa …

The visit around the villa is now complete but you cannot leave without visiting the gardens that surround the house and overlook the sea.

3 Now read the annotations and questions around the script, which will help you to identify and explore some of the techniques used.

4 Classify the techniques and devices that you have identified under the headings 'Grammatical and cohesive devices' and 'Phonological features'.

It is often assumed that using **adjectives** is the key to successful descriptive writing. Activity 36 should have shown you that adverbs, adverbial phrases and **proper nouns** are also extremely important in presenting perspectives on places – don't neglect them in your own writing.

Writing the script for your audio guide

The word limit for your coursework text for a listening audience is 750 words so you only need to write an extract. The extract from the Villa Kerylos script is 375 words long, which gives you some guidance on how much to write.

Activity 37

1 Write the text for two minutes of an audio guide to a place that you are familiar with or one where you can do some careful research, eg a local gallery, museum, historical site or building of architectural interest. Your guide could be aimed at children, teenagers or adults.

2 Record the text yourself or ask someone to record it for you.

3 Test it out on other members of your group and ask for feedback on the success of the linguistic and structural techniques you have chosen.

4 Write a short summary of what you have learned from this experience.

Choosing, planning and writing your audio guide script

Below are the key issues you need to consider in choosing, planning and writing a successful audio guide script. Make notes on your decisions as you make them, so that you can explain the process of your work in your commentary.

1 How will your audio guide develop from, or relate to, your chosen topic? The links with your topic must be clear. For example, if you are studying Gothic and Supernatural, you could write a guide to a gothic building or to an exhibition of paintings on a gothic or supernatural theme.

2 What will the subject, content and purpose be?

- Do you want to inform and interest? (eg leading a visitor round a national heritage site like a castle)

- Do you want to inform and persuade? (eg a guide to the climate change section of the Natural History Museum)

- Do you want to stimulate interest in scientific discoveries and encourage young people to pursue the study of science? (eg a guide to a display in the Wellcome Foundation for medical research)

- Do you want to raise awareness of critical events that shaped history? (eg a guide to the site of Ground Zero (9/11) in New York)

- Does your audio guide have an essential practical application? (eg a guide to a sensory garden for blind people)

3 How are you going to structure your guide? Your plan should include: an introduction, a series of sections with more detailed information, and a conclusion, which may contain suggestions for further research or exploration or invite the listener to take advantage of other facilities, purchases and places of interest. (Revisit your work on rhetorical speeches (pages 130–133) to remind you of the techniques that will be most effective in achieving your purpose.)

4 Draft your script. Then record and test it as you did in Activity 37.

5 Revise and edit your script.

Writing your commentary

Include details of any recording and testing in your commentary, and keep notes of any feedback that you receive from your audience, so that you can demonstrate both the process and your attempts to have your work evaluated.

Activity 38

Working with a partner, review each other's audio guide scripts, by completing a table like the one below. Show how the script has addressed each of the criteria. If you add brief quotations, this will also give you some material for your commentary.

Criteria	Comments on success	Evidence
Awareness of audience and purpose (AO1)		
Writing fluently and confidently (AO1)		
Variety of literary and linguistic techniques and strategies (AO4)		
Creativity in production of text (AO4)		
Use of literary and linguistic approaches, drawing on insights from literary and linguistic studies (AO4)		

4   Radio and TV scripts

Writing a script may be a task that appeals to you and there are a number of interesting possibilities. The script could be exclusively for a listening audience, as on radio, or for an audience who may be listening and watching the television, for example. Writing a script for these purposes is not as easy as it may seem at first, so consider your options carefully.

In this section you will focus on the concept of register, or formality. 'Register' is a term used to describe the level of formality in a text. The extent to which language is formal or informal is determined by the function of the language in a particular situational context, for example, a public political speech or a witness testimony in a court hearing will differ from a dialogue in a TV soap opera or a dramatic monologue. When you are considering a suitable register for a text, you need to select linguistic and literary techniques to match the context, purpose and intended effect of your text, and the relationship you wish to establish with your audience.

Think about formality as a continuum, with very formal at one end and very informal at the other, with all the variations in between. Very few texts would fall right at either end of this continuum; for example, many formal texts use techniques to soften or reduce the level of formality. Get used to looking for 'threads' of formality or informality throughout spoken and written texts and be aware of shifts in register.

You have explored two examples of formal texts – Gordon Brown's speech and the audio guide to Villa Kerylos – but many of the texts designed for listening audiences are relatively informal. Now you are going to investigate the features used to establish an informal register by studying a script for a TV series.

What do you think are the characteristic features of scripts for TV series and soap operas? Programmes of this type aim to create a world that viewers can believe in and relate to. Scriptwriters therefore aim to create a **rapport** with the audience. Character and plot are clearly important, but the key to creating successful characters and situations, which the audience can relate to, is the language used. The focal point is the dialogue, which aims to imitate or replicate spontaneous real-life speech. (To remind yourself of the linguistic features associated with spontaneous speech and informality, return to Unit 1, pages 12–15.)

Writing your commentary

If you want to discuss the register of your script in your commentary, you need to be very specific in stating your intentions, giving brief quotations as examples and pointing out any shifts in register or softening of a formal tone to a more informal, relaxed one.

Key term
rapport

The specific features to look out for are:

- the context of the dialogue and how it influences the level of formality
- **adjacency pairs**
- colloquial vocabulary
- non-standard grammatical expressions
- minor sentences
- ellipsis
- discourse markers
- repeated idiolectical expressions
- use of hedges and deliberate vagueness.

Activity 39

1 Working with a partner, read the extract below from the American TV series *Seinfeld*, each playing one part and taking note of its register.

FADE IN:

Ext. Coffee shop-Establishing shot-Day

Int. Coffee shop-Late Afternoon

A typical New York coffee shop. It's not rush hour but there's activity and we hear that
5 *unmistakable din. Jerry and a longtime friend, George, are sitting at a table. George, slightly insecure, has an opinion on everything. He lives life at a higher intensity level than Jerry.*

Jerry

See, now to me that button is in the worst possible spot. The second button literally makes or breaks the shirt. Look at it, it's too high, it's in no-man's-land. You look like you live with your
10 mother.

George

Are you through?

Jerry

You do, of course, try on when you buy.

15 **George**

Yes, it was purple, I liked it. I don't recall considering the button.

Jerry

Oh, you don't recall.

George

20 *(using pen like a microphone)* No, not at this time.

Jerry

Well, Senator, I'd like to know what you knew and when you knew it.

A waitress, Claire, approaches the table. Obviously over qualified, she always gets the joke. She pours coffee from two pots of coffee.

25 **Claire**

Mr Seinfeld—Mr Costanza

George

Are you sure that one's decaf? Where's the orange indicator?

> How would you describe Jerry's opening utterance?

> Jerry repeats George's utterance for satirical purposes – find another example of this technique.

> This is an example of a deictic reference – find two other examples.

Claire

30   It's missing. I have to do it in my head. 'Decaf left, regular right.' It's very challenging work.

Jerry

Can you relax? It's a cup of coffee. Claire's a professional waitress.

Claire

Trust me, George. No one has any interest in seeing you on caffeine.

35   *Claire exits.*

George

How come you're not doing the second show tomorrow?

Jerry

Well, there's this woman might be coming in.

40   **George**

(Taken aback) Wait a second, wait a second, what coming in? What woman is coming in?

Jerry

I told you about Laura. The girl I met in Michigan.

George

45   No, you didn't.

Jerry

I thought I told you about her. Yeah, she teaches political science. I met her the night I did that show in Lansing. *(Tries to pour milk)* There's no milk in here, what is the story, what–

George

50   Wait, wait, what, what is she like?

Jerry

Oh, she's really great. She's got like a real warmth about her, and she's really bright, and really pretty, and, uh, and the conversation though, I mean it was – talking with her is like talking to you but, you know, obviously much better.

55   **George**

So what happened?

Jerry

Oh, uh, nothing happened, you know. But it was great.

George

60   Oh, nothing happened, but it was – Well, this is great.

So, you know, she called and she said she wanted to go out with you tomorrow night? God bless. Devil, you.

Jerry

Yeah, well, not exactly. I mean she said – you know, she called this morning and she said she had
65   to come in for a seminar and maybe we'd get together. So–

George

(Whistles for Jerry to stop) Yo, whoa, whoa, whoa – 'had to?' 'Had to come in?'

Jerry

Yeah....

Short, regular exchanges maintain the pace – find another example.

A common non-standard expression – find other examples.

What is the effect of the repetition here?

What is the effect of Jerry's repetitions and incomplete utterances?

How would you describe Jerry's utterance?

George

'Had to come in?'

Jerry

Yeah, but.....

George

75　'And maybe we'll get together'? 'Had to' and 'maybe'?

Jerry

Yeah ────────────────────────────────────

Comment on the effect of the increasingly rapid adjacency pairs.

George

No. No. No. I hate to tell you this. You're not going to see this woman.

80　**Jerry**

What? Are you serious? (*Not convinced*) Why, why did she call? ────

What is the dramatic effect of Jerry's series of questions?

George

What do I know? Maybe, you know, maybe she wanted to be polite.

Jerry

85　'To be polite'. You are insane. ────────────

How would you describe Jerry's statement? What is his purpose?

George

Alright, alright. I didn't want to tell you this, you want to know why she called?
You're a back-up. You're second line, a just-in-case, a 'B' plan contingency....

Comment on George's intention here. Why does he repeat his point in several different ways?

Jerry

90　Oh, I get it. This is about the button.

Why does the scriptwriter return to the button?

2　Re-read the script, addressing the annotations and questions around it, to identify the techniques used to create an informal register and engage a listening audience.

3　How would you describe the level of formality, and why is it appropriate? Think about how it reflects real speech and uses shared knowledge.

4　Although the *Seinfeld* dialogue sounds very realistic and would make the audience feel that they were listening to a real conversation, you know that it has actually been carefully shaped and crafted by the scriptwriter, who has used dramatic devices, appropriate language and regular turn-taking.

Make a list of features which suggest that this is not real spontaneous speech but has, in fact, been skilfully crafted.

Activity 40

1 Record a two- or three-minute conversation between two people. It might be a good idea to give the people involved a topic to talk about and allow them a minute or so to think about what they might say. You don't want them to plan the conversation, but you don't want them to be totally lost for words either.

2 Make a transcript of the conversation.

3 Then shape it into a short dialogue suitable for a radio or TV audience, using some of the techniques you have just explored.

Writing your commentary

Remember to keep notes on any research that you do as it will be helpful to refer to it in your commentary. Also keep any practice writing, with annotations, to include in your appendix to show work in progress.

Independent research

Watch a variety of TV dramas – regular series, soap operas, one-offs. Record and transcribe short extracts so that you can study the linguistic and structural features in some detail. Add to this research by reading a range of scripts for television or film; published copies should be available from major bookstores or your library. Practise writing short stretches of dialogue based on themes from your chosen topic.

Take it further

Record 2–3 minutes of both a TV drama and a radio play (a good source of radio plays is BBC Radio 7). Make a transcription of each recording and compare the stylistic techniques used in them. Are there significant differences between the TV drama, which has viewers as well as listeners, and the radio drama, which is exclusively for a listening audience?

Choosing, planning and writing a TV script

Your script could be based on an incident that you have researched or on a particular issue in one of your literature texts, and could be either contemporary or historical. For example, you might write a script on the topic of 'Women's Lives', exploring an aspect of a dystopic society or presenting a poem in dramatic form. Whatever you eventually choose, you need to consider the following key issues before making that decision, and planning and writing your script.

1 What are your reasons for choosing a TV script as a coursework task for a listening audience? What have you enjoyed or found interesting about the TV scripts you have read and the scripted programmes you have watched?

2 How will the subject and theme of your script relate to your chosen topic?

3 What is your purpose in writing the script? Although an element of any TV script is to entertain the audience, there may also be other purposes, such as to make a social comment, raise awareness of issues, present historical material in a new way or dramatise real-life events, etc. Be clear about your purpose and the effect you wish to have on your target audience.

4 Be selective about what you include in your script, including the number of characters. With a limit of 750 words, two or three characters are all you will need.

5 Remember that your script is written to be performed, so it has two audiences – the television audience and the actors. You need to set the scene and include **stage directions** for the actors.

6 Write your draft script and then arrange to have it read and recorded.

7 Ask for constructive criticism from other members of your group and make any necessary decisions about editing your script.

8 Now write the final version.

Key term
stage directions

5   Monologues

Key terms

monologue
dialogue
soliloquy
pragmatics
dramatic irony
foreshadowing

According to the *Oxford English Dictionary*, a **monologue** is 'a long speech by one actor in a play or film … or broadcast programme' in contrast to a **dialogue**, which is 'a conversation between two or more people [in a] book, film or play'. So keep reminding yourself that a monologue is a text that is written to be performed in front of an audience. A monologue could be delivered when the character is alone on the stage or could be a completely self-sufficient script, as in Alan Bennett's *Talking Heads*. (Look back at your exploration of one of Bennett's monologues on page 37 of Unit 1.) Unlike a dialogue, a monologue reveals the inner thoughts of the character in a direct way, in a similar way to **soliloquies** in Shakespeare's plays.

The key feature of a monologue is that language is used to create a specific persona, or character. In successful monologues the character seems to be completely alive and credible, although they should not be entirely predictable. Much of the impact derives from the apparent spontaneity and similarity to real speech, but although writers do employ features of spontaneous speech, the monologue is actually carefully crafted to achieve a particular effect. So you need to explore how theatrical techniques can be integrated with specific language choices to create a convincing persona. (Recap on your studies of persona in the poems of Duffy and Fanthorpe on pages 45 and 48 of Unit 1.)

Real speakers often unintentionally reveal aspects of their personality through their language choices. In the same way, a well-crafted monologue can reveal aspects of a character to the audience. This means that you need to consider the **pragmatics** of language – the implied meanings and what the speaker is really saying. The writer also attempts to capture the individual 'voice' of the speaker by creating a particular idiolect, also described as a kind of 'linguistic fingerprinting' because it reveals the particular speech habits that make the speaker unique.

However, the writer of a monologue needs to do more than simply create a persona who unburdens their private thoughts and anxieties; there must also be some kind of structure and development to hold the listener's attention. Something needs to happen in the monologue, such as a major revelation for the audience or for the speaker.

Dramatic irony and **foreshadowing** are also useful techniques for the monologue writer. Dramatic irony allows the audience to be aware of something that is not known to the character, for example, what they say about their relationships with other characters may indicate how they perceive themselves in contrast to how they are perceived by others. Foreshadowing allows the audience to see clues about what may happen later.

If you choose to write a monologue for your coursework task, you will be able to demonstrate your ability to create character and use your study of dramatic techniques. Now let us look at the characteristic features and techniques in action.

Activity 41

Working in a small group, one person should read aloud the following extract, which is the opening of a monologue.

From 'The Guid Sisters' by Michel Tremblay

The first time I seen him I thought he was ugly. At least, I didnae think he was guid-looking tae start wi. When I opened the door he took off his hat an said tae me. 'Would the lady of the house be interested in buying some brushes?' I shut the door in his face. I never allows a man intae ma hoose. Ye
5 never know what might happen … The only one 'at gets in is the paper boy. He's still ower young to get any funny ideas. Anyhows, a month later back he came wi his brushes. It was bucketing outside so I let him stand in the lobby. Once he was in the hoose I started to get jittery, but I tellt masel he didnae look the dangerous type, even if he wasnae very bonny tae look at … But he ayeways looks that smart. No a hair oot ae place. Like a real gentleman. And he's ayeways that polite. Well, he selled me a couple
10 a brushes an then he showed me his catalogue. There was something 'at I wanted but he didnae have it wi him so he said I could order it. Ever since then, he's come back once a month.

1 Individually, note the features that help to create the persona of the speaker. Look for evidence of the speaker's idiolect, informal speech features and the pragmatics or implied meaning of what the speaker says.

2 Share your findings with the rest of your group and list all the features you have identified. Present your findings in a table like the one below. Some features have been listed to get you started.

3 When you have listed the features, use the second column to comment on their effects.

Linguistic features	Effects
Imitation of the Glasgow regional accent	
The meaning of what she says	Suggests her distrust of men

4 Now return to the text and look for any dramatic devices that help to create the personality of the character and suggest the development of the action. Can you identify any foreshadowing, a suggestion of how the action might develop? Use a similar table to the previous one to present your findings.

Dramatic techniques	Effects
The immediate, intriguing opening 'The first time I seen him'	Implies there are going to be other times

5 Discuss and agree on what might encourage the audience to continue listening.

Activity 42

1 Choose one of the following short activities to develop your own skills in writing a monologue.

  a Write an extract of monologue for the brush salesman referred to by the character in the extract in Activity 41, presenting the situation from his perspective. Will he have the same dialect or a different one? What will his perspective suggest about possible developments?

  b Complete the original monologue in the previous extract in approximately 250 words.

2 Share your monologue with other members of your group and ask for feedback on its effectiveness.

Writing your commentary

Make a note of the features that you used in writing your monologue. It might be helpful to classify them in the following way: grammatical and structural features to give the text cohesion; lexical and phonological features, eg indications of idiolect; dramatic devices.

Activity 43

The text below is an extract from a monologue. It was stimulated by the novel *Nausea* by Jean-Paul Sartre and was a response to the topic Entrapment.

Working with a partner or in a small group, one person should read the monologue aloud.

Jean-Paul Sartre

The clock in the hallway begins to chime. But I do not really hear it – it is in the distance like the echo of a far away funeral bell. Not here. You are here lying on the floor but you are also not here. You are far away from me just like you wanted and far away from life. You are not here so I cannot really see you and
5 cannot see what I have done. It was like a red wave of anger and frustration and you made it come and take me. Your cruel words built up and up, swelling like the tide until they were crashing over me like the sea, the sound of the sea roaring in my ears making me deaf to all other noises and all other thoughts except for the crashing and the anger and the nauseating feeling. You could have stopped
10 me but instead you went away. You left me! They will judge me now but they will not judge you, as innocent as a lamb. I couldn't hear or see I couldn't understand and the red waves came crashing and then it was over. You are lying on the floor but you are gone forever.

Sirens in the distance but I would not hear them. I would be far away, floating
15 on the calm blue sea, away from you lying on the shore and the red waves that did this to you, the red waves that took you away. I would be drifting slowly away, never to return, like a rowing boat lost in an endless blue ocean.

2 Consider the following features.

   a What are the implications about past action?

   b How does the language used convey the state of mind of the speaker?

   c What is the effect of the literary techniques such as similes?

3 Write a short commentary, explaining why you think the writer made particular choices and the effects achieved, quoting evidence from the text to support your points.

Independent research

Listen to and read a wide variety of monologues; don't restrict yourself to contemporary ones, but study examples in earlier literature too. Good choices to investigate include:

- William Shakespeare; look particularly at key soliloquies in *Hamlet* and *Othello*
- Alan Bennett often creates isolated middle-aged/elderly women, but there are many other interesting possibilities
- Franca Rame; her collection *A Woman Alone* and her monologue 'Medea', a contemporary version of the classical Greek play by Euripides
- Jean Marlow; her series of books on audition speeches.

Take it further

Make a close investigation of monologues featured in stage plays. For example, study the monologue delivered by Serafina Pekkala in Part 2, Act 1 of the stage play adapted from *His Dark Materials* by Philip Pullman. Then contrast it with Catwoman's monologue in Act 1, Scene 3 of *By the Bog of Cats* by Marina Carr.

Choosing, planning and writing your monologue

Below are the key issues you need to consider when choosing, planning and writing your monologue.

1 Think about what you would like to use as the stimulus for your monologue and how it relates to your chosen topic area.

2 Decide on the persona you want to portray – their age, gender, social class, idiolect, dialect, etc.

3 Plan the structure of your monologue. With a limit of 750 words you might choose to write an extract, in which you will need to plan the sequence of the whole monologue and then decide which part to write.

4 How will you indicate developing action? For example, if you choose to write the introduction, you can include elements of foreshadowing.

5 You may want to include a scene setting and stage directions.

Here are some different approaches that you might work with.

Literary option

Choose a relatively minor character from your chosen prose fiction text or from a poem you have studied, which features a particular character or persona. Write a monologue for that character, presenting their perspective on events.

You will need to reshape details from the fiction text and use first person narrative to create the voice of your character. As far as possible, you should relate the details of the character to the impression that has been developed in the novel or poem, although you may wish to introduce new details of your own.

Historical option

Choose a famous person in history and do some research into their private life by reading biographical accounts, diaries, archive newspaper articles, and watching TV programmes. Select one aspect of the person's life and create a suitable scenario to give their reactions to a particular event, while also revealing other details about their beliefs and attitudes.

Real-life option

Create a character from life around you. Use your observations of people and their linguistic habits. Ordinary informal conversations can be a good starting point. Do not attempt to copy or imitate a specific person, but instead develop a fictitious character using your skills of observation and your knowledge of literary and linguistic techniques.

Independent research

Alan Bennett said that he got ideas for his monologue voices by listening to ordinary people and noting their use of idiolect. Do the same for your research – be observant, be a good listener and take a notebook with you everywhere to jot down ideas.

Writing your commentary

Whichever task you choose for your coursework, you need to show in your commentary the influence of the stimulus texts to demonstrate what you have learned about monologue techniques. So you need to make reference to your study of your texts and your study of the monologue genre. This does not have to involve a close analysis of the texts, but should highlight some of the literary and linguistic features and narrative or dramatic approaches that inspired you.

D Writing your commentaries

In this section you will look at how to write the commentary on each of your pieces of original writing – an important part of your coursework that needs careful planning. Each commentary should be a maximum of 500 words in length and together can earn you up to 32 marks of the total 80 marks available for all your coursework.

1 Meeting the assessment objectives

The purpose of the commentaries is to explain the process of your own writing and to make clear links between your stimulus texts, your wider reading and your choice of coursework tasks. In order to do that, you need to explore and explain:

- why you chose a particular topic and why the task interested you
- the context of your text and your target audience and purpose
- how you did your research into your chosen genre and style models
- how you were inspired and given ideas by your stimulus texts and wider reading
- why you chose specific language and literary techniques to shape your text and what effect you intended them to have; in order to do this you need to identify the features in your text and use short quotations from your text to illustrate and support your points
- the feedback you received from your audience and how and why you made significant revisions.

It is important to have a logical, organised approach and to collect material for your commentaries while you are planning, drafting and editing your coursework tasks. Keep a notebook to record details of texts you read and decisions that you make while researching and working on your original writing. Keep your notes and any drafts of your work in a folder so that you can refer to it when you begin to write your commentaries.

Each commentary should be organised in three sections: introduction, analysis and conclusion.

Assessment objectives

The criteria you need to meet for your commentaries are expressed by the examiners in two assessment objectives like this:

AO2: Demonstrate detailed critical understanding in analysing the ways in which structure, form and language shape meanings in a range of spoken and written texts. (16 marks)

AO3: Use integrated approaches to explore relationships between texts, analysing and evaluating the significance of contextual factors in their production and reception. (16 marks)

2 The introduction

Make sure your introduction sets the scene, and discuss:

- the title of your text and how it is linked to your chosen topic
- the type of task and the genre you have chosen
- the context, audience and purpose of your text.

Activity 44

Read the extracts from commentaries below. Annotate copies to show how they address the points in the list on page 146.

Introduction 1

My dramatic monologue was inspired by the topic Women's Lives. It would be broadcast on either television and radio and its purpose therefore is primarily to entertain. While writing my monologue I focused on a selection of Alan
5 Bennett's 'Talking Heads' monologues. The theme of my monologue is loneliness and isolation: I became interested in this theme after reading 'The Well of Loneliness' as my chosen novel.

The audience for my monologue is wide but is probably most relevant to female loneliness. Elderly people in particular may be able to relate to what my
10 protagonist Iris says.

Introduction 2

The purpose of my autobiographical text was primarily to entertain but also to record what it was like to be young in the 1990s.

I felt I would like to write about my own life after reading the autobiography 'Bad
5 Blood' by Lorna Sage and the 'Baghdad Burning' blog, which both present intriguing and moving pictures of the lives of young girls. I had also read 'Faithfull', the autobiography of Marianne Faithfull, which gives a vivid snapshot of life in the 1960s and this gave me the idea of attempting a similar approach with the 90s. My idea came from my main topic Women's Lives. My source texts were influential in terms
10 of literary and linguistic techniques but the approach in my autobiography was mainly through comic language and anecdotes, which contrasts with the more sombre and anxious tones of some of my stimulus texts.

Introduction 3

As my chosen coursework topic was Dystopia I decided to write an election speech about addressing inequalities in wealth in our society. My speech is aimed at an audience of university students. The purpose of it
5 is to persuade them to vote for me. I have used many different forms of personal pronouns. I did this to make the audience feel that I was interacting with them. Examples of this are 'You won't simply be electing me as your President, you will be electing yourselves too.'

3   The analysis

Your analysis should be a critical, technical discussion of your work. In it you need to discuss and explain what you learned about the different genres you explored, how you used your research and why you chose particular linguistic and literary techniques.

As the word count for each commentary is only 500 words, you cannot afford to adopt a line-by-line approach. Instead, be selective and highlight significant or interesting aspects, for example, mention some ideas you got from your stimulus texts, highlight significant literary and linguistic choices, give examples and explain the effects you intended to have.

You might want to mention some ideas that you gained from your stimulus texts and how you found them useful as style models, either in your main analysis or your introduction, depending how much you want to say. For example:

> I called my monologue "Trapped by the sickness" in response to the topic Entrapment, which it relates to. The idea of 'the sickness' was inspired by the novel 'Nausea' by Jean-Paul Sartre.

You could also explain your research into your chosen genre. For example:

> In order to accurately write the speech I did some research into existing speeches to study the genre. This informed me of the conventions. As an example of a political speech I used the 'War on Iraq' speech by Tony Blair to the British public. In this he explains the reasons for war and tries to persuade them that it is a good idea.

A good starting point for your main analysis might be to consider the particular voice and tone of your text. For example:

> The purpose of my speech is to persuade my audience to vote for me so I tried to maintain a dramatic aspect to my speech by using sentences such as 'I hope we are passionate enough to fight for a better future'.

You would then look at the specific techniques you used to achieve your purpose – in the above case, the use of grammatical techniques such as second person pronoun and literary techniques such as metaphor. For each technique you identify, you must give evidence from your text by quoting a brief example and then comment on the intended effect. For example:

> Imperatives, a common feature of speeches, such as 'Imagine', help the audience to put themselves into the situation and therefore to support what the speaker is saying.

You will probably have something of interest to say about each of the four categories below, although only some of the features in each category will be relevant to your texts. Use the lists as a checklist, adding to them and adapting them to suit your own texts. At the end of each category, extracts from commentaries offer ideas about possible approaches.

Vocabulary

Aspects of vocabulary (lexis) to consider include:

- voice and tone
- semantic fields
- technical **jargon**
- **emotive words** and phrases.

> Lexis is used to support recurring themes and ideas throughout the monologue. Lexis in the semantic field of the sea is threaded throughout, eg 'a red wave of anger', 'swelling like the tide', 'sea roaring', 'drifting' are used as a metaphor for the character's inability to control her emotions or actions.

> In my anti-smoking speech I used nouns phrases such as 'this season's look' from the semantic field of fashion and emotive phases like 'nasty yellow slime' and 'smell like an ashtray' from the semantic field of health.

Grammar

Aspects of grammar to consider include:

- types of sentence
- ellipsis and elision
- pronoun
- repetition
- tripling
- contrasting pairs
- adverbials to mark time or structure the text.

In analysing my work I can see how grammar helped me to create a distinctive style in my monologue. I have used many active verbs in the non-finite form, eg 'crashing', 'swelling', 'roaring', 'floating'. This gives the impression of a strange, eternal present, where events are slightly suspended. My repeated use of the second person pronouns, eg 'You' and 'Your', focuses the attention on the implied listener. I have used structural techniques to create parallels and contrasts, eg 'They will judge me now but they will not judge you', 'You are lying on the floor but you are gone forever'.

In my speech declaratives present opinions as facts, eg 'most students do not come from a rich family'. Tony Blair did this in his speech on the Iraq war when he said 'Removing Saddam will be a blessing to the Iraqi people'.

Key terms
jargon
emotive words
assonance

Literary techniques

Techniques to consider include:

- figurative language
- alliteration
- rhythm and word patterning
- **assonance**
- narrative voice.

The literary framework is also highly relevant when discussing my dramatic monologue. The extended metaphor of the protagonist being out at sea presented her feelings of confusion and turmoil and her lack of control. I used similes such as 'innocent as a lamb' and 'like a rowing boat' to create shifts in mood and to lessen the tension.

Rhetorical features are common in my speech with lists of three, repetition and direct address. An example is 'a better future for students, for ourselves and the students of the future'.

Cohesion, structure and presentation

These aspects provide the signposts, which, among other things, guide your reader through the text, and include:

- paragraphing
- discourse markers
- indications of foreshadowing
- layout features.

The transition between past, present and conditional tenses in my monologue helps to convey changes in mood.

Sound references feature throughout, eg the opening contrast between the 'chiming' clock and the funeral bell introduces a sinister element and this moves seamlessly into sounds of the sea which distance the protagonist from the world of reality.

Her victim complex is shown through the use of negative constructions, eg 'You left me', 'gone forever', 'never to return' – this is intended to present her feelings of self-pity. The reference to the 'funeral bell' at the beginning of the monologue foreshadows her eventual suicide.

Discourse markers are a feature of speeches that allow the audience to know where the speaker is in his or her argument. I used the adverbs 'Most', 'Almost', 'Often' at the beginning of utterances to guide the audience through the points in my speech.

Writing your commentary

Do ensure that any comments about your use of graphological or layout features are clearly linked to the purpose of your text and your language choices.

Activity 45

When writing your commentary, your approach should be to:

- identify and discuss the literary and linguistic features you have used
- explain why they were used and what effect was intended
- use short quotations from the text to illustrate
- comment on the influences of the stimulus texts, showing how they helped in the production of the original writing

Look again at the extracts and identify how, and if, this approach has been carried out.

4   The conclusion

Your conclusion should be brief and may only be a couple of sentences long, but it gives you the opportunity to reflect on your creative writing. Depending on the task you chose, a successful conclusion might refer back to your topic and stimulus texts, sum up what you hoped to achieve and point out anything significant that you learned through your preparation for writing.

Your conclusion certainly should not be just a summary or repetition of points you have already made. Also avoid explaining what you would have written for your coursework task, if you had had more time or more words, and do not say how successful you think your creative writing is – the moderator will assess the success of your work.

Read the concluding paragraph from a commentary below, which is a good example of a succinct, purposeful and thoughtful conclusion.

> I was inspired to write my persuasive speech from my study of the Dystopia topic. A speech seemed the best way of conveying my ideas and a rhetorical framework was particularly suitable as I could incorporate lots of features to involve the audience and to provoke them to think about the implications of smoking. My speech was planned and so this allowed me to deliberately include a number of literary and linguistic techniques.
>
> My study of political and persuasive speeches really developed my understanding of the differences between spontaneous and crafted speech and also made me aware of the power of rhetoric.

5   Acknowledging and referring to sources

As part of your coursework folder, you have to include a **bibliography**. It does not have to be very lengthy, but should include any particularly influential texts. Split the bibliography into two sections: chosen texts and wider reading, listing the books, articles and websites you have referred to in your commentaries or which gave you ideas while planning your original writing. Within each section, list texts and sources in alphabetical order – the books and articles according to the first author's surname and the websites according to the address. Here is a good example:

Key terms
bibliography

Chosen texts

Tremain, R – *Restoration* (Sceptre, 1995) ISBN 0340530448

Winton, T – *Cloudstreet* (Picador, 2002) ISBN 0330322699

Books

Wider reading

Dalrymple, W – *In Xanadu* (Flamingo, 1990) ISBN 0006544150

Ravenhill, M – The Daily Play, *The Guardian*, 9 August 2007

Newspaper article

www.bl.uk/learning/index.html (the British Library)

www.timesonline.co.uk/tol/news

Explain which website it is if need be.

6   Assessing your commentaries

Practise writing and assessing commentaries before you write the final ones for your coursework folder. You could start by writing short commentaries on some of the model texts you have explored, then on your own writing activities, and, if possible, on a partner's work. The next activity shows you how to assess commentaries so that you can feed back to your partner. The more you practise, the more you will increase your confidence and skill.

Activity 46

1   Working with a partner, read the first extract from a commentary below. Then read the annotated comments around it which assesses the level of achievement against assessment objectives AO2 and AO3.

Commentary 1

Like the stories of Angela Carter, my story aimed to portray female figures in an unconventional way to how they are often presented in traditional fairy stories and in fiction and the media. I wanted to make my female characters strong and in control, not vulnerable and naïve. To do this I have deliberately presented the male figure of the father as weakening and losing his power by describing him with the similes 'transparent as water' and 'worn out like an old nightshirt'. Context is also important in this kind of traditional narrative and I have placed him in a context where he is dominated and threatened by the natural world, eg the lake is like 'poisonous mercury' and twinkles 'evilly like a witch's eye'.

As a contrast to my reading of Carter I read a number of traditional fairy tales and I have retained the classical themes and images: images of colour are typical and I have contrasted 'silver' and 'blood-red' to create visual contrasts. I have also tried to imply the opposition between good and evil by contrasting the attractive and threatening features of nature, eg 'the wide silver lake' and 'velvet blanket' as opposed to 'the blackness', 'sinister', etc.

References to 'the castle', 'the shadowy pine trees', 'the witch's eye' all re-create the conventional contexts of fairy stories. This is deliberate to fulfil my readers expectations but at the same time to subvert them as my intention is to make the reader look at things differently. As I am writing for an adult audience the message should become clear through my use of stylistic techniques. I wanted to get the attention of my readers immediately so I began with an adverb 'Next' and then introduced the 'melancholy' castle: personification is a typical feature of fairy stories and I have used this technique as a cohesive device throughout my story, eg the lake being sinister and evil. I also wanted to give a real sense of the landscape like in animated films of fairy stories so I used the verb 'loomed' to suggest almost that the castle was moving: this reinforces the sense of threat to convey my theme of entrapment.

[1] AO3: understands conventions of genre

[2] AO2: explains use of similes

[3] AO3: reference to genre conventions

[4] AO2: explores use of imagery

[5] AO3: explains influences on own writing

[6] AO2: explains intended effect of stylistic techniques

[7] AO3: clear discussion of purpose

[8] AO2: aware of how literary devices create meaning

[9] AO2: links... language choices to effect

[10] AO3: refers back to original topic

2 Then use the following approach to assess the remaining two commentaries on page 153. You will need to refer to the mark scheme, which has four bands for each assessment objective.

  a Read each commentary and annotate it with comments.

  b Look for evidence of AO2 and provisionally place the work in a band.

  c Repeat the process with AO3.

3 For each commentary identify the features that work well and any areas that could be improved.

You are not expected to give actual marks but your task is to investigate the commentaries for evidence of AO achievement.

Assessment criteria for AO2

AO2	Demonstrate detailed critical understanding in analysing the ways in which structure, form and language shape meanings in a range of spoken and written texts.
Band 1 0–3 marks	• Acknowledge and make an attempt to explain more obvious literary and linguistic choices in stimulus texts and in own writing with some evidence of critical understanding. • Show some awareness of how form and language shape meaning.
Band 2 4–7 marks	• Identify and discuss some clear and relevant examples of literary and linguistic techniques in stimulus texts and own writing. • Show awareness of how form and language shape meaning.
Band 3 8–11 marks	• Examine a range of literary and linguistic techniques in stimulus texts and own writing. • Demonstrate knowledge and understanding in discussing how form and language shape meaning, showing well-developed critical understanding.
Band 4 12–16 marks	• Explain and comment on an interesting range of literary and linguistic techniques in stimulus texts and own writing. • Demonstrate some sensitivity and perception in discussing how form and language shape meaning, showing detailed critical understanding.

Assessment criteria for AO3

AO3	Use integrated approaches to explore relationships between texts, analysing and evaluating the significance of contextual factors in their production and reception.
Band 1 0–3 marks	• Indicate some awareness of the significance of contextual factors in relation to literary and linguistic choices. • Identify and make some relevant comments on the influence of stimulus texts on own writing.
Band 2 4–7 marks	• Offer some relevant comment on the significance of contextual factors in relation to literary and linguistic choices. • Provide some explanation of the influence of stimulus texts on own writing.
Band 3 8–11 marks	• Explain in some detail the significance of contextual factors in relation to literary and linguistic choices. • Explore and make some comment on the influence of stimulus texts on own writing.
Band 4 12–16 marks	• Show awareness and explore the significance of contextual factors in relation to literary and linguistic choices. • Explore and offer detailed comment on the influence of stimulus texts on own writing.

Commentary 2

In my election speech for the NUS presidency I have used many features of rhetoric employed by politicians and other public speakers.

To do my research I read a number of famous speeches, eg the wartime speeches of Winston Churchill, Tony Blair's 'War on Iraq' speech and speeches by Martin Luther King and Nelson Mandela.

I was inspired to write a persuasive speech by reading around my topic of Dystopia and because I feel strongly that there are inequalities in our society. I wanted to focus on the issue of student poverty so the best way to do this was to target a student audience in an election speech to the NUS.

Like other public speakers who aim to gain the support of their audiences, I have repeatedly used the personal pronouns 'I' and 'me'. I have used rhetorical questions and groups of 3 (this is a stylistic device often used in public speaking as it has been shown to be memorable). I have also tried to include emotive abstract words like 'passion', 'hope' and 'stress'. I wanted to involve my listeners and make them feel that they had to respond so I used the imperative form of the verb in 'Imagine how much easier life could have been'.

Commentary 3

My aim in writing this speech was to persuade young teenagers not to smoke or to give up if they had already started.

My target audience would be about 12/13 years old as I feel this is the time when most young people want to be seen as part of a social group.

I felt the best way to do this was to use the metaphor of fashion and get them to think about the repulsive aspects of smoking. To do this I employed vocabulary from the semantic field of fashion, eg 'Hot off the catwalk', 'style', and to make my point I contrasted this with the unpleasant reality, using premodification like 'nasty yellow' (slime) and 'empty' (wallet).

I also aimed specifically at this age group by using an informal register with colloquial expressions they could relate to like 'seriously bad', 'that boy or girl you fancy', 'trying to pull', 'look like an idiot'. The opening of my speech imitates the kind of language used in fashion shows or glossy magazines. I deliberately used ellipsis 'Hot off the catwalk' to achieve this effect.

I got my idea for this approach by studying charity adverts and government campaigns where language is used to make the audiences feel guilty or ashamed in some way.

Glossary

AAVE [page 73]
African-American Vernacular English, a variety of American English (see also Black Vernacular English, BVE)

adjacency [page 75]
something being next to something else

adjacency pair [page 138]
the term in conversation analysis for the two halves of an interaction between speakers, the first turn and the response

adjective [page 135]
a word or phrase that modifies a noun

adverb [page 129]
a word or phrase that modifies any part of language apart from nouns

adverbial phrase [page 129]
a word or phrase modifying a phrase or clause, typically indicating time, place or manner

agenda [page 14]
a list of things that need to be discussed or acted upon

alliteration [page 45]
the usage and grouping of words beginning with the same letter or sound, for literary effect

archaic [page 69]
old-fashioned

assonance [page 149]
the repetition of vowel sounds to create rhymes within a phrase or sentence

autobiography [page 115]
an account of someone's life, written by that person

auxiliary verbs [page 32]
verbs that are used to form the tenses, moods or voices of other verbs

bias [page 115]
a preference for a particular point of view, reflecting preconceived ideas rather than fact

bibliography [page 150]
a list of the books and other sources used or referred to in a work

biography [page 115]
an account of someone's life

blog [page 123]
an informal abbreviation of weblog – a website on which items are posted on a regular basis and displayed with the most recent items at the top

blogger [page 123]
a person keeping a blog

catalyst [page 109]
an event or person in the narrative, whose presence suddenly causes a conflict or problem

clarity [page 134]
the nature of something being made easy to follow and understand

clause constructions [page 70]
the ways in which clauses are created by authors to portray message and style

cohesion [page 101]
something being a united whole and having clear meaning

colloquial language [page 9]
informal, everyday language typically used in speaking

compound sentences [page 77]
sentences containing more than one subject or clause with a verb related to the subject

common nouns [page 17]
the names of real objects

constructive criticism [page 104]
giving someone feedback about their work to help them to improve it

context [page 94]
the circumstances of the text

contextual factors [page 11]
the circumstances that exist in which an event occurs and which help to explain the nature of the event

contraction [page 9]
the shortening of a word or words to reflect spoken usage, indicated by an apostrophe

cooperative principle [page 21]
the idea that participants in a conversation communicate effectively by working together to reach common goals

coordinating conjunctions [page 17]
the words that link together clauses within a sentence

CPR [page 11]
contexts, purposes, receivers – factors that help with the analysis of a speech encounter

cue [page 14]
the signal indicating that something should happen

deictic language [page 17]
words or expressions that rely on context to give them meaning

deixis [page 17]
a term for words or expressions that rely on context to give them meaning

dialect [page19]
a form of language with its own distinct choice of words, grammar and pronunciation, often found in a specific region

dialogic [page 27]
the adjective for a conversation between two or more people

dialogue [page 142]
a conversation between two or more people

direct speech (DS) [page 17]
the exact words uttered by a speaker, presented within quotation marks

discourse marker [page 25]
word or phrase that marks the divisions between the parts of a communication

dominant speaker [page 14]
the person who is in control of a conversation

dramatic irony [page 142]
the dramatic term for the mismatch between what the audience realises and what the character fails to understand

elision [page 29]
the joining together of words, leading to the omission of a syllable when spoken or written

ellipsis [page 17]
the omission of part of a sentence that can be understood from the context

embedded dialogue [page 36]
reported conversation contained within an utterance

emotive words [page 149]
the use of particular words in a text that are designed to produce a certain emotional response from the receivers

e-text [page 123]
literally, electronic text – text that is available in an electronic format, such as a posting on the internet

ethnic [page 19]
belonging to a group of people sharing cultural and social habits

exchange [page 9]
things that are passed between people, such as the elements of a conversation

exposition [page 109]
the crucial information about situation, plot and character that is given to the audience

face theory [page 21]
the idea that participants in a conversation wish to preserve their status, and respect other participants' 'face' in order that they are respected in return

fact [page 115]
something that is true without dispute; in a story, an event that happened in reality

figurative language [page 32]
words that are not used literally, such as in metaphors or similes, often suggesting a comparison between two things

filler [page 14]
sounds (er, um) or words (y'know) that are spoken to fill potential gaps in utterances

flash fiction [page 112]
a type of fiction that is extremely brief, usually about 150 words

foreshadowing [page 142]
the hints and clues in a story about what is going to happen

formality [page 129]
the way people adjust the tone of their language to suit the situation they are in (see also register)

framing narrative [page 75]
the overall narrative of a story, within which dialogue is contained

function categories [page 12]
the groups into which things are placed according to their different purposes

genre [page 30]
a style or category within a broader form of art or media

genre-blending [page 109]
the use of elements from different genres to create a new style of writing

graphological features [page 105]
the elements of the visual aspects of a text

graphology [page 25]
the study of the visual aspects of texts

hedge [page 14]
a word or phrase that softens the force with which something is said

heightened language [page 70]
language that for literary effect is more stylised, or emotionally or linguistically more intense

homophones [page 25]
words that sound the same but which have different spellings or meanings

idiolect [page 19]
the term for an individual's language or speech patterns

idiom [page 17]
an informal expression whose meaning cannot be derived from the words that make it up, but which is understood by the group that uses it

imperative [page 69]
a grammatical form conventionally expressing an order

incomplete construction [page 9]
speech that is not grammatically whole but which reflects the way people speak

informality [page 129]
a manner of communication that is spontaneous, private and reliant on the context of the participants' relationship

interact [page 11]
how things or people behave towards each other

interior monologue [page 109]
the presentation of a character's thoughts in a narrative text, enabling the reader to understand the character more fully

interrogative [page 69]
a grammatical form conventionally expressing a question

intonation [page 13]
the rise and fall of the voice in pitch in speaking

jargon [page 149]
words or expressions specific to particular subjects, often precise, complex and difficult to understand

juxtaposition [page 72]
the setting of things next to each other, for literary effect

layout features [page 105]
the elements of how a text is presented visually and how this shapes meaning

letter writing conventions [page 72]
the commonly accepted ways of writing letters, for clarity of communication

lexis [page 9]
the total set of words in a language, often called the 'vocabulary' of a language

linguistic devices [page 105]
the methods by which an author's choice of language creates meaning

linguistic framework [page 9]
the toolkit used to examine the way spoken and written language works

literary [page 45]
the adjective for literature, often referring to its study

literary devices [page 105]
the methods by which an author's style of writing creates meaning

maxims of cooperation [page 75]
the principles of cooperation by participants to achieve an effective conversation, especially quality, quantity, relevance and manner

metaphorical language [page 45]
words that are not used literally, where one thing is conceived of as representing another, often a concrete idea representing an abstract notion, eg 'the point of the argument'

micro-fiction [page 112]
another term for flash fiction, a type of fiction that is extremely brief

micropause [page 9]
a pause of less than one second in reported conversation

modifiers [page 77]
adjectives or adverbs, qualifying the sense of nouns or verbs respectively

monologue [page 142]
a discourse of one speaker, ranging from a person alone speaking to themselves, to one person addressing a large public audience

narrative tension [page 117]
the methods by which an author uses the reader's lack of knowledge about what is coming next in the story to maintain their interest in the narrative

neologism [page 107]
the term for a new word or expression

non-fluency features [page 79]
aspects of spontaneous speech, such as false starts, fillers and hesitations, that indicate it is unplanned

omniscient narrative viewpoint [page 55]
a third person narrator, telling a story from the outside and knowing both everything that occurs and the internal workings of all the characters

onomatopoeia [page 45]
the formation of a word reflecting the sound of the object or action to which it refers

opinion [page 115]
a person's point of view about something

overlapping [page 9]
where one speaker starts before the previous speaker has finished

'over the shoulder' narrative viewpoint [page 55]
a third person narrator, telling a story from the outside, but focusing on the viewpoint and internal workings of one particular character

paralinguistic features [page 18]
the elements of non-verbal communication: a speaker's gestures, posture and facial expressions

participants [page 9]
the people taking part in an event

persona [page 29]
an aspect of someone's personality that is presented to others, either to make a specific impression or defined by a particular situation an invented personality

perspective [page 115]
the way that a writer views something; his/her point of view

phonetic [page 73]
the adjective for the sounds of speech

phonetic spelling [page 79]
the spelling of words by how they sound

phonological features [page 79]
features relating to the study of speech sounds

podcast [page 129]
a collection of digital media files, distributed over the internet, which can be played on portable media players or personal computers

politeness principle [page 21]
the theory that participants pay attention to the other's face needs in order for a conversation to succeed

position [page 117]
the way in which an author presents information and opinion in order to persuade the reader to share his/her point of view

possessives [page 73]
nouns or pronouns that denote possession

postcard fiction [page 112]
another term for flash fiction, a type of fiction that is extremely brief

pragmatics [page 142]
the study of how meanings are conveyed in the social contexts of language use

proper nouns [page 135]
nouns that represent unique entities (eg John), rather than a class of entities (eg person)

prosodic features [page 18]
the way that a speaker communicates: volume, pitch, tone, pace and stress

prosodic techniques [page 129]
using the skills of verbal communication to help to convey a message

rapport [page 137]
the positive connection between people or groups of people

receiver [page 11]
the person with whom the speaker is communicating

recipient [page 70]
the person or object receiving something

regional [page 19]
belonging to a specific geographical area

register [page 12]
a form of language appropriate to a particular situation or context

reported speech [page 17]
the communication of what someone else has said, often with the tense changed; also referred to as indirect speech

resolution [page 109]
how a story finishes, finding an ending/solution to the conflict the story sets out

revelation [page 112]
the moment when something previously unknown becomes understood

rhetoric [page 130]
the technique in which grammatical and linguistic features are used to try to persuade and create emotion in an audience

rhetorical question [page 69]
a question raised to emphasise a particular point where the speaker already knows the answer

salutation [page 72]
a greeting, for example at the beginning of a letter

scripted drama [page 36]
a play created in written form, with dialogue, directions for the actors and stage instructions

scripted speech [page 30]
an utterance or conversation that has been written for speaking in a drama

semantic field [page 32]
a group of words drawn from a particular area of experience, eg food or colours

sentence constructions [page 70]
the ways in which sentences are created by authors to convey message and style

sentence types [page 25]
the different sorts of sentences, reflecting the purposes for which they are constructed: declarative, imperative, interrogative and exclamatory

sequencing [page 134]
the placing of objects in a logical order to achieve an effect

shape [page 109]
the form of a story, the structure of a narrative

short-shorts [page 112]
another term for flash fiction, a type of fiction that is extremely brief

signing off [page 72]
the writer's name at the end of a communication

signposting [page 134]
the use of clear signs to enable the receiver to find their way around something easily

simulate [page 9]
assume the appearance or copy the style of something

social language [page 49]
language used by a particular social grouping

sociolect [page 19]
the term for a particular social group's language or speech patterns

soliloquy [page 142]
the dramatic device whereby a character alone on stage utters his/her thoughts and feelings aloud

specialised lexis [page 32]
the words that are understood in context to refer to a specific situation

speculation [page 115]
a theory about something without firm evidence

speech encounter [page 11]
a verbal communication between people; this can take various forms

spontaneous conversation [page 9]
unplanned talk between two or more speakers, also termed 'live conversation'

stage directions [page 141]
the pieces of text in a play that tell the actors how they should move around on the stage

subject–verb–object [page 77]
a basic sentence structure, where the subject is followed by an active verb and then by the object, and which can be used for literary effect

syntactic parallelism [page 130]
repetition of the same grammatical structure, used for rhetorical effect

syntax [page 13]
the rules that apply to the construction of sentences

taboo language [page 21]
language that is considered forbidden within a certain social circumstance because it is highly inappropriate

tag question [page 13]
a short interrogative structure attached to a declarative,
eg 'Nice day, isn't it?'

tags [page 79]
labels, for example to introduce an utterance

term of address [page 25]
the manner in which someone refers to another, reflecting
the nature of their relationship

tone [page 12]
the character of a voice; the way it expresses feeling

topic management [page 14]
the subject of a conversation, and how it is developed as
the speakers interact

topic shift [page 25]
a change in the focus of a communication

transcription [page 9]
a printed version of a conversation

triadic structure [page 130]
lists of three, used for rhetorical effect

turn-taking [page 14]
the ways speakers manage to exchange turns in a
conversation without speaking at the same time or
leaving awkward pauses

utterance [page 12]
the physical realisation of a sentence in its spoken or
written form

vague language [page 17]
language that uses words without precise meanings

verbose [page 69]
an adjective for using more words than are needed

vernacular [page 79]
an everyday form of language, specific to a region
or country

voice [page 107]
an opinion or attitude uttered by someone that reflects
that person's identity

weblog [page 123]
a website on which items are posted on a regular basis
and displayed in reverse chronological order, with the
most recent items at the top

written discourse [page 69]
a formal written text, often implying communication
or debate

Published by:
Pearson Education Limited
Edinburgh Gate
Harlow
Essex CM20 2JE

© Pearson Education 2008

First published 2008
10 9 8 7 6 5 4 3 2 1

ISBN 978-1-84690-251-2

Printed in Great Britain by Henry Ling Ltd., at the Dorset Press, Dorchester, Dorset

The Publisher extends grateful thanks to Barbara Bleiman for her consultancy in respect of Unit 1: Exploring Voices in Speech and Writing.

Pearson Education Limited accepts no responsibility for the content on any third party Websites to which a link from this book is provided or for any use of personal data by the third party operating such a Website. The links are provided 'as is' with no warranty, express or implied, for the information provided within them

In the interest of providing support across the range of set texts for Edexcel GCE Language and Literature at AS Level, this Student Book includes extracts from texts whose content is at times sensitive and explicit. Inclusion is based on the educational purpose for which this A Level resource is intended, and in consultation with centres through the review process.

Picture Credits
18 Alamy Images: Ingram Publishing (Superstock Limited). 26 Alamy Images: Flashpoint Pictures / Ian Miles. 30 Alamy Images: Jack Carey. 47 Alamy Images: Janine Wiedel Photolibrary. 58 Ben Ramos Photography: Photographers Direct. 66 Corbis: Corbis Sygma / Alain Nogues. 92 Corbis: Francis G. Mayer. 96 Corbis: Envision / Steven Mark Needham. 99 Reuters: Trevor Leighton. 122 Vicky Clarfelt. 130 Corbis: Hulton-Deutsch Collection. 144 Getty Images: Roger Viollet

All other images © Pearson Education.

Picture Research by: Ann Thomson

We are grateful to the following for permission to reproduce copyright material:

10 Downing Street for the speech by Gordon Brown on 27 June 2007 Crown copyright; A&C Black for an extract from Blood Brothers by Willy Russell, reproduced with permission of A&C Black; The Agency (London) Ltd for an extract from The Dogs by Hanif Kureishi, first published in 2004 copyright © Hanif Kureishi reproduced by permission of The Agency (London) Ltd. All rights reserved and enquiries to The Agency (London) Ltd 24 Pottery Lane, London W11 4LZ info@theagency.co.uk; Anvil Press Poetry for the poem "Boy" by Carol Ann Duffy from The Other Country by Carol Ann Duffy published by Anvil Press, 1990. Reprinted with permission of Anvil Press Poetry; Ben Atkinson for an extract from his blog from November 2007 www.getjealous.com/benandjess, reproduced with permission; Ellie Barnard for an extract from her blog on 20 February 2008 yellowhighheels.blogspot.com, reproduced with permission; Bliss Magazine for an extract about junk food published in Bliss Spring 2007 copyright © Bliss Magazine 2007; Bob for an extract from his blog on 8 August 2006 ibosblog.blogspot.com, reproduced with permission; Bloodaxe Books for the poems "Single Parent" by Connie Bensley from Choosing to be a Swan, 1994; and "Arrival 1946" by Moniza Alvi from Split World: Poems 1990-2005, 2008 reproduced by permission of Bloodaxe Books; Cambridge University Press for an adaptation of "Differences between speech and writing" from The Cambridge Encyclopedia of the English Language 1995 by David Crystal published by Cambridge University Press 2003 © David Crystal 2003, reproduced with permission; Casarotto Ramsay & Associates for an extract from the play Outlying Islands by David Greig copyright © David Greig 2002. All rights whatsoever in this play are strictly reserved and application for performance etc., must be made before rehearsal to Casarotto Ramsay & Associates Ltd, 7-12 Noel Street, London W1F 8GQ. No performance may be given unless a license has been obtained; Cengage Learning Services Limited for an extract from The Language of Conversation by Francesca Pridham published by Routledge 2001; Vicky Clarfelt for an extract from her blog on 3 February 2008, http://imanaccounthandlergetmeoutofhere.com, reproduced with permission; Culturespaces for an extract from Villa Kérylos audioguide comment, www.villa-kerylos.com/en/kerylos copyright © Culturespaces; David Higham Associates Limited for extracts from 'Flowers' by Alice Walker from In Love and Trouble published by Orion 1984; The Color Purple by Alice Walker published by The Women's Press 1983; and Cloudstreet by Tim Winton published by Picador 1982. Reproduced with permission of David Higham Associates; Faber and Faber Ltd for extracts from The Caretaker by Harold Pinter 1960 published by Faber and Faber Ltd; Vernon God Little by D.B.C. Pierre published by Faber and Faber Ltd and the poems 'Take One Home for the Kiddies' by Philip Larkin from Collected Poems; and 'Preludes' by T S Elliott from Selected Poems published by Faber and Faber Ltd copyright © The Estate of Philip Larkin; U.A. Fanthorpe for the poem "Waiting Gentlewoman" by U.A Fanthorpe, reproduced with permission; Guardian News & Media Ltd for extracts from "The Daily Play" by Mark Ravenhill published in The Guardian 9 August 2007; "Climate change blog" published in The Guardian 20 September 2007 and "Newspaper report about Tornadoes in UK" published in The Guardian 25 September 2007 copyright © Guardian 2007; Help the Aged for an extract from the Rajasthan Water Appeal May 2007, reproduced with permission of Help the Aged; Hodder and Stoughton Limited for an extract from Spilling the Beans by Clarissa Dickson-Wright published by Hodder 2007, reproduced with permission of Hodder and Stoughton Limited; ICM Talent for an extract from Death of a Salesman by Arthur Miller, 1949 copyright © ICM Talent on behalf of Arthur Miller; Independent News & Media Ltd for an extract from "The Gossip band newspaper performance review" published in The Independent 26 February 2007 copyright © The Independent 2007; ITN Source for a transcript of the news report "Tornadoes wreak havoc across UK" aired on Channel 4, 24 September 2007 copyright © ITN Source, reproduced with permission; Mslexia Publications Ltd for extracts from a Man describing his thoughts whilst at Heathrow by Christie Watson and an extract on The art of writing by Kirsty Gunn originally published in Mslexia, the magazine for women who write www.mslexia.co.uk, reproduced with permission of the author and Mslexia Publications; Nelson Thornes Ltd for the transcript of the 'Hairdresser Conversation' from Real and Scripted Talk ISBN 0748-731946 first published in 1998, adapted with the permission of Nelson Thornes Ltd from Ron Norman.; Pan Macmillan for the poem "Driving to the Hospital" from Newborn by Kate Clanchy copyright © Kate Clanchy 2004; and an extract from the poem "You are the bread and the knife" from Nine Horses by Billy Collins copyright © Billy Collins 2003, reproduced with permission of Pan Macmillan, London; Penguin Group for an extract from Notes on a Scandal by Zoe Heller published by Viking 2003, Penguin Books 2004 copyright © Zoe Heller, 2003. Reproduced with permission of Penguin Group; PFD for the poem "I could have been a builder" by Benjamin Zephaniah © Benjamin Zephaniah reproduced by permission of PFD (www.pfd.co.uk) on behalf of Benjamin Zephaniah; The Random House Group for extracts from Talking Heads by Alan Bennett, published by BBC Books; Notes from a Small Island by Bill Bryson, published by Doubleday; and Paddy Clarke Ha Ha Ha by Roddy Doyle, published by Secker & Warburg. Reprinted with permission of The Random House Group Ltd; Rogers, Coleridge & White Ltd for an extract from The Bloody Chamber by Angela Carter first published by Vintage 1979 copyright © 1979 Angela Carter. Reproduced with permission of the author c/o Rogers, Coleridge & White Ltd; 20 Powis Mews, London W11 1JN; RTÉ for an extract from the radio phone-in broadcast Liveline&# 8221; presented by Joe Duffy, courtesy of RTÉ Radio, RTÉ is the National Public Service Broadcaster of Ireland; Shairpo West and Castle Rock Entertainment for an extract from The Seinfeld Scripts The First & Second Seasons copyright © Shairpo West and Castle Rock Entertainment 1998; Sheil Land Associates for an extract from Restoration by Rose Tremain published by Sceptre copyright © 1989 by Rose Tremain, reproduced by permission of Sheil Land Associates; Stuart Thompson for an extract from his blog http://mrwhatshisface.blogspot.com on 28th October 2005, reproduced with permission; and Town House TV Productions Ltd for a transcript from Trisha broadcast on Channel 5 in July 2007.

Every effort has been made to trace the copyright holders and we apologise in advance for any unintentional omissions. We would be pleased to insert the appropriate acknowledgement in any subsequent edition of this publication.